RIVERS OF GOLD

PLACE IN RETURN BOX to remove this checkout
TO AVOID FINES return on or before date due.

DATE DUE	DATE DUE	DATE

ZAMBEZIANA: Vol XXII

A SERIES ON CULTURE AND SOCIETY

IN ZIMBABWE

RIVERS OF GOLD

by
H. ELLERT

MAMBO PRESS

Gweru

ZIMBABWE

MAMBO PRESS
P.O. Box 779, Gweru, Zimbabwe
Tel: 263-54-4016
Fax: 263-54-51991

DT
2942
.E44
1993

RIVERS OF GOLD

First Published 1993

Copyright © 1993 H. E. Associates

Line illustrations : Mike White

All rights reserved. No part of this publication may be reproduced, stored in a
retrieval system or transmitted in any form or by any means, electronic, mechan-
ical, photocopying, recording or otherwise without prior permission from the
publisher and the copyright holder.

ISBN 0 68922 529 4

Printed and published in Zimbabwe
by Mambo Press, Senga Road, Gweru
1993

To Albert Bruno Plangger—
who first encouraged me

Frontispiece from: *Ethiopia Oriental* by
Fr João dos Santos

CONTENTS

Acknowledgements

I wish to record specific thanks and sincere appreciation to Father Albert Plangger, the ex-Director of Mambo Press for his encouragement and enthusiasm for this project which I first discussed with him many years ago. I also wish to acknowledge my friends in the Prehistory Society of Zimbabwe whose companionship I have enjoyed over the years. In particular I mention Val Botes (now in Canada) who shared my enthusiasm in the search for Masapa, Innocent Pikirayi, Robert Soper, Linda Kelly, Lorraine Adams, Peggy Izzett and others. To the Director and staff at the Queen Victoria Museum, Harare, Zimbabwe, the Director and Staff of Bulawayo Museum, Mr. Cran Cooke of the same institution, the Director and staff of Livingstone Museum, Livingstone, Zambia, the Director of Fort Jesus Museum, Mombasa, Kenya, *Museu Naciona da Arte Antiga*, Lisbon, Portugal, *Museu da Cidade*, Lisbon, Portugal, Mr. D. Hein and Ms R. Harper (Museum of Western Australia) for assistance in identification of Chinese stoneware jars, to R.S. Calado of the *Museu Nacional da Arte Antiga* for discussion on Portuguese faience wares, to Mike White for illustrations, to Angus Shaw and Louis-Marie Tattevin for certain photographs (acknowledged), Carolyn Boyd-Clarke for correcting my English, Pru Lamy and her father Alan Taylor for maps and to innumerable contributors and friends who have helped me realise this project. Last but not least, I also owe a debt to John Haasbroek of Mambo Press for the final editing, the design and lay-out of what was something of a medley of pictures and text. Finally, I hope that all sources of published material have been adequately acknowledged in the footnotes. I take concluding responsibility for all and any errors or ommisions.

Preface

This book explores historical events of the sixteenth and seventeenth centuries within the geographic region of the Zimbabwean highveld known to the Portuguese as the Rivers. An area largely delineated by the present day gold-fields of Zimbabwe. The reader will detect a strongly Portuguese perspective – this is deliberate – yet, it also covers, albeit very briefly, Portuguese-Shona relations during this crucial period and the subsequent two centuries until the advent of British colonial interests in the late nineteenth century.

It is important for the reader to understand that my use of the word *Portuguese* is extremely generous, encompassing as it does all persons of Lusophone cultural expression and within the context of this book applies equally to Europeans, Asians, Africans and successive generations of coloured progeny. It may also be taken, in a general sense, to mean the *vashambadzi* or Portuguese trading agents and emissaries. The *vashambadzi,* as we shall learn, played a crucial role on behalf of the foreigners. These intermediaries assimilated the cultural norms of their masters and were the forerunners to the later so-called *assimilados* of twentieth century colonial Mozambique. Portugal could only spare a few European Portuguese for their African *conquistas.* Undoubtably, some were *fidalgos* or aristocrats or clergymen in positions of power and privilege but the vast majority were common folk. Because of the shortage of manpower in Portugal and the awful wastage rate during the outward passage and tropical fever, the ranks were supplemented by *degradados* or transported criminals. Very few Portuguese women ventured to the East and inevitably miscegenation occurred throughout *Asia Portuguesa* and no less so in Mozambique and the Rivers of Gold beyond the western mountains. My use of the term *muzungu* is also expansive and may be taken to mean virtually any non-African Portuguese speaking person – this would include Europeans, Indians, Chinese or any coloured offspring. The Shona lexicon defines *muzungu* simply as a Portuguese.

Born of my own abiding interest in Portuguese maritime expansion during the Age of the Discoveries, *Rivers of Gold* is really a specialist contribution in many ways, but, hopefully it will also appeal to a general readership. The work is the result of many years of general research and numerous expeditions into the bush.

It may be difficult to communicate the excitement and elation at finding a tiny fragment of blue and white porcelain at a suspected historial site. This happened one day in the early 1980s during a field trip to the supposed site of the Portuguese *feira* of Masapa in the company of friends from the Pre-History Society of Zimbabwe.

The discovery of evidence that a thriving Portuguese settlement had once existed in the *brachestegia* woodlands above the Mkaradzi river valley in the shadow of Fura mountain, — fired me with renewed zeal to search out and catologue all that I could about the Portuguese in the Rivers of Gold. I have also experienced that special feeling which comes from identifying place names on old Portuguese maps and walking along river banks in the footsteps of the Portuguese. Each chapter opens a different window to the past and allows us to explore those fascinating and bizarre events, many of which date back nearly four hundred years. Over the past decade I have embarked on a journey which has taken me from Portugal to Mozambique, Zimbabwe, India, Thailand and China. Finding stoneware jars, identical to those brought by the Portuguese to Zimbabwe, in dusty vaults beneath the *Museu Nacional da Arte Antiga* in Lisbon were important discoveries for me as I undertook this work. Equally significant were those special moments of quiet reflection inside the monastery of *Jerónimos* and the *Torre de Belém* on the Tagus river where the Portuguese embarked. The same feeling is rekindled once inside the tiny chapel of *Nossa Senhora da Baluarte,* the second earliest Christian edifice south of the equator (the oldest being the cathedral of São Salvador which, in its ruined state, is located in the Angolan province of Uige). With its classic Manueline style vaulted stone ceilings, this church, on Mozambique Island, aroused in me the very essence of the Portuguese saga and their quest for the Rivers of Gold.

Journey's End was atop a small hillock which formed the central feature of Maramuca, the westernmost known *feira* of the Portuguese. Surrounded by flowering *msasa* trees, so distinctive of *brachystegia* woodland and the earthwork outline of the old Portuguese settlement, there was an overwhelming sense of timelessness as I was gripped by the same emotions. Still further to the west, at the Kame ruins site museum, a piece of blue and white porcelain is a vibrant reminder of Rozvi-Portuguese trade. Lastly, numerous visits to museums and archives researching and comparing artifacts, porcelains, and other evidence have completed my work.

Professor David Beach who has been good enough to read my text suggested a number of corrections and these have been incorporated in the text. He has also submitted that because Professor Erik Axelson stopped his summaries of the Portuguese in south-east Africa at the date 1700 there has been a general tendency for anglophone works on this subject to end here. He is right of course. Beach argues for a much longer perspective bringing the story of the Portuguese in Zimbabwe to a more logical conclusion.

It is no coincidence that 1700 marks a turning point in Anglophone investigation of the Portuguese on the Zambezi during the subsequent two centuries. Original documents covering this period do exist but they were largely written by semi-literate backwoodsmen and the task of adequately translating these papers is extremely daunting, to say the least. Some scholars, notably Axelson, Bhila, Isaacman, Newitt, Beach and Mudenge have all touched upon them in their works which contribute towards our understanding of this interesting period in Zimbabwe's history. I have drawn from many of these secondary works in constructing this different perspective of history. I have not had the luxury of time to complete this task in full measure. Nevertheless, I have endeavoured to make this account as complete as possible but accept there is still much to be said about this important period so closely related with Portuguese settlement on the Zambezi and with the Chikunda and the Rozvi of Zimbabwe during the eighteenth and nineteenth centuries.

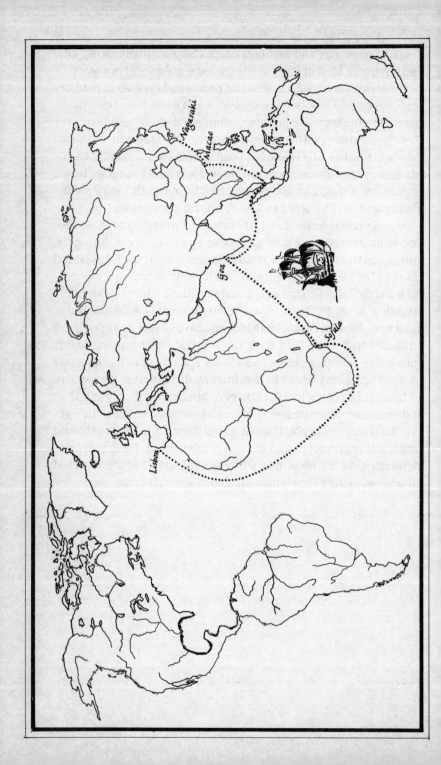

CHAPTER 1

The Historical Background, 1498-1693

The appearance of Vasco da Gama's flotilla off the south-east African coastline at the turn of the sixteenth century marks the beginning of the colonial period in the history of Mozambique and the starting point for our story. Inevitably, as the Portuguese stumbled across evidence of Swahili-African trade, their interests focused on the Swahili bazaars where this exchange took place. Before long the Portuguese learned that the gold came from the mines of the interior and this set the stage for the arrival of Lusitanian adventurers on the Zimbabwean highveld in the opening decades of the sixteenth century.

In 1504, the noted Portuguese poet and goldsmith, Gil Vicente, fashioned a splendid piece of religious art which is now considered a classic artifact in the Gothic-Manueline style. This was the celebrated Monstrance of Belém wrought from gold brought to Lisbon in 1502 by Vasco da Gama after his second triumphant voyage of discovery to India.(1) The golden tribute from the Sheik of Kilwa gave Portugal a glimpse of an African eldorado – greater perhaps than Elmina on the west coast of Africa – for Vasco da Gama had word that the precious Kilwa gold came from mines in the African interior beyond Sofala in the *lands of Zanj* – the lands of the blacks.

From the east African coastal entrepôts of Malindi, Mombasa, Zanzibar, Kilwa and Mozambique the trail led down through a series of small island settlements to Angoche and Sofala where traders struck inland on annual caravans in search of gold and ivory in exchange for cloth and beads. For the Portuguese, the discovery of the golden hoard at Kilwa was the beginning of a journey of exploration and exploitation which lasted nearly 150 years before ending in ignominy in the late 1690s.

The coming of the Portuguese to the east coast of Mozambique in 1497-98 appears to be contemporaneous with the gradual dispersal of the Great Zimbabwe society across the highveld of Zimbabwe which was completed by the sixteenth century leaving only a residual population in possession of the old city. Radio-carbon evidence has demonstrated that the process of demographic expansion of this culture preceded its collapse by at least two centuries.

The uplands of Zimbabwe were the domain of several chiefdoms; those of the Manyika, the Mocaranga and the Abatua. These States warred with each other but for most of the Portuguese period (1500-1698) the Mutapa or Monomotapa exercised only nominal suzerainty over parts of Manyika and Mocaranga. Certainly, the Mutapas had no claim to Abatua, a much wealthier and more powerful society in the west. These lands, extending no further west than the Munyati river, became known to the Portuguese as the Rivers (2), an apt description indeed.

From the central watershed of the Zimbabwean highveld the major river systems drain north, south and east. Many of these rivers with their auriferous sands, the Mutari, Revue and Ruenya of Manicaland; the Mazowe, Nyadiri, Manyame and Angwa of Mashonaland; were panned by Africans for alluvial gold hundreds of years before the arrival of the Portuguese. The Portuguese reached these lands by trekking along winding bush paths and discovered the highlands of Manicaland and Mashonaland where the open woodland savanna with its plentiful game and permanent water provided a welcome relief from the oppressive climate of the lowveld.

The first Portuguese were hospitably received in accordance with traditional African custom. The Lusitanians soon learned that Muslim-Swahili traders regularly attended *bazaars* or trading fairs where gold and ivory were exchanged for beads and cloth of Indian manufacture (3). Brightly coloured glass beads and cotton textiles were in demand in the African Iron Age society. Chiefs and headmen received these foreign visitors and concluded business in the time-honoured way, involving considerable and protracted discussion, haggling and final agreement.

It was into this region – the Rivers of Gold – that these adventurous Europeans, the *Muzungos* (4) came in the early sixteenth century. In so doing they connected with a long established pattern of trade which linked this gold-producing region of Zimbabwe with a string of semi-autonomous Swahili settlements along the east coast of Africa, the Gulf entrepôts of Muscat and Ormuz and the Indian provinces of Gujerat, Malabar and Coromandel — a veri-

table triangle of trade. Yet within 150 years these *Muzungos* wrought social and political havoc by over exploitation of resources, demographic upheavals and political manipulation. The story of the Portuguese in the Rivers of Gold is at once fascinating and intriguing and is deserving of a wider audience than that of scholars and historians alone.

Our journey into the Rivers begins with the excitement at the Portuguese court caused by the return of Vasco da Gama and his treasures from Africa. Clearly, Sofala was a flourising yet unhealthy settlement in 1501 when Pedro Álvares Cabral sent Sancho de Toar to bring greetings to the resident Swahili Sheik. The Portuguese emissary presented the Swahili leader with gifts of trinkets, mirrors and glass beads which evidently delighted the people of Sofala. In exchange he received a string of gold beads worth one thousand *Cruzados* confirming the golden promise of the interior (5).

In 1505, King Manoel ordered the construction of the fortress of São Caetano on the site of the old Swahili settlement at Sofala and on 21 September the same year Pêro de Anhaia who, once he had successfully crushed Swahili resistance, started work (6). In late 1505 a Portuguese expedition ventured up the Buzi river making contact with the African people but the elusive gold was slow in coming, and not before May 1506 did an emissary of the Mutapa finally reach Sofala (7).

3

Pêro de Anhaia soon fell victim to the terrible climate of the steamy mangrove swamps and succumbed to fever. He was replaced by Manuel Fernandes, the Sofala Factor, who continued the thankless task of building the fortifications and developing trade with the Africans. The arrival in the same year of two ships with reinforcements and supplies boosted flagging morale and helped the Portuguese to complete part of the original fort using blocks of stone carried from Lisbon as ballast in the Naus and Caravels. The work was never completed and when Portuguese authority transferred to the more strategic coral island of Mozambique it was constantly neglected. By the beginning of the twentieth century most of the old fort had disappeared and the final blow to Sofala came when the stone was broken up and transported in barges to construct public buildings in the modern port city of Beira on the Pungwe estuary.

The Portuguese suffered in the disease-ridden and pestilential climate which surrounds Sofala. They also had to contend with another Swahili rising but this was suppressed and ended with the death in September 1506 of the old Sheik Yusuf and his replacement by a more compliant vassal named Sulliman. The passing of old Yusuf brought to an end the Muslim rule over Sofala dating back to the tenth century when Omani seafarers travelled as far south as *Sofalah* at the extremity of the lands of Zanj. The Baghdad-born Arab traveller, Al Mas'udi, sailed these waters in 926 and has provided us with a fascinating second-hand account of the people of Sofala, their use of iron and their trade in gold and ivory which was much sought after in China for gaming pieces and dagger handles. (8)

King Manuel appointed António de Saldanha as Captain of Mozambique and Sofala in 1507 and on 26 August, 1509 he arrived at Mozambique to take up the appointment. (9) In 1510 Saldanha sailed to Sofala where he learned that the gold trade had fallen considerably, due, according to the official explanation of the Portuguese at Sofala, to the activities of the Swahili at Angoche Island north of the Zambezi delta and to interior wars. (10).

In reality, rampant misappropriation by the Portuguese officials, gross over-estimates and the inability to make contact with the interior were to blame. Certainly, the Swahili, having been denied access to the Sofala route had instead relied on the Zambezi and

Save river routes. Neither did the Portuguese have the right assortment of trade goods – the Africans were conditioned to the Cambaya Indian beads and Gujerati textiles, *Bertangil vermelho*, red coloured cotton cloth made in Surat and Cambay and exported to Africa mainly via the port of Diu and Damão, and were not particularly interested in the Portuguese mix of European trinkets like brass pisspots and mirrors. Another factor which mitigated in favour of the Swahili was their innate understanding of African custom and social mores —the Swahili had intermarried in coastal communities and spoke vernacular languages fluently. (11) Saldanha was faced with a formidable task indeed — how was he to achieve success in the face of Swahili dominance of the gold trade.

In July 1511 the Portuguese Captain decided that might would prevail and he sailed on Angoche island north of the Zambezi delta. Attacking the Swahili settlement he took prisoners who revealed, under torture, information about the *Cuama* or Zambezi river route to the interior and the Rivers of Gold. (12) Saldanha learned how the Swahili living on Angoche regularly travelled up the Zambezi via Quelimane. They travelled in dugout canoes along river systems until they reached the main stream of the river where they hoisted sail, navigating the river as far as Sena. Here in later years, the Portuguese built the fortress of São Marçal. From Sena, the river is still navigable as far as Tambara where rapids necessitate an overland journey until the river is again passable to Massangano and Tete. Traders then followed inland paths along the Ruenya and the Mazowe to the highlands. Other traders struck south-west to Manica.

This was important intelligence and Saldanha immediately instructed a *degredado* named António Fernandes to make a journey overland from Sofala to the gold mining regions of the interior. From written records discovered by Professor Eric Axelson in 1939 in the National Archives of Lisbon we have a graphic account of two journeys by Fernandes in 1511 and again in 1513-14. Fernandes was certainly illiterate, so his experiences were subsequently committed to parchment by the person whose name appears on the manuscript, Gaspar Veloso. (13) Fernandes travelled with African companions who introduced him to the local customs and etiquette.

He must have learned something of the local languages, been

possessed of an iron hard constitution and had great tenacity of spirit to survive the rigours of such an epic journey. Fernandes journeyed to the eastern districts of Zimbabwe visiting many of the gold-producing regions of Manicaland and Mashonaland provinces before returning from his first expedition with a retinue of Africans who brought one hundred *mithqals* of gold as tribute and nine hundred for trade. On his second and much longer trip, Fernandes visited Manicaland, Mashonaland and then ventured further west into the lands of Abatua and through many of the highveld gold – bearing regions before returning to Sofala. Fernandes achieved this incredible success yet he was soon forgotten and there is no record of what became of him; yet for the Portuguese the significance of António Fernandes was considerable. He had discovered the route to the gold-producing regions, determined the potential for trade in gold and ivory and brought stories of the healthier plateau which compared favourably with the climate of Portugal. The winter months were said to last from mid-May until the end of August when the bush would flower and become green with the arrival of spring in September and October. (14) This description corresponds exactly to the seasonal rhythm of Zimbabwe today.

When travelling by foot the practice was to march during the cool hours of morning until noon when the party would halt and spend the afternoon preparing food and collecting thorn scrub to secure the camp perimeters from wild animals at night. Certainly Fernandes and subsequent Portuguese adventurers would quickly have followed local dietary traditions, based on stiff porridge or *sadza* made from ground and boiled millet, sorghum and other grains as the staple food. This would be supplemented by vegetables, game or beef, wild fruits from the bush, honey and fermented beer.

Fernandes is likely to have been received in the manner described in 1620 by Father Júlio Cesar who visited the Mutapa's *Zimbabwe* encampment. (15) As Fernandes entered a new area he would have visited the local chief to *hombera* or pay his respects, exchange gifts and receive the traditional hospitality. Often the chief would instruct his *svikiro* or spirit medium to consult ancestral spirits for their advice before Fernandes was free to continue his journey through tribal lands. By faithfully following this established custom, Fernandes was made welcome throughout his travels but in the years ahead Portuguese failure to abide by these rules was to cost them dear.

By October 1512 Simão Miranda de Azevedo had succeeded Saldanha as Captain of Mozambique and Sofala (16), and he made effective use of the Antonio Fernandes reports by deciding that the Zambezi river route offered the most promise. In 1513, the Captain learned from the Sofala Factor, Pedro Vaz Soares, that profits from the gold trade hardly covered expenses. Control of the gold trade had not yet been wrested from the Swahili who continued to dominate this important commerce. As Sofala languished in its steamy tropical miasma the Swahili settlements at Angoche prospered and ocean-borne trade from Mogadishu, Lamu, Malindi and Mombasa continued. Realising this, Miranda de Azevedo built a small trading post on the Luabo channel near Quelimane and started trading in opposition to the Angoche Swahili. (17) Swahili-Portuguese competition for the gold trade with the interior continued but around 1600 the Muslim traders were concentrating on the southern Sabi river route to the interior. By taking the back door into the Rivers they were able to continue their lucrative trade with the southern Torwa – the forerunners of the Rozvi – of Abatua.

An intriguing feature of the Sabi-Swahili hypothesis is the existence of isolated African communities in the Gutu and Chinyika districts who, in 1961, were discovered to practice male circumcision, eschew the flesh of swine and have decidedly Muslim family names (18) These people are ethnic *Varemba* who live in scattered communities all the way from the upper Save to Venda in the northern Transvaal province of South Africa. The *Varemba* are probably seventeenth century descendents of Islamicised Shona and therefore not clearly linked with the much earlier Swahili trade on the Sabi. There is some conjecture that the Save river water levels were much higher in the sixteenth and seventeenth centuries making navigation by shallow-bottomed craft possible for considerable distances inland. This conjecture is supported by unconfirmed reports of steel pegs or rings fastened into rocks along the Save.

Under Miranda de Azevedo's direction the fortunes of Sofala improved and in 1513-14 Pedro Vaz de Soares purchased 25 029 *mithqals* of gold and 25 000 kilos of ivory. This success was

7

achieved largely because of Miranda de Azevedo's policy of honesty and adherence to local custom in paying tribute to the Chiefs in whose lands his men traded. He boosted the export of gold from Sofala and Mozambique to India by 20 000 *Mithqals* in 1514. (19) This brief period of economic revival at Sofala came to an end when Miranda de Azevedo died in September 1515 at Sofala.

His successor, Cristovão de Tavora was largely instrumental in making repairs to the fortresses of São Caetano and São Sebastião on Mozambique Island. He also sent an ambassador to the Mutapa at Nembire, near the north eastern Mvuradona mountains, and this resulted in further improvements in relations, trade and travel. However in 1519 the fortunes of Sofala declined again because of the interventions of an African chief named Inhamunda of Manyika who blocked communications between the coast and the plateau lands of the Mutapa. Some historians suggest that Inhamunda was an early Teve ruler and others that he was a Danda chieftain. Attempts to placate Inhamunda were unsuccessful and he responded to Portuguese entreaties by executing messengers and keeping any tribute. Inhamhunda effectively blockaded Sofala until the early 1540s when internecine wars between him and the Mutapa ended. (20)

Vicente Pegado was appointed Captain of Sofala in 1530 and because of the rampant private trade and smuggling he was forced to embargo all such commerce by Crown employees. Pegado requisitioned bolts of cloth from the *Vedor da Fazenda* or Royal Treasury in Portuguese India specifically for the Rivers trade but because of a cash shortage he was forced to pay his officials in kind rather than coin and this unwittingly stimulated unofficial trade.

In 1531 Pegado complained to the Viceroy about the non- arrival of trade goods and also the habit of passing Indiamen of dumping *degredados* or transported criminals at Sofala, as this human flotsam did little to improve the quality of society in this unhealthy Portuguese outpost. (21)

In 1540 João de Sepulveda was appointed Captain of Sofala and in 1541 during an expedition against the Turks he captured two foists off Malindi. (22) Sepulveda made effective use of these vessels for annual trading expeditions along the coast. Returning to Sofala in 1542 after a foray against the Turks off Mogadishu the previous year, Sepulveda received an ambassador from the Mutapa who offered friendship explaining that the wars which had disrupted trade in 1519 were now over. The Mutapa invited the Portuguese to send their own representative to his lands and establish trade. For this mission, Sepulveda chose Fernão de Proença who was a clerk at Sofala and despatched him to the Mutapa with gifts and instructions to establish trading relations. (23) This initiative came at a most opportune time for the gold trade at Sofala had dwindled and the only worthwhile commodity was ivory.

Alongside these official Crown expeditions into the lands of the Mutapa were numerous private or unofficial excursions by Portuguese deserters, *degredados* and traders. Many of these men intermarried and were absorbed by the African communities. The progeny of this miscegenation were known as *mwanamuzungo* (24) by the Shona speaking people and literally meant Son of the Portuguese. Lusitanian libido and the sexual behaviour of the Portuguese in the tropics, particularly in Goa was well documented by the Dutch traveller J H Van Linschoten who visited between 1580 and 1590 and the Englishman Peter Mundy in 1637. There is no reason to assume otherwise in the case of the Rivers (25). António Pinto de Miranda's graphic 1766 description of the *Senhores* and *Donas* of the Zambezi *prazos* leave little to the imagination. The self-indulgent and indolent lifestyle was characterised by entertaining and gambling. Miranda says that:

> apart from their own wives, they use other women. They have in their households a hundred and more slaves and, having had affairs with some of them or dying leave them still captive. They (the women) have 40 or 50 man slaves with whom they amuse themselves by dancing rather improperly and unclothed.

These *mwanamuzungo* spoke the vernacular, understood local custom, and whilst retaining the ability, in some cases to speak Portuguese, were able to interact between both worlds.

In 1551 João de Barros, eminent Portuguese chronicler of the sixteenth century wrote in his *Decadas* of alluvial gold in the Ruenya, Nyadiri, Mazowe and Manyame rivers thereby evidencing the extent of Portuguese knowledge of the interior. De Barros also mentioned the *Symbaoe* or Zimbabwe of the Mutapa, relying upon the information of those who had visited the Rivers. It is possible that António Fernandes may have visited the stone-walled *Zimbabwe* of the Mutapa known as *Rusvingo waKasekete* near the Kadzi river in the Dande region of north–eastern Zimbabwe or a number of other similar stone structures on the highveld but there is unfortunately no definite evidence that he did.

Inextricably linked with the quest for gold and ivory was the Catholic mission in search of souls. The crusading zeal to bring Christianity to the heathen was as vigorously pursued in Africa as it was in Asia and the Americas. The Jesuits and the Dominicans, many of whom were over-zealous and impetuous, played an important role in the spread of Lusitanian influence in the Rivers. Some priests, certainly not all, were educated and lettered men of distinction and frequently had considerable influence befitting this six-teenth century estate. They kept written records noting details of African custom and chronicled the experiences of their lay contemporaries.

Some outstanding literary works, notably *Ethiopia Oriental* (26) of João dos Santos, have become classics but others are nothing more than pure panegyrics or gross exaggeration based on rumour. Dos Santos wrote faithfully in the style of Fernão Lopes (27) whilst others opted for the style of Gomes Eannes da Zurara and his Guinea Chronicles (28) singing the praises of his royal patron at Sagres.

One of the first Portuguese to bring Christianity to the Zambezi was a fanatical Jesuit, Father Gonçalvo da Silveira who baptised the ruling Mutapa giving him the christian name of Sebastião. Silveira was then living at the Mutapa's royal kraal close to the Msengezi river in the Dande district below the Mvuradona Mountains of north–eastern Mashonaland. The stone wall enclosures still to be found near the Kadzi river may be associated with the Mutapa although there is no decided confirmation of this supposition. It may well be that the Mutapa was living at Zvongombwe and similar sites in the Centenary District immediately above the Zambezi valley floor and still in relatively close proximity to the upper reaches of the Msengezi river.

Whether the Mutapa's conversion to Christianity was ever taken seriously by the African ruler we cannot be certain but for the

Swahili rivals in the gold trade the presence of the Infidel priest posed a serious threat. It has been speculated that the Muslims made it known to the *n'angas* and *svikiros* who attended the Mutapa that the Portuguese priest was practising evil, that he was a *muroyi* or wizard. Silveira was also accused of being a Teve spy but as the historian David Beach points out in his definitive Shona history, Francisco Barreto had been talking of an invasion into the Mutapa's lands, and the unfortunate Silveira may have suffered the consequences.

Portuguese documentary accounts of the circumstances leading to the Priest's death are likely to have been clouded by religious and commercial bias at the very least. The *hakata* or divining tablets were cast and Silveira's fate was sealed - certainly the *n'angas* who advised the Mutapa would also have had reason to mistrust the Portuguese and his strange religious influence over their Lord. (29) On the night of 15 March 1561, the Mutapa ordered that the priest be killed and his body cast into the crocodile-infested Msengezi river.

The hapless Silveira achieved more in death than in life for his execution was seen as martyrdom by the Portuguese authorities and as a direct challenge to the Crown. In 1569 King Sebastião (1557-1578), the inexperienced boy King, whose conquest ambitions of the 1560s were the direct cause of his death on the sands of Alcácer-Quibir in 1578, named Francisco Barreto as *Capitão-mor* or Captain-General of a punitive expedition to avenge the killing of the cleric. Barreto raised a large body of idealists who were fired by exaggerated stories of gold and glory in the lands of Monomotapa and Prester John, the mythological Christian king of Ethiopia. Some 600 men joined the Barreto force which sailed from the Tagus in April 1569 bound for Mozambique. (30) Barreto left Lisbon armed with a royal capitulation granted by King Sebastião appointing him as Governor of Sofala and Mozambique and as Lord of the Monomotapa.

The outward passage to Mozambique took its normal toll and the depleted adventurers finally arrived at Mozambique in May 1570. On 4 November 1571 the Barreto campaigners left Mozambique for the Zambezi delta (31) where the expeditionary forces transferred to smaller river craft or canoes which took them to Sena.

The decision to follow the pestilential fever-plagued Zambezi route was forced upon Barreto by the strong-willed priest, Father Francisco de Monclaro, (32) who invoked the name of God in his argument against Barreto's more sensible choice of the overland route from Sofala. The interference of the priest was to have catastrophic repercussions for the Portuguese and doomed the mission to failure.

Men in heavy leather or quilted cotton jerkins, on horses, camels, oxen and a large retinue of camp followers were forced to endure the appalling heat and humidity of the Zambezi lowlands around Sena in the wet season. The men, skins soaked by the tropical downpour, (33) bitten by tsetse flies (34) and mosquitoes (35) developed huge septic ulcers. Men collapsed and died from malaria and dysentery; others simply dropped in their tracks exhausted and fatigued by the oppressive heat. It was a senseless beginning to a disastrous campaign. Lacking leadership with the resolve of a Pizarro or Cortes the *conquistadores* were mired at Sena. Barreto despatched a trader named Miguel Bernardes (36) to the Mutapa requesting him to send an ambassador for talks. Whilst he was away, the unhealthy conditions in the garrison continued to decimate Barreto's men (37) and many of the horses died of trypanosomiasis.

Endeavouring to raise the morale of his men, Barreto ordered an attack on a Swahili settlement near Sena but this little *divertissement* proved temporary and before long Barreto was engaged in a series of inconclusive skirmishes with the forces of an African chief named Samungazi. (38) These forces of the Samungazi were to bear the brunt of the fighting against the Barreto invaders during the dry season of July-September 1572. In a major engagement between the Tonga and the Portuguese, Samungazi is credited with the use of the classic half-moon infantry formation against the Europeans. (39) By employing this strategy, Samungazi nearly succeeded in breaking through Portuguese lines on this and other occasions. Only sustained volley fire from the *Arquebusiers* was able to halt the Tonga. This and the judicious use of sharp-shooters to pick off *n'angas* who exhorted and encouraged Tonga warriors by spreading *muti* or magic, reputed to turn the *Muzungos* blind and make the Tonga impervious to bullets, finally blunted the African leader's numerical advantage. (40)

The Portuguese were unable to press any advantage and abandoned their march towards the highland stronghold of the Mutapa. From their manoeuvres against the Tonga they returned dispirited to Sena where yet another emissary, Francisco de Magalhães, was sent to parley with the Mutapa (41). In the interim, Barreto left for Mozambique on 4 December, 1572 leaving Vasco Fernandes Homem in command of the garrison. Barreto returned to Sena early the following year but died in May, a broken man. Homem took command of the tattered remnants of the Barreto expedition and withdrew to Mozambique to refit. In 1574 Homem's forces embarked for Sofala. (42)

The Homem initiative was not more successful in military terms. The journey started from Sofala and made its way along the Buzi to Manicaland and the Chimoio plateau. As with Barreto before, Homen encountered stiff opposition from the forces of a Mutapan ally named Sachiteve. Homem managed to fight his way through Sachiteve's lands before reaching Manica where he was welcomed by the Chikanga. Whilst in Manicaland, a mining surveyor named Agostinho Sotomayor, was able to inspect several rivers where alluvial gold panning was taking place — possibly the Revue and the Mutare. (43)

This expert determined that a considerable investment in men and machinery would be necessary to develop mines if significant gold recovery was to be realised. The Portuguese were more than a little disappointed at this bleak prognosis for they could see for themselves that recovery of gold involved back-breaking, slow and laborious effort—there were no legendary gold mines and no quick eldorado.

News that the Mutapa was mustering a large army against the Portuguese decided Homem to quit Manicaland and head for Tete by way of Sofala and the Zambezi with the objective of investigating the alleged existence of silver mines near Chicoa on the banks of the Zambezi. (44) Homem delegated the search for these mines to António Cardoso de Almeida plus some two hundred men. This expedition also proved a failure as the cunning residents of Chicoa lured the Portuguese into a fatal trap killing many of their number. (45) Only a little silver was ever found and this had apparently been planted in salted mines to confuse the *Muzungos* and by 13 March

1577 the combined Barreto-Homem expedition against the Mutapa was abandoned. But for the Mutapa who had so cleverly manipulated his allies and used them as cannon fodder for the Portuguese guns this was to prove a phyrric victory. The Mutapa had indeed won the battle but he was to lose the war as hordes of greedy and ruthless adventurers started to invade his ancestral lands of eastern Mashonaland.

The Barreto-Homem expeditions facilitated the influx of hardened profit seekers, the lands of the Mutapa were brought into sharper focus as the lure of golden riches gained fame throughout the Portuguese world. Before and after the campaigns of the 1570s many Portuguese traders had established themselves at Sofala, Sena and Tete and were making personal visits to the gold-producing regions of Manicaland and Mashonaland or sending their agents, the *vashambadzi*. The Mutapa must have recognised the inevitable and the *Muzungos* were soon able to travel and trade freely, provided the customary tributes were paid.

The flourishing trade that quickly developed was based on the age-old commodities of Indian beads and cloth for gold and ivory. Many of the old trading places were designated by official *regimento* as *feiras* and captains were appointed to protect Crown interests, liaise with local African chiefs and to levy a tax on all Portuguese traders. Masapa, which was known to the Swahili as *Aufur* (possibly a corruption of Fura which is the name of an imposing mountain feature which overlooks a gold-producing area near Mount Darwin village) was perhaps the earliest and most important Portuguese settlement. The three principal *feiras* were Luanze, Bocuto and Masapa (46) and although the date of the official regimento establishing these settlements is not known with certainty it would have been no later than 1574 by which time the *feiras* were being recorded in contemporary Portuguese reports. (47)

In 1583, Nuno Velho Pereira became captain of Mozambique and set forth on a journey up the Zambezi to interview traders about gold, silver, copper and ivory. (48) Between 1580 and 1590 Father João dos Santos visited Sena and Tete where he noted, amongst many other things, that traders headed westwards to the *feiras* of Luanze, Mazowe and Masapa. He observed that the Captain of Masapa was responsible for the collection of a levy from Portuguese traders of one bolt of cloth in twenty. Each new appointment to Masapa was obliged to pay the Mutapa a tribute or *Kuruva* (known in Portuguese as Curva) valued at 3000 *Cruzados* in cloth and beads .(49) In return the Mutapa granted freedom of travel and trade. Priests learned the vernacular languages and built churches near the *feiras*. (50) Independent traders and merchants entered the Mutapa's lands; some certainly took African concubines and fathered children, the *mwanamuzungo*. The extent of Portuguese knowledge of the highveld was broadened as merchants ranged further inland in search of gold and ivory. The geography of the region was well mapped.

A series of charts showing the Rivers of the Cuama was published in 1630 in Pedro Barreto de Resende's *Livro do Estado da India Oriental*. The maps illustrate the position of Luanze, Masapa, Dambarare and Matafuna *feiras*. In a 1677 map by João Teixeira Albernaz II the more archaic name for the Zambezi river has been dropped. The maps also show the fairly accurate location of the Mazowe, Ruenya, Ruia, Nyadiri and their various tributary streams. Luanze, Mount Fura, Masapa and Matafuna are all marked. In one of a series of seventy maps published by João Nunes Tinoco of 1663 it is possible to plot the location of Luanze, Masapa and Dambarare as *feiras dos mercadores de ouro*. Evidently Matafuna was a rich source of gold for it appears prominently on most maps of the seventeenth century.

In an eighteenth century map by the French cartographer Rigobert Bonne (1729-95) of the east coast of Africa it is possible to define the position of Luanze, Massapa, the *Mocaras* or Mkaradzi river, Dambarari and the Angwa *feiras*. The famed map maker was obviously relying on Portuguese sources for much of this topographical intelligence.

By the end of the sixteenth century the Portuguese were firmly entrenched at *feiras* in Manicaland and Mashonaland. It was to be the Mutapa's fate to see his lands occupied by the foreigners. Although he had halted the Portuguese he was now to witness the relentless annexation of his ancestral lands by the forces of foreign commerce. By 1596 this Mutapa, whose name is not known for certain, was replaced by Gatsi Rusere, an erstwhile senior commander of the Mutapa's forces and a veteran of the campaigns

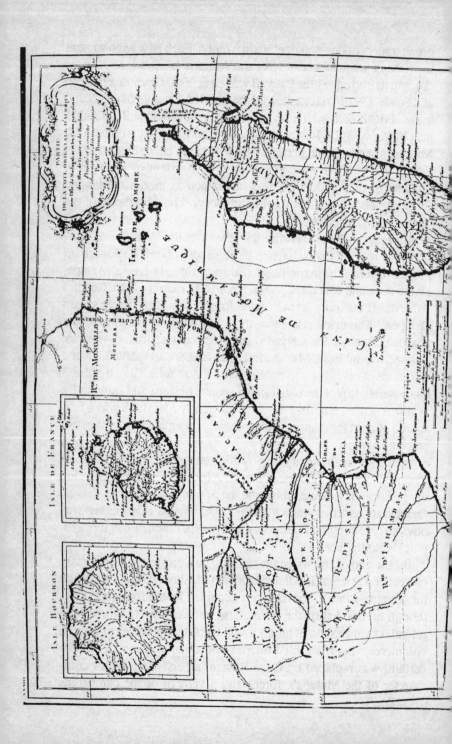

against the Portuguese. The exact date of succession is not certain but 1589 is the earliest date.(51)

The Portuguese recognised an opportunity to expand their sphere of influence with the new Mutapa Gatsi Rusere when, in 1607, they assisted him to quell a challenge to his authority from the lower Mazowe valley region. (52) In the *quid pro quo* for this favour done, the *prazeiro* Diogo Simões Madeira whose military muscle had been employed on the Mutapa's behalf, received rights to directly mine for gold. This important title set the stage for significant Portuguese expansion in the early seventeenth century. The Notarial Deed describing the formal granting of the rights to mine gold, copper, iron, lead and tin was documented by António Bocarro in his *Decadas* where he relates that the colourful event included a parade along the banks of the Mazowe river on 1 August, 1607.

The Mutapa also acquiesced to Dominican requests to build churches and freely proselytise. It would appear that Gatsi Rusere was particularly grateful to Madeira for he entrusted him with the education of two of his sons. (53) The eldest boy was baptised Filipe by Father Jerónimo Baptista and the youngest son was given the christian name of Diogo by Father Francisco do Avelar. (54) Filipe was educated in European ways and later presented to his father by Madeira. Gatsi Rusere was, by all accounts, unhappy at the transformation and the conversion of his son into a black Portuguese. He ordered Filipe to remove his silken robes and attire himself according to African custom. (55) Unfortunately, the Portuguese credo had been deeply inculcated into Filipe and he was reluctant to change his lifestyle and fled from his father's camp.

In 1615, Filipe was reported to be assisting the Portuguese locate the Chicoa silver mines. (56) The Portuguese were obsessed by a new *Potosi* in Africa and their search for silver is well documented in contemporary records. For Filipe, it was as if he had repudiated his people but clearly he was a pawn in the hands of the Portuguese. Meanwhile, Gatsi Rusere's youngest son, Diogo, had been sent to Goa where he was acclaimed a good Christian and fluent in the Portuguese language but there is no record of his ever returning to Africa. (57)

Only a few Africans were sent for such specialised purposes and the vast majority of Africans who embarked from Mozambique did so as slaves. In 1608 a royal decree was promulgated forbidding the embarkation of slaves from Mozambique to Goa where the Africans were much in demand as household servants. (58) The edict ordered that slaves could only be used for galley service because of the disruptive influence they had on Goan society. Despite this command, many Africans were transported to Goa and some to Macau as slaves although the traffic did not reach such epic proportions as it did in the trans-Atlantic trade. This early trade cannot be compared with the much larger scale embarkations of African slaves for the Indian Ocean islands in the eighteenth century. Many anonymous slaves were to achieve considerable renown in the military service of Portugal. Particularly noteworthy is the case of Africans who distinguished themselves during the defence of Macau in 1622 when a major Dutch assault was repelled largely due to the efforts of African slaves. (59) In 1561, the Governor of Macau specifically requested *reinois* (European born Portuguese) and Negro slaves and not *mesticinhos* or, literally, "weakling Eurasians," to reinforce the Portuguese enclave in China. (60) In Goa too, African slaves were much in evidence as Ladies of important households flaunted power and position with ostentatious retinues of household slaves and servants, many of whom were Africans. (61)

Portuguese manipulation of Gatsi Rusere's son Filipe greatly angered the Mutapa and inevitably contributed towards a decline in Mutapa-Portuguese diplomacy. Portuguese fortunes worsened during the tenancy of Estevão de Ataíde, who as General of the Mines of Monomotapa, failed to pay the *Curva* when it was due in 1610 — the year in which he took up his position in Mozambique. Ataíde later despatched a trader named Diogo Carvalho to the Mutapa to question him about silver mines and pledge his intention of paying the tribute. (62)

Whilst he was staying at Masapa, Carvalho built a stockade large enough to garrison fifty people. Foolishly Carvalho embroiled himself in a local conspiracy against Gatsi Rusere which resulted in the death of some of the Mutapa's men. This rank stupidity on Carvalho's part was to have serious implications for the Portuguese as the Mutapa declared an *empata* or open hostilities against the Portuguese who were now forced to retreat from the *feiras* and withdraw to the safety of Tete. (63)

Estevão de Ataíde was recalled to Mozambique Island in July 1613 where he received a written admonishment accusing him of dereliction of duty and incompetence. In September that year he died in disgrace. (64) Diogo Simões Madeira was immediately nominated his successor (65) and in 1615 he sent news to Lisbon via India by hand of Francisco de Avelar (66) that silver had been found along the Msengezi river. The evidence for this report is not known and was probably based on rumours alone. In March, the same year, Gatsi Rusere sent a force of several thousand men to attack the Portuguese who came in search of the reported silver but it was repulsed by superior firepower. (67)

Madeira quickly proposed the reinforcement of the *feiras*, the construction of forts at Manica, Quiteve and Barue (on the route from Sena to Manica) and that a peace treaty should be concluded with the Mutapa. Madeira's reports were communicated to Lisbon and Goa but in the interim a general lull settled over the Mutapa's lands. Gatsi Rusere was aging and there was a contemporary account concerning his use of the narcotic (68) *mbanje (Cannabis sativa)* which may have hastened his end. Gatsi Rusere was succeeded by his son Nyambu Kapariridze (1623-29) around 1623. Portuguese documents record this Mutapa's name as *Inhambo Caprasine*. (69)

Crown action in support of Madeira's recommendations came in 1617 with the appointment of Nuno Álvares Pereira as Governor and Conquistador of the Rivers and the Lands of Monomotapa. (70) A grand title indeed for a man who was to prove himself worse than his predecessor. Pereira arrived in Tete in July 1619 after recruiting men in India to assist with Portuguese administration of the Rivers. Pereira did not pay the customary dues to the Mutapa and it was only in 1628 when he returned to the Rivers that he made arrangements to pay the required *Curva* to the Mutapa. His captaincy was characterised by mismanagement and weakness and Portuguese traders roamed the Mutapa's lands without administrative controls.(71)

When Pereira finally made an effort to pay the *curva*, possibly written as *kuruva* in Shona orthography, he sent his representative Jerónimo de Barros to placate the Mutapa and pay the *curva* or customary tax. (72) De Barros arrived at Masapa where he met captain André Fernandes who joined him in his mission to the Mutapa's *dare* or court on 17 November 1628. When the Portuguese emissaries arrived, the Mutapa was in no mood for pleasantries and he summoned de Barros to the royal enclosure where the luckless Portuguese was hacked to death.

André Fernandes must have learned of what had transpired and he fled into the night. A seasonal thunderstorm enabled him to make good his escape and reach the safety of the Masapa stockade. (73) It is not known why Kapariridze ordered this killing which would have inevitable repercussions in terms of Portuguese response but he may well have acted as he did in the belief that the Portuguese were conspiring to replace him with his uncle Mavhura. (74) He had decided to take the initiative and confront the Portuguese thereby asserting his authority.

At the stockade, Fernandes mobilized the defence and for seven days successfully withstood the Mutapa's forces. The surrounding countryside was plunged into turmoil and the Portuguese abandoned the *feiras* for Tete once again. The Mutapa declared his *empata* or *mupeto* and a state of general hostility came into existence. (75) News of the chaos in the Rivers reached the Portuguese Viceroy in India and ultimately Lisbon and by royal decree Nuno Álvares Pereira was suspended in 1631, his family connections notwithstanding, and in the same year he died. (76) In an effort to restore Portuguese authority, Diogo de Sousa de Meneses coordinated two military campaigns against the belligerent Mutapa. In the second and final battle near the Feira of Luanze in May 1629, a significant element of the Mutapa's forces switched allegiance and supported the rival Mutapa, Mavhura.

The Portuguese forces were also bolstered by African troops recruited from outside this theatre of conflict. (77) By June 1632, Nyambu Kapararidze had been driven into exile north of the Zambezi river where he continued to pose a threat to Portuguese designs.

During the wars against Nyambu Kapararidze, one of his sons was captured by the Portuguese and baptised as Miguel. The young Miguel was placed in the care of the incompetent *fidalgo*, Nuno Alvares Pereira, who sent him to Goa in the personal custody of the newly appointed Viceroy, Dom Miguel de Noronha, the Count of Linhares, who was then wintering at Mozambique in 1629 whilst en- route for India. Miguel, son of the Mutapa, was educated at royal expense and later ordained as a Dominican priest and in 1664-65 was reported to be at the convent of Santa Barbara of Mercy at Chimbel, Goa. Miguel died at Goa but not before achieving the diploma of Master of Theology in 1670. He lived out his final years as the parish priest of Santa Barbara.(78)

Whatever scheme the Portuguese might have been considering for Miguel to succeed his father, it was never realised as the Dominicans had been carefully cultivating the old Mutapa's uncle Mavhura (1629-52), baptised Filipe .(79) When the Portuguese installed him as their vassal king they secured unfettered access to all his lands. No longer obliged to pay the *Curva* or be accountable under African customary law for their transgressions, increasing numbers of Portuguese entered the lands in search of gold. Portuguese authority was vested in the Captain of the Gates resident at the *feira* of Masapa which was considered as the administrative entrance to the Mutapa's lands. (80)

In reality the Captain of the Gates exercised little or no jurisdiction over the traders who wielded enormous power and marched at the head of large armed parties searching for gold and ivory. These *prazeiros* or prazo-holders won their concessions either directly from the Portuguese Crown (although not many interior concessions were granted by the Crown in the seventeenth century) or by private treaty with the Mutapa or local sub-chiefs. Other *Muzungos* seized large tracts of countryside by sheer force of arms. So great was the impact of the prazo-holders that the term *prazo* has arguably been borrowed into Shona with the modern day phonetic equivalent being *purazi* meaning a farm or lands. (This derivation is not certain for the term may stem from the Ndebele *amaplazi* and the Afrikaans *plaas* meaning farm).

António Gomes SJ, in a report of 2 January 1648 written at Salcete, Goa, reported a Chinese *prazeiro* leading a force of 4000 men and an African *prazeiro* named António Camello described as a brave captain under whose standard many Portuguese were proud to fight. A mixed band of adventurers indeed.

For most of Mavhura's reign he was surrounded by his Dominican mentors and acolytes. Chief amongst them were Fathers Manuel Sardinha and Luis de Espirito Santo who brought the fortunes of their church to greater heights than ever before (81). The years between 1629-1652 bore witness to a phenomenal rise in the numbers of Portuguese who came to Zimbabwe in search of gold. It is extremely difficult to assess exact numbers because their impact was considerably enhanced by attendant forces of African recruits assembled through the *prazo* system, a unique institution created by the Portuguese in the seventeenth century. (82)

The terms of the system, which provided Crown grants of land to white Portuguese women on the express condition that these women married only white Portuguese, was probably formalised much later. Continued title to the *prazo* could only pass to female offspring on the understanding that they in turn wed white Portuguese. Marriage to a mulatto, failure to reside upon the estate or neglect would result in forfeiture of the *prazo*. In reality, hardly any of these conditions were observed and the female heiresses usually married mulattoes and over the years a class of coloured *prazeiros* emerged in the Zambezia, Tete and Manica provinces of Mozambique. Some of these *prazeiros* laid claims to vast tracts of land above the eastern escarpment of Zimbabwe in addition to their own lands in Mozambique. The *prazo* system appears to have become formalised in the late seventeenth or early eighteenth century but it certainly appears to have its origins in the early or mid-seventeenth (83) when men like Sisnando Dias Bahão (whose Shona nick-name was *Mossuampaca*), a former captain of Manica, and Antonio Lobo da Silva (known in the Shona vernacular n*yembe,* meaning the insignia of a chief), exercised considerable authority in both Mozambique and Zimbabwe. (84) It was during the Mutapa Mavhura's reign that Portuguese adventurers or *prazo*-holders roamed across much of Mashonaland and parts of the Midlands provinces building fortified wooden stockades as bases for trade and private military operations. They seized cattle in raids and coerced local people into revealing the localities of the gold mines. (85)

Sisnando Dias Bahão may have been the first Portuguese to attempt an extension of Portuguese influence into the lands of Abatua which was also known to the Portuguese as *Mãe d'ouro* or Mother of Gold, beyond the Mupfuri river. The Portuguese became aware, in the 1640s, that the ruler of the Torwa enjoyed independent trade with Muslim Swahili following the Zambezi river route. Shards of Wan-li porcelains found at Kame during archaeological work substantiate this contention. Bahão was certainly involved in military operations in *Abatua* or the lands of the Torwa in western Zimbabwe but in 1644 he died at the Luanze *feira* after being poisoned by jealous rivals and Portuguese initiatives into this region ceased. (86)

In an endeavour to improve the exploration and administration of the Rivers, the Portuguese Viceroy, the Conde de Linhares appointed Pedro Álvares Pereira as Captain of the Rivers in 1633. Pereira secured this lucrative appointment soon after the Captain of Mozambique, Diogo de Sousa de Meneses, had won a decisive military victory over Mutapa Kapararidze on 24 June 1632 resulting in the restoration of trading rights and the reopening of the *feiras*. The Conde de Linhares had little time for Meneses and by dint of his powerful position at the seat of Portuguese power in Goa was able to engineer the dismissal of the Mozambique captain replacing him with his own favourite, Pedro Álvares Pereira. (87)

Pereira set about preparing a complex report recommending that the Rivers be settled by volunteers who should restrict themselves to commerce and refrain from meddling in African politics. This advice was so obviously ignored and continued involvement in local politics and Mutapan successions aggravated Luso-African relations and ultimately proved one of the major reasons for the expulsion of the Portuguese in the late seventeenth century as shall be demonstrated later.

Partly in response to Pedro Álvares Pereira's counsel but perhaps more as a measure to stimulate gold production from the Rivers, the Portuguese monarch ordered João da Costa and a Spanish mining engineer with Peruvian experience, Andres de Vides y Albarado to the Rivers in 1633. (88) After his arrival in the Rivers, Albarado, officially known as Administrator and Assayer of the Gold and Silver Mines, confirmed the existence of gold in Manicaland and Mashonaland. Albarado urged mass Portuguese immigration as the most effective strategy to exploit the mineral resources. (89)

The scheme met with the approval of the Viceroy, the Conde de Linhares, who endorsed a fanciful scheme for the settlement of a thousand married families, the posting of missionaries and the construction of a Customs House. The plans, although welcomed at court were never implemented. The waning of Portuguese influence, the threat of Dutch attack and the chronic shortage of human resources contributed to this. (90) The 1633-34 settler plan also depended upon proving the extent of gold in the Rivers and the evidence was inconclusive. The scheme may also have been deliberately sabotaged by the incoming Viceroy, Pero da Silva, who conducted his own appraisal of the Rivers. He relied on the advice of the newly appointed Captain of Mozambique, Lourenço de Sotomayor, who had no interest in sharing his monopoly with thousands of immigrants and painted a very grim picture of the Rivers, while highlighting the pathetic state of Mozambique Island and the inadequate fortifications of São Sebastião. (91)

As early as 1511 the gold trade, officially the Royal monopoly, was being grossly abused by Crown officials and in particular captains or governors who secured their appointments by royal favour or purchase from the Viceroy. These officials made fortunes from the contraband trade. Blame was habitually laid at the door of the perfidious Swahili but this was not altogether true.

Clearly, a large percentage of this golden wealth was spent in Goa (92) which at this time was known as the " Rome of the Orient" because of the richly decorated churches where gold leaf and fili-gree were conspicuously evident. Nor were the pleasures of Goa purely spiritual for the capital of Portuguese India was also famed for its fabulous and tempting assortment of goods which would fetch high prices in Portugal and finally the " Houris and Sharab " (prostitutes and wine) the ever present temptation of all seaports. (93)

The snail-like pace of the Crown administration was notorious and functionaries and clergy alike were habitually paid *tarde, mal e nunca*: late, badly or never (94), and more often than not these wages were paid in goods rather than cash. The Portuguese crown condoned private trade by its officials. (95) In later years the shortfall in gold production was blamed upon the *Banyans* or *Canarins* from Portuguese India, but in reality corrupt officials, who enriched themselves whilst they had the chance to do so, were responsible.

The years of the vassal king Mavhura brought exploitation and the misery of the African population to a high point. From the third quarter of the sixteenth century onwards successive Mutapan rulers had permitted the encroachment of the Portuguese upon the Shona economy because it suited them to do so. The Portuguese trade brought valuable goods and therefore this activity was encouraged. Inevitably, Portuguese dominance asserted itself, and during the period 1576 to the mid-seventeenth century Portuguese military strength and ecclesiastical manipulation took on a tight stranglehold and the traditional balance of Shona power was broken. The Portuguese capitalised on political crises and succession feuds which bedevilled the Shona during this period.

Mavhura, a victim of Portuguese intrigues, had taken the baptismal name of Dom Phillipe in honour of the ruling Portuguese monarch. Mavhura was reputedly so devoted to his Dominican teachers that in 1643 he was known as "the Black man of the Portuguese" (96) and while he enjoyed the relative comfort of his court, events elsewhere in his lands were having terrible consequences upon his people. The Portuguese had spread throughout the highveld, building settlements close to the major goldfields. Gold production rose during the mid seventeenth century but at enormous cost to the delicate balance of traditional African society. (97)

Whole communities were driven from an established pattern of life into a sordid and wretched economy based on gold and cloth. Imported Indian textiles were sold on credit and defaulters were forcibly pressed into the service of the merchants and robber barons. Agriculture was often abandoned as families were forced to spend time panning rivers for alluvial gold to pay for their purchases. Portuguese settlement near the *feiras* reached its greatest extent during the Mavhura administration, pushing European influence to the far corners of the Mutapa's lands. Villages were raided for cattle and slaves and eventually even the seemingly acquiescent Mutapa declared that :

> They, the Portuguesee, do great harm to the people killing some, wounding others, stealing sons and daughters and cows of their herds so that each day I have complaints in this my Zimbabwe. (98)

The wretchedness prevailing in the Rivers prompted Pêro da Silva, then Viceroy of India, to write to King João IV in 1644 imploring him to bolster Portuguese authority (99) but his pleas were unheeded because of the chronic shortage of manpower throughout the Empire. The captaincy of Mozambique Island passed from one to the other in quick succession and it was not until 1643 when Júlio Moniz da Silva assumed the office, that some semblance of order was restored at Mozambique and the Rivers. (100)

During this period traders who roamed across the countryside of Mashonaland paid scant heed to the captains. A general state of lawlessness prevailed. Portuguese traders squabbled over title to mines and the attack upon the *feira* of Maramuca, the property of Gonçalvo João, by rivals jealous of the nearby gold fields, is a case in point. (101)

When the Mutapa Mavhura died in 1652 he was succeeded by his son, *Kupisa,* identified in Portuguese documents as João and *Cupiça* (102) later baptised by Dominican priests on 4 August taking the name of Dom Domingos. The new Mutapa was suitably enthroned by the Portuguese and in the early stages of his rule they were still free to preach, build churches and attend the Mutapa's *dare* as scribes. But before long the Portuguese detected a more hostile demeanour in the new Mutapa. As long as the Portuguese were able to influence political succession and bend their vassals to their will, they were free to continue their unrestricted abuse. However in the second half of the seventeenth century gold production declined and only the *feira* of Maramuca reported an increase in yields. The Jesuit chronicler Manuel Bareto observed in 1667 that the African population was seriously depleted, infant mortality on the increase and the land ravaged by plagues of insects. Wars and slavery were taking their grim toll.

King Pedro II abolished the exclusive trading concession hitherto enjoyed by the Captain of Mozambique over the Rivers. From 1671 onwards divers Portuguese were free to trade against payment of taxes and customs dues. Pedro also favoured a new scheme for settlement but this was never achieved because of the manpower shortage in the overseas *conquistas* or colonies. (103) By 1678 there were very few Portuguese at the major centre of Dambarare and three years later there were virtually none living in the feiras on a permanent basis. The important feiras of the late seventeenth century were Dambarare, Angwa, Tafuna and Chitomborwizi but these were only being worked by Indian traders described by the Portuguese as *Banyans* and *Canarins* (104) from Diu, Damão, Chaul and Goa.

The success of the Indians attracted the enmity of the Portuguese who jealously accused them of being unprincipled engrossers, enriching themselves at the expense of the Portuguese, and demanded that they be repatriated to India. Padre Gomes S.J., writing in the seventeenth century held a different and more realistic view, arguing that the Indians made much better settlers than their European counterparts and that immigration to the Rivers should be encouraged provided they brought their families with them. (105)

Before Kupisa's authority was completely established there was a period of uncertainty when the Portuguese backed other pretenders. One of these was a man named Filipe who had the support of the *prazeiro* António Lobo da Silva but by 1683 Kupisa was in power and continued to rule his lands until around 1694 when a man named Nyakunembire (106) came to power. As the Mutapa state was racked by tribal intrigues, Portuguese inspired dissent and manipulation, a new African power was being forged in the west. The low ebb of the Mutapa state contrasted with the rise of a remarkable man who in a short time rose to become *Changamire* or chief of the Rozvi.

This man established himself as a new dynastic leader in the history of the Rozvi–Torwa people whose great stone enclosures may be seen to this day at Nandare (Nalatale), Danangombe (Dlodlo) and Kame. Known as Dombo, this man built a rival force to that of the Mutapa. This became and remained the dominant power in central and western Zimbabwe until the early nineteenth century, when it foundered in the face of the invading Nguni *impis* who were moving north during the *mfecane* or period of great tribal upheavals in South Africa. (107)

The last quarter of the seventeenth century witnessed a rapid decline of Portuguese influence and the Mukombwean Mutapa, as noted, grew far more independent of the *Muzungos* than any of his immediate predecessors. It may be argued that the Mutapa feared that the Portuguese plotted to depose him in favour of a Portuguese client and for this reason he decided to form an alliance with the Changamire. (108) This tactical move corresponded with a surge

27

of African resentment against the Portuguese. Clearly too, the Mutapa had recognised that Rozvi ascendancy would inevitably affect his own position and he quickly resolved to ally himself with the new power on the highveld. The Portuguese were the logical focus and in diverting Dombo's warlike ambitions against a common adversary he was able to make plans for political survival.

The final scene in this story of the Portuguese in the Rivers is set in June 1684 when the Rozvi met the Portuguese in battle at Maungwe near a small trading settlement in Manicaland. Although the Changamire's forces were numerically superior and on several occasions nearly broke through Portuguese defences the African yeomen were no match for the Portuguese *arquebusiers*. Powder and shot inflicted serious injuries on the Changamire's ranks and by dusk he ordered a retreat.

Relying on the graphic account of this battle by Father António de Conceição who accompanied the Captain of the Rivers, Caetano de Melo e Castro, we learn of a highly effective stratagem employed by the African chief under cover of darkness. The Changamire ordered women to cut brushwood and in the early hours of the morning the Portuguese woke up to find their lines surrounded by large fires. Panic and confusion spread like wildfire and many of the Portuguese African troops fled into the dark. The Changamire pressed home his advantage by leading forays into the Portuguese camp where he captured many prizes. (109) These clever tactics demoralised the Portuguese to such an extent that they withdrew to Macequece leaving the Changamire a psychological victor of these final hours.

Caetano de Melo e Castro immediately realised the gravity of this defeat and recommended to the Viceroy that urgent reinforcement of the Rivers was necessary to avert complete disaster. He also recognised that the remote *feiras* were especially vulnerable and arranged for the fortification of Dambarare which was considered the central administrative point. However the only forces that could be mustered were a group of eighteen *Canarins*, the much maligned Indians. (110)

It is important to emphasise that the Portuguese were extremely thin on the ground at the best of times and numbered perhaps no more than a few dozen permanent residents in total. By 1688 the

Changamire's forces posed such a threat that many Portuguese abandoned the Rivers for the sanctuary of Tete. The void was filled by *Canarins* who replaced the fleeing Portuguese at the *feiras* and by the 1690s gold production was restored at many of the traditional *feiras*. The Indians were adept at fostering good trading relations with the Africans and perhaps carrying out mining on their own account. Many of these Indians had mining experience and gold yields were boosted at both Angwa and Chitomborwizi.

It cannot be established with certainty when Nyakunembire succeeded Kupisa although this was around 1694 but he obviously felt equally vulnerable to Portuguese and Rozvi political ambitions. For this reason he also made the decision to invite the Changamire's assistance against the Portuguese. Suddenly, in November 1693, (111) the Changamire's warriors fell upon Dambarare with a ferocity unequalled in the 150 years of Portuguese experience in the Rivers. The attackers achieved complete surprise and during the savage onslaught Indian traders, settlers and priests were killed. Buildings and churches were plundered and razed. Priests were reportedly flayed alive and their flesh and skins carried away to be used as *muti* or magical charms against the African followers of the Portuguese.

The Changamire was held in awe by his followers for his ability to work magic. (112) Learning of Dambarare's destruction, the Indians at Chitomborwizi and the Angwa river wisely withdrew to Tete. (113) Much of the booty from Dambarare was probably carried away to the Rozvi strongholds in the west and in the late nineteenth century many relics of Portuguese origin were unearthed by European prospectors who were excavating the old stone ruins in search for golden artifacts. This linkage with the destruction of Dambarare is not altogether certain for these items may have been acquired by trade as noted earlier.

The Portuguese strove to contain the Changamire's threat and in 1695 sent an expedition commanded by the newly-appointed Captain of the Rivers, Jose da Fonseca Coutinho, against him. (114) This initiative proved a complete disaster for the Portuguese - the morale of their African troops, upon whom considerable reliance was placed, was extremely low and many of them had deserted after hearing about the powerful *muti* made from the flesh of the dead *muzungos*. These magical charms are known in Shona as *mazango* and may consist of various roots, pieces of human skin or certain organs all pounded together and stitched to a string worn around the upper arm to ward off evil or bring good fortune. A green vegetable known as *tsunga* in Shona and cooked like spinach has historically been mixed with human flesh and then eaten as a stew which fortifies against injury or harm.

Rigid belief in the power of the *n'anga* and witchcraft were deep rooted in contemporary African society and any of these practices would have had decided psychological impact. The Portuguese discovered they could no longer command the same authority over their African troops and the Fonseca Coutinho forces withdrew. The Changamire then swept down upon the isolated settlements of Manicaland and finally on Macequece itself. (115)

With Macequece laid waste in the late 1690s the Portuguese occupation of Manicaland and Mashonaland was over. In the eighteenth century, Chipangura, as Macequece was known to the Manyika, was reoccupied by itinerant Portuguese or their *mwana-muzungo* who continued to exploit the lucrative gold trade made possible by the riches of the Revue river valley alluviums.

Zumbo, on the confluence of the Zambezi and the Luangwa rivers, enjoyed greater prominence in the eighteenth century and became the focus of the Zambezi valley trade. Most of the old *feiras* of the Rivers were completely forgotten although it is possible that the Angwa settlements may have been worked by Portuguese Indians at some stage during the eighteenth century.

In 1737 Tomás da Rosa Freire observed that if the *feiras* were to be re-established then Masapa should be considered a priority because it was close to Tete. He also emphasised the importance of paying the traditional tax to the Mutapa in the form of gunpowder and cloth. This report of the early eighteenth century suggests that the Africans of the highveld were now experienced in the use of muzzle-loaders for which they required the gunpowder.

The Rivers of Gold had yielded their treasures grudgingly and during their 150 years of occupation the Portuguese never succeeded in finding their Eldorado or a new *Potosi*. In 1696, a Portuguese Indian, Domingos Carvalho (116) reported the discovery of silver but this was not able to contribute to a reversal of

Portuguese misfortunes in the Rivers. Francisco Barreto had failed where Pizarro's *conquistadores* had succeeded. It may be claimed that the African climate was a debilitating factor - indeed it was, but the Spaniards also faced adverse weather and inhospitable terrain which did not prevent them from conquest in the Americas. Quite simply, the Portuguese were stretched too thin, they were much further from home and although vast quantities of gold were won from the Rivers between 1502 and 1667 (estimated around US$ 250 million) (117) it never built a lasting Lusitanian presence in Zimbabwe.

The Portuguese failed to achieve the potential for settlement and trade, and succeeded only in slowly antagonising the African people. They interfered with the delicate fabric of the iron-age economy where seasonal agriculture, hunting and mining were vital elements for a stable society which was in harmony with nature. They provoked serious economic upheavals by forcing upon society a cycle of foreign supply and demand where increasing amounts of gold and ivory were required to pay for the imported beads and cloth.

Cultivation was forsaken as women and children were forced to pan the rivers or tunnel deep into narrow shafts and pits for gold ores. Communities were visited by the ravages of unknown diseases like smallpox and other apocalyptic ills. Yet, somehow, this traumatised society recovered rapidly enough evidencing an African resilience, a capacity to yield, absorb and finally overcome by attrition, the foreign invader. Similarly, Catholicism never endured and it was only in the late nineteenth century with British colonial occupation that this Christian faith was re-established. As the Spaniards steadily advanced in the New World the Portuguese Empire in the East declined and the fragile settlements in the Rivers reverted to bush.

The Portuguese never mustered sufficient energy to colonise and develop the Rivers as they did in Brazil where tobacco and sugar fuelled economic prosperity. Their best hope had come with the 1667 settlement scheme but this opportunity was squandered because of Empire fatigue and the Portuguese prediliction for *murmuração* or backbiting and squabbling. In Africa, it appeared that gold was so plentiful that it could be had in exchange for beads and cloth.

No proper mines were ever developed as the geological formations in which the gold occurs would have been extremely difficult to exploit using sixteenth and seventeenth century techniques. The Portuguese failed to grasp the fundamental truth — the Africans had the right technology for their times and this involved painstakingly hard work and gold production could not exceed these historical levels. No lasting colonization or alternate economic activity was ever attempted as there was a seemingly inexhaustable supply of alluvial gold and vast herds of elephant still roamed over most of the land so that tusks were plentiful. Even the distinct advantage offered by superior firepower mattered little in the final analysis. Illustrative of this was an incident which occurred in the late 1680s when Antonio Lobo da Silva and seven companions together with a force of *chikunda* African troops killed an African chief and a number of his followers who posed a threat to their trading interests.

Within an hour of the carnage the Portuguese sat down at their Zambezi river camp to amuse themselves, gambling and joking. With musket and shot the Portuguese were able to terrorise the people of the Rivers yet this awesome technological advantage was never effectively applied and the highveld *Conquistas* were lost to the Portuguese.

As previously noted, Portuguese-speaking Indians were to prove themselves extremely adept at trading in the Rivers. The Portuguese could not really match their innate commercial cunning and financial strength. (History has a cruel tendency to repeat itself and in many East African countries the business acumen of the Indian communities has provoked the same prejudices in the twentieth century as it did all those years ago.) In fact, for some time until 1694 when the ill-fated and financially disastrous Portuguese Trading Company was established with a royal monopoly of trade in *Asia Portuguesa*, Gujerati *Banyans* enjoyed rights to free voyage between Diu and Mozambique and the Rivers where they plied successful and profitable trade .(118) Certainly Indian economic influence grew from 1686 after the formation of the *Companhia dos Manzanes* in Diu. The shareholders were rich Indian merchants and arms dealers who quickly established a monopoly on trade between Diu, Mozambique Island and to a certain extent the Rivers. (119) The Diu merchants who financed the annual voyages to Mozambique built a profitable trade supplying beads and textiles from Cambaya and Surat. This lucrative commerce was the very life-blood of this Portuguese enclave. In addition, the Gujerati vessels offered the most reliable and regular passage between India and Mozambique and many Portuguese officials and merchants took advantage of the service. The wealthy reputation of Diu spread far and wide and during the meteoric rise of Omani sea power in the 1660s the city was raided and a vast booty carried off .(120)

The introduction of the Portuguese Trading Company, heralded as the answer to the declining fortunes in the East, proved a complete failure and it was scrapped in 1699 when the former rights were restored and resumed by a leading Diu merchant named Macandagi Sacar .(121) Unfortunately for the Portuguese, Diu was never to regain its former economic importance.

Some Portuguese did appreciate the bitter irony of their fate and lamented that all their efforts had been for the benefit of India because the gold went there sooner or later. The gold was dug from the African soil only to be transported to India where the Hindu buried it again.(122) True enough, but the Portuguese had their halcyon days when Goa was transformed into a dazzling seat of Empire. *Goa Dourada* was a rich paradise indeed during the late sixteenth and early seventeenth century and many Portuguese who came were content to remain for,

Quem viu Goa dispensa de ver Lisboa. (123).

This was the same vile and wicked Goa so aptly described by Luis de Camões on his arrival in 1553 as,

Mae de vilões e ruins e madrasta de homens honrados (124)

The story of Portugal in the Rivers was to end as Camões had predicted in 1570 when he published his great epic poem of Portugal, *Os Lusiadas,*

> *Ali, Cafres selvagens poderão*
> *O que destros imigos no puderam,*
> *E rudos paus tostados sós farão*
> *O que arcos e pelouros não fizeram.* (125)
> (Canto X.38)

33

Camões endured seventeen long years in *Asia Portuguesa* from 1553 until his final return home in 1570. He embarked from Goa in 1567 penniless but clutching his manuscript and spent the next two years languishing on Mozambique Island. Here he would have become well acquainted with the chaotic situation in the Rivers and therefore confident in his writings that Portugal in Africa would fall at the hands of black savages armed only with fire-hardened clubs. Camoes accurately predicted the fall of the *feiras* and the expulsion of the Portuguese from the Rivers.

Several of these *feiras* were occupied intermittently for decades during the sixteenth and seventeenth centuries and a closer look at these settlements, or what little remains of them now unfolds in our story of the Portuguese in the Rivers of Gold.

References

1. Custódia de Belem, Museu Nacional de Arte Antiga, Lisbon, Portugal. Height : 73mm,weight approx. 6,350 kg. According to the testament of King Manuel dated 7 April, 1517 the workmanship is ascribed to Gil Vicente, *" Mando que se dê ao mosteiro de Na Sa de Belém a custódia que fez Gil Vicente para a dita Casa......"* (A.N.T.T., gaveta 16, maço, número 2.)

2. There are numerous Portuguese documents describing the " Rivers of Cuama " or the Rivers of the Zambezi and notable amongst them are reports by Fr. António da Conceição of 12-12-1696 and Fr. Filipe de Assumpçao of 1698.

3. Virtually all cloth was manufactured in the Cambaya region of Gujerati province Western India. From Gujerati, the textiles were shipped to Africa via Diu and Goa. *Bertangil vermelho* - red, heavy cotton cloth, was a typical export. Bertangil was also produced in a variety of other colours and stripes.

4. The term *Muzungo* was common currency for a European and occurs in Swahili and in most autochthonous languages of South East Africa. In Shona, for example the word *Murungu* for a white man occurs. There are numerous contemporary Portuguese references to *Muzungos*.

5. Dickinson R.W., *Rhodesiana*, No. 19, December, 1968, p.39. Sofala.

6. Axelson E., *Portuguese in South East Africa, 1488-1600*, p 46., C. Struik (Pvt) Ltd., 1973. See also; Dickinson R.W., Sofala-Gateway to the Gold of Monomotapa., *Rho desiana*, No. 19, December, 1968 p 33-47., Lobato A. *A Expansao Portuguesa em Moçambique*, 1498-1530. Vol I p 51-150 for origins and details of initial years at Sofala.

7. *Documents*. Vol I., 1497-1506., p 507. Pêro de Andaia ordered that cloth and beads be given to an emissary of the Monomotapa who visited the fort. Report dated 19 May, 1506.

8. Burke E.E., " Some aspects of Arab contact with south-east Africa "., *Historians in Tropical Africa.*, UCR, 1962.

9. *Documents*. Vol. II., p.381.

10. Axelson E., *Portuguese in south east Africa, 1488-1600*. p. 75.

11. Boxer C.R., An African Eldorado: Monomotapa and Mocambique, 1498-1752. *C.A.H.A., No. 2*, 1960. p. 2-3.

12. Axelson E., op. cit. p .77-78.

13. Lobato A. *Expansão* Vol II, p. 219-220,223. Tracey, Hugh., António Fernandes-Rhodesia's first pioneer. *Rhodesiana* No. 19, 1968, p. 1-26.

14. Tracey H., op. cit.

15. Mudenge S. *A Political History of Munhumutapa.*, ZPH., 1988, p .244. See also António Bocarro's *Década* in Theal's *Records* Vol. III, p. 404 with a description of the welcome accorded to Diogo Simões in 1614 when arriving at Chitima (adjacent to the present border of Zimbabwe–Mozambique)

16. Lobato A., *Expansao* II p. 27-28.

17. Axelson E., op. cit. p. 84-86.

18. Mandivenga E.C., *Islam in Zimbabwe*, Mambo., 1983, p .30 the names include Sharefi, Bakari, Maisiri, Ali and Mustafa. The link with sixteenth and seventeenth century Swahili traders requires further investigation.

19. ditto.

20. Axelson E. op. cit. p. 88-90.

21. Axelson E. op. cit. p. 125-132.

22. Foist, a light galley driven by oars and sail.

35

23. Axelson E. op. cit. p. 133-135.

24. Fr. António da Conceiçao., Treatise on the Cuama Rivers, 20 June, 1696 to Fr. Diogo da Conceicão, Goa. Various references to *Mwanamuzungo* inhabiting Portuguese settlements.

25. Boxer C.R., *Seaborne Empire*, p. 307-309 on Portuguese sexual behaviour with female slaves and concubines.

26. João dos Santos, *Ethiopia Oriental*, Évora, 1609.

27. As Crónicas de Fernao Lopes. c. 1387-1459. Fernão Lopes is the foremost Portuguese chronicler of any age and his commentary on the life and times of Pedro, Fernando and John are considered classics of Portuguese literature.

28. Gomes Eannes d'Azurara, a panegyrist of the Infante Dom Henrique and the early voyages of exploration and the Guinea coast. Crónicas da Guiné.

29. Beach D.N. The *Shona and Zimbabwe.*, Mambo, 1980, p. 93,123, Mudenge S. op. cit. p. 64-68

30. Axelson E. op.cit. p. 152-154.

31.. Axelson E. op. cit. p. 158.

32. *Documents* Vol. VIII, p. 259,263. Barreto had earlier sent ships with provisions to Sofala but after the priest had prevailed Barreto ordered that the vessels be recalled to the Zambezi and Sena. Axelson E. op. cit. p. 158

33. *Breve Monografia Agraria*, Ministry of Agriculture, Moçambique, 1977, report indicates that the rains in the Zambezi valley area start in October-December and continue until January-June with a maximum of 8 months and a minimum of 2 months regular precipitation. The average rainfall in this region is between 1000-1400 mm, extent of season 5-6 months, average annual temperature 26 degrees celcius, (maximum 34-36 degrees) and the average annual relative humidity percentage being 75%.

34. The lower Zambezi valley is dominated by the distribution of *Glossina mortisans* and *Glossina pallidipes* whilst the upper valley to the west of Tete is infested by *Glossina mortisans* tsetse fly.

35. There are approx. 100 species of mosquitoes (family *Culicidae*) in the lower and upper Zambezi and the regions traversed by Barreto are zones of year-round endemicity for Malaria and various other diseases hosted by mosquitoes such as philaria, yellow fever and dengue. Albino Manuel Pacheco reported on the incidence of diarrhoea and syphilis in the Chetima district during 1861. He also remarked on the occurance of *hydrocele,* a medical condition characterised by accute swelling of the testicle or scrotum. During 1974, the writer visited Makombe on the Zambezi river in the Mazoe area of Tete where an Army medical doctor stationed with Rhodesian troops in Mozambique reported treating such cases hitherto only encountered in his textbooks on tropical medicine. Territorial Army doctor to H. Ellert, 1974.

36. Axelson E. op. cit. p. 158.

37. Axelson E. op. cit. p. 158. Axelson reports that Barreto habitually rode wearing chain mail. It is likely that others were similarly attired contributing in no small measure to their discomfort in the oppressive heat of the Zambezi valley.

38. Monclaro, Francisco de., *R.S.E.A.* Vol III, p 186-7, see also Axelson E. op. cit. p 158-159.

39. Axelson E. op. cit. p 159.

40. *Documents* Vol VIII., p. 289,291, for an account of this battle including a description of the female *nganga* who strode ahead of the African warriors spreading about *muti* from a gourd before she was blown apart by shot from a light artillery piece or *falcão*.

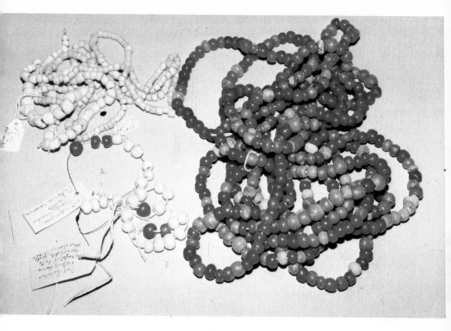

Plate 1

Plate 2

Plate 3

Plate 4

Plate 5

Plate 6

Plate 7

Plate 8

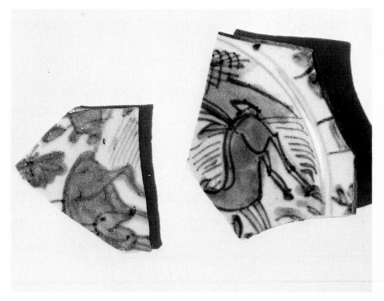

Plate 9

Plate 10

Plate 11

Plate 12

Plate 13

Plate 14

Plate 15

Plate 16

Plate 17

Plate 18

Plate 19

Plate 20

Plate 21

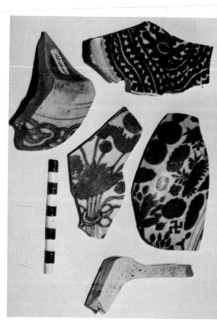

Plate 22

41. Axelson E. op. cit. p. 160, also Monclaro, *R.S.E.A*, Vol III., p 195-7; Homen to Silva, Leite, p. 387-8.
42. Axelson E. op. cit. p. 160-161.
43 . Mudenge S. op cit. p.219. Axelson E., op. cit. p .162 for further details of Souto mayor's assaying results.
44.   Axelson E. op. cit. p. 162.
45. Axelson E., op. cit. p. 163.
46. *Documents*. Vol VIII p. 271,273 for details of the three principal fairs of the Portuguese.
47. *Documents*. Vol VIII p. 249 report dated 1573 with details of the principal fairs suggesting establishment prior to that date.
48. Axelson E., op. cit. p. 169
49. Mudenge S., op. cit. p. 184.
50. Jesuit missionaries in Brazil spoke Indian vernacular and it is assumed that their Dominican counterparts did the same in S.E. Africa and the Zimbabwean mission.
51. Beach D.N., op. cit. p. 125-126. Beach records Gatsi Rusere as having Mutapa status in 1601. Abraham's argument for the succession of Gatsi Rusere by 1589 remains sound and this contention is endorsed by Beach. see History Seminar Paper No. 79, 1990, *The Changing traditions of the Mutapa dynasty*.
52. Beach D.N., op. cit. p. 126
53. António Bocarro, *Decada, R.S.E.A.,*, p. 369.
54. Bocarro, op. cit., p. 371-2.
55. Bocarro, op. cit., p. 406-7.
56. Bocarro, op.cit., p. 407.
57. Mudenge S., *Christian Education at the Mutapa Court.*, ZPH., 1986. p. 15, quoting a report of Francisco do Avellar about silver mines dated 1617 published in *Moçambique* XXXIX, 1944, p. 74.
58. *Documents*, Vol IX p. 115-116
59. Boxer C.R. *Portuguese Seaborne Empire*, 1973, p. 304.
60. Boxer C.R. op. cit. p. 304-305.
61. Boxer C.R. op. cit.
62. Axelson E., *Portuguese* 1600-1700., p. 36
63. Axelson E. op. cit. p. 36-37
64. Axelson E. op. cit. p. 39
65. *Documents* Vol. IX p. 251
66. Axelson E. op. cit. p. 46
67. Mudenge S. op. cit. p. 240
68. Mudenge S. op. cit. p. 224, for details of Gatsi Rusere's use of the drug *mbanje*.
69. Beach D.N. op. cit. p. 128. Beach argues that the succession took place in 1623.
70. Axelson E. op. cit. p. 55-56-57, see also "voyage by Fr. António Gomes, SJ., to the Monomotapa Empire" 2 January, 1648, António Gomes to Fr. João Marachi.
71. Gomes, Viagem.
72. Axelson E., op. cit. p. 69
73. Gomes, Viagem.
74. Beach D.N. op. cit. p. 128
75. Beach D.N. op. cit. p. 128
76. Axelson E., op. cit. p. 76
77. Mudenge S. op. cit. p. 256
78. Mudenge S. *Christian Education at the Mutapa Court.*, ZPH., 1986, p. 16,17,18.
79. Beach D.N. History Seminar Paper, No. 79.,1990, p.2

80. *Documents.* Vol IX p. 125

81. Fr. Louis, 3-2-1630, *R.S.E.A.*, Vol. II, p 427-8.

82. Boxer C.R., *C.A.H.A.*, No. 2, 1961, a report that Manuel Barreto SJ., in his account of Zambezia in 1667 evidences that the *prazo* system was already in existance although Padre António Gomes makes no mention of it twenty years earlier.

83. Boxer C.R., op. cit.

84. Beach D.N., *Shona*, p. 130-169.

85. Beach D.N. op. cit. p. 130,131,176, 200-201.

86. ditto

87. Axelson E., *Portuguese 1600-1700,* p. 97-98.

88. Axelson E., op. cit. p. 99.

89. ditto

90. ditto, p. 109-114

91. ditto

92. Boxer C.R., *Port. Seaborne Empire*, p. 151

93. ditto, p. 307

94. Boxer C.R. op. cit. p. 78

95. Boxer C.R. op. cit. p. 325

96. Mudenge S. *Christian Educ. at Mutapa Court.*, 1986., see also report in AHU Cxa. de Moçambique — Monomotapa — Mamvura dated 4-3-1643.

97. Beach D.N. *Shona*, p. 129-130

98. Axelson E., op. cit. p. 125

99. ditto, p. 115

100. ditto, p. 116

101. Abraham D.P., in *JAH.*, Vol II, 1961, p. 218. Manuel Barreto, 1667.

102. Beach D.N. History Seminar Paper No. 79, 1990, *The changing history of the Mutapa dynasty.* p. 2

103. Axelson E., op. cit. p. 144

104. Boxer C.R., *Portuguese Seaborne Empire*, p. 257, 389. The term *Canarin* applies to Konkani-Marathi inhabitants of Portuguese India. The word later took on a pejorative sense.

105. Boxer C.R. *CAHA*, 1960, African Eldorado : Monomotapa and Mozambique., p. 7. See also Axelson E., *Port. 1600-1700.*, p. 180-81.

106. Beach D.N. op. cit. quoting original Portuguese documents states that the Mutapa was known as *Nhacunimbiri.*

107. Beach D.N. *Shona.*, p. 264.

108. ditto, p. 140.

109. Fr. António da Conceição to Fr. Diogo da Conceição, 1696, *Treatise on the Rivers of Cuama,* Goa, in a translation of Portuguese documents by D.N. Beach and H. de Noronha Vol. I, 1980.

110. ditto, p. 209-210.

111. Beach D.N. *Shona,* p. 140.

112 Mudenge S. *Pol. History of Munhumutapa.* ZPH, p. 290. Axelson E. Port. 1600-1700., p. 182.

113 Beach D.N. op. cit. p. 140. António da Conceição, op. cit.

114 Axelson E. Port. 1600-1700, p. 185. António da Conceição, op. cit.

115   Axelson E. op. cit. p. 184

116   ditto, p. 184-85

117   Various estimates, best available, see R. Summers in *Ancient Mining of Rhodesia*,1969, Museum Memoirs.

118   Fernades A.P. Port. Trading Coy., 1694-99, *Journal Goan Archives* Vol II, No. 2, 1985, p. 15.

119   ditto, p. 16

120   Boxer C.R. op. cit. p. 136., Diu was raided in 1668.

121   ditto, p. 24

122   A reference to the adornment of Indian women folk with gold and subsequent internment upon death.

123   Mario C. Leão, Reflexo de Portugal na Cultura Goesa. Boletim Centro de Estudos Maritimos de Macau, 1989, p. 74

124   ditto

125   Camões, Luis de, *Os Lusíadas,* Canto X 38.

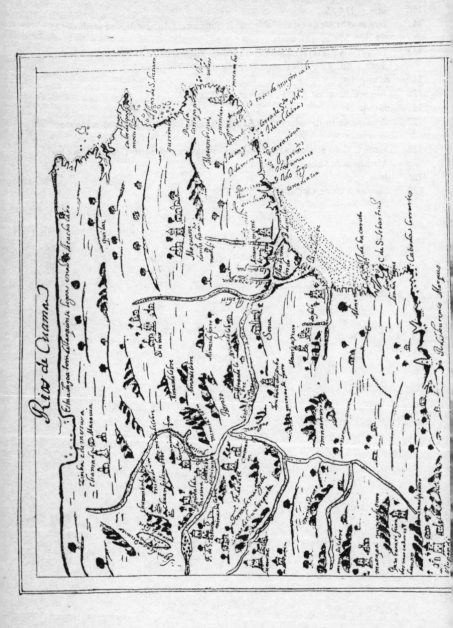

Rio de Osama

CHAPTER 2

Feiras

Description and historical perspective of settlements on the highveld

> They are three in number the trading fairs where the
> Portuguese go trading their cloth and beads for gold.

The famed Portuguese soldier chronicler, Diogo do Couto, writing
his account of the ill-fated Francisco Barreto expedition to the lands
of the Mutapa in 1570, described the three principal *feiras* of
Luanze, Bocuto, and *Masapa* in some detail. From Manuel Barretto's report on the Rivers of Cuama written in 1667 we learn that:

> In Mokaranga, as the empire of Monomotapa is called,
> there are several minor captains, such as the captains of
> Dambarare, Ongoe, Luanzi and Chipiriviri, with their
> chief captain, who resides at Zimbaoe or at the court of
> the emperor, with a garrison.... (1)

These *feiras* were pivotal in the spread of Portuguese influence in
eastern and central Mashonaland during the sixteenth and seventeenth centuries. Virtually all the *feiras* were located at the cross-
roads of inter-communal trade, close to perennial water and in the
proximity of goldfields or other significant mineral deposits such as
copper or precious stones. The relative salubrity of the climate in
the highlands of Mashonaland was also a welcome relief from the
unhealthy lowveld of the Zambezi valley.

> Mokaranga is very healthy, fertile and verdant, with
> numberless rivers and fountains. (2)

At one stage the most promising of the *feiras* was *Masapa* where:

> not so long ago a piece of ore was dug out from which
> over 400 Cruzados were extracted. The veins of gold so
> forcibly break up from below the ground that they were
> found to crop through the roots of trees and from one of
> them broke a piece of gold which weighed 12 000
> Cruzados like unto a big yam. (3).

The Portuguese *Cruzado* was a gold coin minted in the early sixteenth century in Lisbon with a mass of 3,5 grams and in 1517 its value was fixed at four English shillings. If one is asked to believe even part of this claim about the golden riches of the Rivers then these nuggets must have represented a fortune and given the Portuguese more than a glimmer of the elusive Eldorado. Finds of giant nuggets were highly likely and many have been found by lucky prospectors and miners even in modern times. Outcrops of almost pure gold have been found in the Gadzema-Giant mine district of Chegutu and at the fabulously rich Globe and Phoenix Mine at Kwekwe where a huge mass of bullion weighing several kilos once jammed the massive ore crushers during milling operations.(4) Engineers working to free the equipment were absolutely astonished to find a solid chunk of gold wedged inside the mill. (5)

When António Fernandes, the illiterate *degredado* made his epic journey, to a certain extent evocative of Francisco Pizzaro's expeditions in Peru, to the lands then known as Quiteve, Mocaranga and Abatua in the early 1500s he effectively pioneered Portuguese settlement in the Rivers of Gold. Following winding footpaths through the African bush, Fernandes visited trading centres with long traditions of African-Swahili commerce. His inauspicious background notwithstanding, Fernandes must have been a remarkable character, possessed of a tenacious spirit and an iron-hard constitution resilient enough to withstand the ravages of fever, dysentery and insect bites.

Without the goodwill of the people through whose lands he journeyed it is unlikely that Fernandes would have returned from his long peregrinations. Yet return he did, and with fabulous stories of strange lands and golden riches. Gaspar Veloso, a clerk at Sofala, committed to parchment all that António Fernandes told him and in 1936 this important historical document was brought to light by the historian Erik Axelson whilst researching in the Lisbon archives. During the early days of the sixteenth century the Portuguese followed the accepted customs

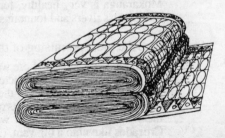

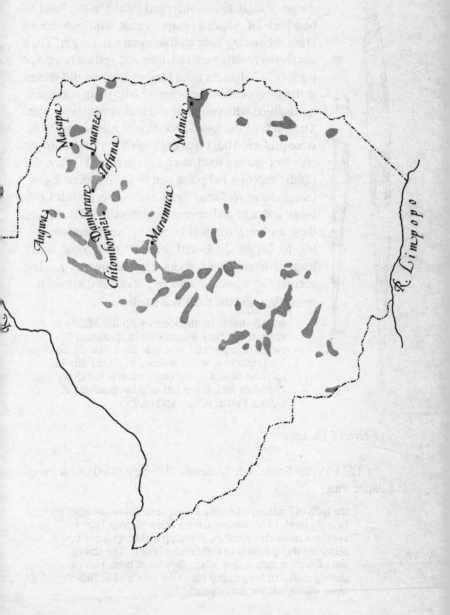

and timed their annual trading caravans to coincide with the seasonal markets of the interior. Travelling, first from Sofala and later from Sena and Tete, the Portuguese or their agents marched inland at the head of hundreds of African bearers laden with bundles of cloth measuring four to five metres in length. They also brought strings of red, blue and yellow beads for trade (6). Villagers from remote areas would gather at the appropriate time bringing with them porcupine quills filled with gold dust and sealed with bees-wax. The quills of the female porcupine, *nungu* in Shona, were preferred but often eagle quills or the hollowed claws of guinea fowl were also used. (7)Today, the plastic cap of a ballpoint pen or similar plastic containers have replaced these ancient receptacles (8). Ivory was also an important commodity. The first of these trading *feiras* was known as *Luanze* and according to Diogo do Couto was situated some thirty leagues from Tete (about 150 kilometres). The second fair was called *Bocuto* about 200 kilometres from Tete and the third was *Masapa* :

> which stands on the journey up the Mazowe river some fifty leagues from Tete and between Bocuto and this fair there stands the long thickly wooded mountain called Fura. In all these places do the Dominican priests keep churches and at the fair of Masapa there resides a Portuguese captain. (9)

Feira of Luanze

In 1634 Pedro Barreto de Rezende (10) described the *feira* of Luanze thus:

> the forts of Luanze, where the Portuguese hold a market, is in the lands of Mocaranga, forty leagues from Tete. It is only a palisade of stakes, filled up inside with earth, allowing those within to fight under cover. The stakes are of such a nature that when they have been two or three months in the ground they take root and become trees which last for many years.

There are several trees commonly used to fence hut enclosures in Zimbabwe and the most popular of these is the *mushamba* or *Livelong* tree *(Lannea discolor).* There are several other likely candidates including *Pterocarpus angolenis* known as *mubvamaropa* in Shona and the *Kirkia acuminata.* Truncheons cut from these trees in October when the sap is rising easily take root and sprout new leafy shoots after planting. (11)

The size of this fort is like a large terrace, being a hundred fathoms (brassas) in circumference, where the captain resides, who is elected by the Captain of Mozambique, and with him the Portuguese and Christians who may be trading in these parts. (12)

There is some speculation surrounding the origins of the name for this *feira* and it may have something to do with the archaic Portuguese word *luanhe* or *luane* describing a dwelling with a walled courtyard of a type common in Zambezia from the earliest times of Portuguese occupation in Mozambique. This *feira* is variously identified on early maps as either *luanze* or *luanhe* but the most likely derivation is an indigenous African place or regional name for Ruanje or Ruhanje as a trading centre located between the Nyadiri and Ruenya rivers.

In Francisco de Sousa's *Oriente Conquistado* and his description of the Rivers of Cuama dated 1696, the *feira* of Luanze was reported upon retrospectively. It was said to have comprised a Dominican church (located at map ref. VS 538 131) and to have been located in a region rich in cattle, chickens, butter and rice. Perennial fresh water springs made the land cool and healthy. This geographic account is accurate and the modern-day visitor to the Murehwa and Mutoko Districts will encounter a pleasant wooded landscape characterised by huge granite kopjes and fertile, well-watered valleys. There are small plantations of rice, maize, sugarcane and vegetables while cattle and other livestock graze in *vleis* (13) and along stream banks.

Frei Gaspar de Macedo's (Vicar of Manicaland) declaration of 1633 (14) concerning the *feira* of Luanze includes an interesting reference to the ruins of a great building said to have been the court of the Queen of Sheba who sought Solomon. Gaspar de Macedo also described a very beautiful river which rises in the lands of Mocaranga and after flowing through many lands rich in gold empties into the sea near Sofala. He named the river as *Sabaya*, obviously a dialectae variation of *Sabi* (Save) which rises on the watershed of Zimbabwe near the Wedza mountains. The Save then flows southeast to its confluence with the Odzi at Nyanyadzi before continuing eastward into Mozambique and the Indian ocean.

The ruins mentioned are certainly likely to be Great Zimbabwe although there is an interesting stonewall ruin near Mutoko (map ref VR 238 765) known as the Mutoko or Tere ruin. In 1929 these latter ruins, situated in a large granite outcrop, were partially excavated and gold leaf and a shard of Chinese celadon ceramic ware were recovered near the foot of a section of decorated walling (15).

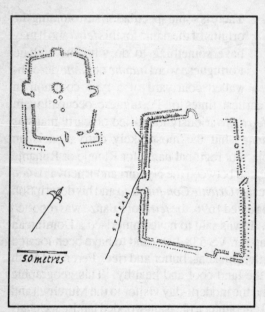

The celadon dates from the fourteenth century and is likely to be contemporary with similar finds at Great Zimbabwe. These ruins are about 45 kilometres by road from the site of the Luanze *feira*. The main features of the Luanze *feira* are two rectilinear earthworks and the ruins of what may have been the Dominican church (map ref VS 538 131). The site of this settlement was discovered in late 1964 by a prospector named N. J. Van Wyk who found glass beads whilst panning for gold in a small stream near the earthworks located at a point (Map ref VS 531 134) which is in the Mudzi communal lands close to the main Mutoko-

Nyamapanda road. A small track at the 212 kilometre peg leads to the site and this is located opposite the junction to the Masarakufa Dam at a distance of 57 kilometres from Mutoko. The largest of the Luanze earthworks was described by the archaeologist Peter Garlake, who visited and examined the site in 1964 (16), as measuring about 111 m by 86 m with an earth wall about 1,5 m high and 4 m wide and an external ditch about 3 m by 1 m deep. He found no visible evidence of any structures inside this earthwork but some 40 metres distant he located a second smaller earthwork with a low central mound about 12 m in diameter which might have been the foundations of a building. One hundred and thirty metres to the east of the largest earthworks Garlake found a stone wall enclosure similar to those on Mount Darwin and of possible nineteenth century construction. Between this earthwork and the enclosure he found a small cemetery consisting of about 25 graves each marked by a single headstone. Two hundred and fifty metres to the north Garlake found traces of hut dahka in a cultivated land which according to a local informant were the remains of an old Portuguese church (map ref VS 538 131).

In 1961 the historian D.P. Abraham (17) reported that Luanze was situated at the north-west end of Chitomba hill near Ranja (Ruhanje-Luanze) village. He also commented on the existence of a stone-lined well which had since been buried by an overburden of river sand near the Nyadota stream at the foot of the Chitomba hill. Attempts to re-discover this old well have not been successful.

Surface finds of broken pottery in the vicinity of the smaller earthworks prompted Garlake to excavate and he discovered shards of blue and white porcelain of the Wan-li period of Ming. These were the most numerous of his finds. He recovered a total of 33 Plate 2 shards from the surface and from the trench and these included 5 shards of buff-coloured Chinese stoneware with a bright green exterior glaze embellished by an overlay of trailed Acanthus leaves and flowers highlighted in yellow. Garlake noted that this distinctive ware was similar to finds at Fort Jesus, Mombasa, Kenya, but not previously found in Zimbabwe. All five shards were from a single vessel which the writer has identified as being a type of jar produced during late Ming. It is a copy of a jar first manufactured during T'ang (618-907) and later popularised for export in the

47

sixteenth and seventeenth centuries. Garlake also recovered shards of a thick, red-coloured earthenware of possible Portuguese origin, black glazed Chinese stonewares, a fragment of Portuguese faience or decorated porcelain and some pieces of black burnished ware with stamped decorations of unknown provenance. Other finds included beads ranging from Indian red to grey-blues and light blues, two lead shot of irregular shape 5mm to 7 mm in diameter and a single gold pellet.

Feira of Makaha

Some distance to the south of Luanze the countryside expands into a series of broad open valleys stretching to the Makaha goldfields and the Ruenya river to the south where alluvial gold panning still takes place. According to a list of known ancient workings, compiled by Roger Summers in his work on ancient mining in Zimbabwe, the Makaha region was extensively mined for gold and copper for several centuries before the arrival of Europeans in the late 1890s (18). These workings are scattered over a wide region and more than 18 have subsequently been developed as modern mines. In 1953 The Rhodesian Commission for the Preservation of Natural and Historical Monuments and Relics published an account of, *The Monuments of Southern Rhodesia*. In this a Portuguese fort is listed as Monument No. 69 describing it as:

> an old fort situated on Lawley's Concession to the left of the road leading to the Ruenya river about three miles before striking the river (19). The building was obliterated many years ago but the north and east sides were still clearly defined. The fort consists of a rectangular enclosure measuring forty yards by forty yards bounded by a stone-and-mud wall about five feet in height. This was loopholed. At the corner on the eastern side are two bastions.

There was no definite evidence to prove that the Portuguese had built this structure but in a written communication dated 11 November 1945, J.D. Pare, a prospector, reported to the Queen Victoria Museum the existence of an earthwork at Makaha similar to those at the Angwa river. Pare, had, at one time, been mining at the Goho claims in the Angwa valley where he became familiar with the

48

Portuguese earthworks known to exist there.

The *Geological Bulletin* covering the Makaha region dated 1935 reveals that between the beginning of the twentieth century and 1934 a total of 322 ounces of gold was recovered from alluvial sands by registered prospectors. The gold was recovered from the Manuchi river which rises near the Radnor Mine before flowing into the Nyamazizi river and the Ruenya river. A survey of the Manuchi river established the existence of at least 1,4 million cubic metres of alluvial sands rich in gold. (20)

The site of this suspected Portuguese earthwork was visited in 1987 by amateur historian Mark Igoe who was investigating an old report dating back to 1964, communicated to him by the priest in charge of Avila Mission in the Katerere district of Manicaland. The priest had told Igoe of an old Portuguese graveyard complete with gabled wall which comprised headstones and inscriptions. All attempts to locate the cemetery failed as the original informants had long since died or left the mission. This unsubstantiated report may relate to probable Portuguese settlement in the Maungwe district. Whilst in the Ruenya valley, Igoe noted that considerable gold panning was taking place and that the industry was a major source of livelihood for the local people who jealously guard their concessions from the unwanted attentions of outsiders. (21)

Feira of Bocuto

The precise position of Bocuto or Bokuto has not yet been determined although shards of blue and white Chinese ceramics were found by Dr Judy Maguire close to the confluence of the Gwatera and Hoza rivers in the Umfurudzi Safari Area (map ref US 895 385) at a spot between a track on the west and a small waterfall on the Gwatera river to the east. There is a stone wall enclosure on Mahomba hill which is close to the confluence of the Mazowe and Ruange rivers and further to the north-west there are reported finds of gold and glass beads near the Beryl Rose Mine at map ref US 76 38. (22)

Bocuto, was the second fair of the Portuguese who wrote that:

> it stands between another two small branches of a river which also come to join together into a big one, and the

fair is some two leagues 10 kilometres) from the nearest
banks of either, and is forty leagues (200 kilometres)
from Tete to this place, and thirteen leagues (65 kilometres) from Luanze as the crow flies.

Yet another Portuguese account fixing the location of Bocuto
concerns an account about the need to construct fortifications on the
Zambezi above Tete, Masapa, Bocuto and Luanze. Of these:

the third fort shall be at a place named Bocuto, where
there is also a *feira*, along the river Manzovo (Mazowe)
where it is met by another river called Inhadire, (the
actual Nyadiri), which is forty leagues from Tete and ten
leagues from Masapa.. (23)

This description provides a conflicting location and further investigation will be required before Bocuto is definitely positioned. The
construction of these forts was contained in a royal communication
to the Viceroy of India, Dom João Forjas Pereira dated 21 March,
1608.)

In 1960, a prospector named Calder, working along the lower
reaches of the Mazowe discovered a long abandoned stone wall
construction close to the confluence of the Nyadiri and Mazowe
rivers (map ref VS 48 52) and he was particularly struck by the
clever use of shaped stone blocks in the walling which was close to
the Mazowe. Calder's discovery (24) appears to substantiate the
1608 Portuguese report concerning the construction of a third fort
at Bocuto near the confluence of the Manzovo and the Inhadire (the
Mazowe and the Nyadiri rivers).

There are various unconfirmed reports about a Portuguese
earthwork in the Umfurudzi but these have never been substantiated. There are a number of ancient gold workings in the nearby
Pfungwe district (25) but the predominant source of gold in this area
is alluvial, and gold panning in the Gwatera and Mazowe is
common.

The Mazowe river is the central geographic feature of this area
and the Portuguese made use of it as a route into the Rivers from
Sena and Tete. During the dry winter months which last from May
until September it provided a permanent source of water on these
journeys. The river was also used to measure the length of the
journey as we have noted above.

Lower down the Mazowe river, Calder discovered galina, lead and silver on the slopes of the Nyakata mountain (map ref VS 682 564). The existence of silver in this mountain evokes echoes of the centuries-old Portuguese quest for the precious metal. The prospector did not find any evidence of ancient workings however. (26) As the Mazowe flows into Mozambique it narrows and passes through the eastern mountain range which forms the edge of the Zimbabwean plateau. There is a stone fort on the slopes of the Nyamatikiti hill (map ref VS 9353) which overlooks Mozambique (27) but no evidence associating this structure with the Portuguese has yet been found.

There are two prominent hill features in the Odzi/Mutare goldbelt named Dambarare and Bokuto respectively and it is tempting to connect these two place names with the two known *feiras* of Bocuto and secondly Dambarare, of which we shall read more later. This is all speculative yet provides an interesting coincidence. (There is a place name of Bokuto in the Mutoko district and further investigation will be required to ascertain any connection with the old *feira*). The Portuguese were extremely active in the Odzi and Mutare goldbelts and these geographic place names may well have been transferred. The same may be said of the Musapa gap in the Eastern Highlands district of Chimanimani which gives rise to the Musapa river just south of the early Portuguese trading *feira* of Bandire. The Musapa river valley was an old trade route to the interior people of the Hera and Mbire in the Sabi and beyond. The name Musapa or Masapa may well have been taken by the Portuguese for their feira near Mount Darwin. There is no local oral tradition to give evidence that Masapa is a local name.

Feira of Masapa

In Francisco de Sousa's description of the Rivers, Villages and *Feiras* of the Portuguese contained in his *Oriente Conquistado* of 13 December 1697, it is noted that Masapa was the third *feira* on the journey up the Mazowe river and located at a distance of fifty leagues (250 kilometres) from Tete. The settlement included a Dominican church dedicated to Our Lady of the Rosary. Masapa was described as being near the great mountain of Fura which was rich

in gold. Stone wall ruins were said to exist on the mountain and flowing from it was the *Mocaras* or Mkaradzi river with its little sands of gold which the *cafres* or Africans gathered .(28) Although this account is dated well after the destruction of the *feiras* it is of importance in fixing the location of the third *feira*. There is a report dated 1631 of a Dominican church at Masapa attended by a Friar. The Dominicans were extremely active and built a number of churches at the various Portuguese *feiras* (29 & 30)

Diogo do Couto's chronicles of 1573 describe Masapa as being the third fair, some fifty leagues from Tete. Masapa was located by Diogo do Couto as close to a long, thickly-wooded mountain called Fura (31). The Swahili knew the mountain as *Aufur* and there has been some hysterical and unscientific speculation by Edwardian writers of the early twentieth century connecting the *aufur* of the Swahili with the spurious legend of Ophir, the Queen of Sheba and King Solomon's mines. Mount Darwin, known locally as Fura is an imposing geographic feature which stands 1 508 metres above sea level.

During a geological survey of the district in 1960 conducted by Major O. Mather, no less than 18 different ancient gold workings were discovered and these were said to be so numerous that they merged one into the other (32). To this day, alluvial gold is recovered from the Mkaradzi river which rises in the mountain. The work takes place when the summer rains have subsided and the water flow is reduced. The sheer extent of these early workings and the level of alluvial gold recovery from the Mkaradzi valley bear strong witness to Portuguese activity in this area during the sixteenth and seventeenth centuries. No positive identification of the Masapa settlements has yet been concluded although in 1932 miners clearing rubble from old gold workings on the south bank of the Mkaradzi river came across shards of blue and white porcelain (33).

These claims, known collectively as the Duke of Cornwall claims were worked in 1917, in 1928-30 and finally in 1932 before being abandoned. In the Mather reports the area around Mount Darwin was described as being largely uninhabited save two mining camps. The thick bush was the home of elephant, rhinoceros and other large game animals but these have since all disappeared. The countryside was well forested with *brachystegia* woodland which thrived in the localised precipitation around Mount Darwin. The ridges overlooking the Mkaradzi valley were covered with Msasa and Mupfuti trees and in the lower-lying areas there were stands of Mahogany which prefer the acid soils of the pegmatites (34). Mather also commented on stone-wall enclosures in the vicinity of

Fura. At the end of his survey work in the district, Mather claims that he found earthworks which he believed to be Masapa but unfortunately his description is so vague that the place cannot be found again.

The writer visited Fura during 1975 and examined a number of stone-wall structures on the western ridge of the mountain.

These circular walls appear to date from the so-called *refuge period* of the nineteenth century when stone encirclements or corrals were hurriedly built by placing rough stones one upon the other in a haphazard fashion.

There is a stone-wall ruin dating back to a much earlier period found on a granite kopje above the Mkaradzi valley (map ref US 553 412). The use of dressed stone and the general architecture distinguish this as a *zimbabwe* or *rusvingo* type of construction which employs the use of shaped and carefully fitted stone blocks often decorated with chevron pattern inlays. Three shards of blue and white Chinese porcelain were recovered from the surface of a midden below a section of walling on the eastern side of this ruin.

There are grounds for attempting to connect this *zimbabwe* with the site of the Mutapa Kapararidze's *dare* of the seventeenth century. Father António Gomes's account of the murder of the Portuguese emissary Jeronimo de Barros of 17 November, 1628 contains one small clue. Andre Fereira, who had accompanied the unfortunate Jeronimo de Barros, refused to heed the Mutapa's summons to attend his *dare* and escaped under cover of a seasonal thunderstorm gaining the safety of the Masapa stockade.

Barely one thousand metres from this ruin there is considerable evidence of Portuguese occupation in the form of blue and white porcelain shards, grey-black stonewares and hut dahka. All this Plate material was found by the writer in a field on farm no. 3 (map ref US 555 415). A short distance away, on farm No. 7 at map ref US 562 422 there is further evidence of Portuguese habitation with surface finds of red Indian Cambaya beads, shards of Chinese blue and Plate white porcelain and stonewares. Fragments of glazed green Plate stonewares with carved ornamental acanthus leaves with Jui borders in yellow similar to those found at Luanze were also recovered.

A more comprehensive search of this field on farm No. 7 revealed surface finds of blue, green and red beads, a plain brass locket and a brass badge similar to artifacts found at Fort Jesus and described by James Kirkman in his account of the 1958 excavations. Still within a general radius of one thousand metres there are other surface finds of imported Chinese and Portuguese wares (map ref US 568 423) including a fragment of a Wan-Li plate. Finds of the common grey-black Chinese stonewares, Portuguese terracotta wares and beads are common alongside hut dahka, *guyo* and *huyo* grinding stones and other evidence of joint African-Portuguese occupation.

The present day residents of these farms all confirm that when they settled the land in the early 1970s and started ploughing the virgin lands, they discovered blue and white porcelain shards in great quantity but thinking nothing of them, ignored and discarded them. The owners of both farms no 3 and 4 indicated the existence of old wells upon their properties which provide water throughout the year. Finds of blue and white porcelain occur at farm no. 2 at map ref US 569 404. The wide distribution of this material points to the existence of Masapa as a complex of settlements over an area of approximately four square kilometres at the very least and to a certain extent similar to the pattern followed at Macequece and Dambarare.

Masapa was deserted in 1693 when the Rozvi razed the old settlement after the destruction of Dambarare.

Feira of Dambarare

This feira of the Rivers was perhaps the most extensive of all the settlements. It is difficult to say when Dambarare was founded although it has been determined by archaeological evidence that the area was settled by the late sixteenth century or early seventeenth century. By 1631 Dambarare was an established *feira* with a Dominican church and by 1667 Manuel Barreto was able to write that Dambarare was a noble settlement with a good-sized town. Diogo de Sousa de Meneses who, in 1635 was Captain of Mozambique, spoke of alluvial gold in the *Manzovo* (Mazowe) river which flows from Dambarari (or nearby). In the 1670s Dambarare's fortunes declined and the region was plagued by locust swarms, drought and disease which seriously depleted the population (35).

The rise of the Rozvi in the 1680s prompted the then Captain of Mozambique, Caetano de Melo de Castro, to appoint Francisco do Valle as Captain of Dambarare in June 1684 with specific instructions to strengthen the *chumbos* as protection against possible attack (36). African resentment of the Portuguese was increasing and

Mello de Castro noted that the *mwanamuzungo* or bastard sons of the Portuguese were untrustworthy and more prone to spying for the Mutapa than remaining loyal subjects of the King. The constant bickering and in-fighting — *murmuração* so prevalent in the Portuguese lines and the callous treatment of the African auxiliaries aggravated the situation.

Fortifications were duly constructed at Dambarare. Almeida y Sousa described one of these garrisons as being located on a terrace which commanded a splendid view of the surrounding countryside which had plentiful water year round (37). The nearby river was the *Marauoza* (present day Murowodzi) and said to be only a stone's throw from the fort. There may well have been several fortifications, including one on a small hill which enjoys an excellent panorama. The top of deeply-embedded stones still trace the rectangular outline of the fort apparently described by Almeida y Sousa (38). Part of Melo de Castro's master plan for the protection of the Rivers included the deployment of between 18 and 20 artillery pieces. Outdated *falcões* (bronze artillery pieces.) were to be sent back to Goa and recast. Eventually, two small artillery pieces were delivered to Dambarare together with an armoury with sufficient stocks of gunpowder and flint.

In the late 1680s the main settlement at Dambarare was nothing more than a pathetic cluster of mud or *taipa* huts within a wooden stockade near the Murowodzi river. In 1698 Fr. Filipe de Assumpção reported that Dambarare, prior to its destruction, comprised mud and wooden walls by the Murowodzi river with a moat which had been constructed by Caetano de Mello de Castro. He also reported the presence of two small artillery pieces. There were no soldiers and an atmosphere of neglect pervaded the place (39).

The stockade was afforded some additional protection with an external ditch or moat. Writing in the 1690s António de Conceição declared that " at Dambarare we used to have a fair with its earthworks, but within, there was nothing more than the Church with its Vicar and Captain, the rest lived in the vicinity at some distance from one another." In November 1693, according to a description by the same writer the inhabitants of this feira were killed before they could reach the safety of the fort, the Church was desecrated, burials allegedly disinterred and Priests flayed alive

(40). After the destruction of Dambarare it may have been temporarily occupied in the early eighteenth century by Portuguese Indians but it was never to resume its former importance.

During the Portuguese occupation of Dambarare many Portuguese planted and cultivated gardens and orchards. Pithy wild lemon trees (41) growing along river valleys in the Mazowe district may date back to groves planted by the Portuguese. These have become the progenitors of lemon and orange trees now extensively cultivated at the Mazowe Citrus Estates in the picturesque valley 30 kilometres north of Harare, the capital city of Zimbabwe.

The first modern reports suggesting the whereabouts of this *feira* came in 1891 when Theodore Bent reported finds of what was then described as "old Delft and Nanking Chinese pottery" near the Jumbo mine. The fertile Mazowe valley and the abundance of gold attracted many European settlers and prospectors in the late nineteenth century. The next link in this chain of scientific detective work comes from the finds of Elizabeth Goodhall of the Queen Victoria Museum who collected finds of imported Chinese ceramics from the surface of the present day site of Dambarare in 1944-45.

The final conclusive evidence was provided by the historian D. P. Abraham who identified the earthworks as being Portuguese (42). In 1966 the archaeologist Peter Garlake was taken to a large earth mound by a prospector, who in 1923, had discovered a human burial in the remains of the old foundations. In the interim, the site revealed to Garlake had been ploughed and cultivated making it almost unrecognisable. Here Garlake carried out his excavations (map ref TR 777 654) in June 1967 (43). Infra-red photography clearly delineated the extent of the earthwork which comprised an enclosure of 90 metres in width from east to west bounded by four straight earth banks about 155 metres in length on the eastern side and 180 metres on the western side.

Garlake found that this earthwork was the largest of four similar structures in the area. Within the confines of all these earthworks he gathered surface finds of Chinese and Portuguese ceramics. He noted that the Murowodzi river contains alluvial gold (44) and that there was an ancient working immediately below earthworks at map ref TR 763 674 , close to the Murowodzi river. These workings contained shafts up to 20 metres in depth with ores assaying around

74,5 dwt. Garlake also commented on an old working with " very regularly cut galleries with arched roofs, quite uncharacteristic of ancient African mining techniques." He observed that this tunnel might have been hewn under Portuguese direction but there was no evidence of gold although iron might have been extracted as the horizontal duct drives into an ironstone outcrop.

Garlake unearthed portions of two separate buildings which were made from sun-dried brick *(taipa)* laid in double flemish bond with the main wall being about 90 centimetres thick. Although the quality of masonry was poor this was compensated for by the width of the walls which were capable of carrying fairly substantial roofing timbers with grass thatching. Several iron nails, contemporary with the building, were recovered from the site. Garlake excavated thirty-one burials from the two buildings leading him to conclude that these had been Churches. The undisturbed skeletons lay extended, full length, with arms crossed about their chest, hands clasped at the waist, or in two cases, clasped to the head. This appeared to follow Christian and not traditional African burial practice. Furthermore, the burials were laid out in an east-west direction. Ten of the remains were of male caucasoids, the remainder being both male and female negroids plus a number of infants. Some of the burials contained grave goods consisting of carved ivory beads, a bronze medallion, bronze and silver aiguillettes, an engraved silver buckle, gold rings, copper epaulettes and various other items of European manufacture (45).

Garlake assembled a collection of 3 182 shards of imported ceramics from China, Portugal and Persia (Iran). The Chinese material included blue and white porcelains, grey-black and green glazed stonewares. The Portuguese shards consisted of faience and terracotta wares.

In endeavouring to determine the duration and extent of European occupation of Dambarare it is interesting to note that a mere two per cent of the buildings in the main earthworks were examined. As Garlake concludes, should the ninety-eight per cent of the area still unexcavated follow the same pattern, it would conceivably contain more than one thousand burials. There is no evidence to the contrary. The majority of the skeletons belonged to European males many of whom were barely mature but had already lost many teeth - not an uncommon occurrence in the sixteenth and seventeenth century and particularly so under conditions of extreme hardship, unhealthy diet and climate. It may be extrapolated from this evidence that Dambarare was a major centre of Portuguese activity in the seventeenth century surpassing even Masapa in importance as the staging post for the outlying *feiras*. Further archaeological investigation of Dambarare is strongly indicated.

An interesting find at Dambarare is a shard of indigenous pottery bearing markings characteristic of the Barwe Tonga of the lower Zambezi valley. Similar material has been unearthed at the confluence of the Mazowe-Ruenya system and the Zambezi — the site of Massangano, a Portuguese settlement dating from the seventeenth century on the Zambezi route from Sena to the *feiras*. Massangano was examined by Peter Garlake and M.D.D. Newitt in 1967 when seventeenth century Chinese ceramic sherds were found. The *Aringa* of Massangano comprised a stockade of wooden stakes surrounding the settlement of mud huts. The ruins are located at the junction of the Mazowe-Ruenya and the Zambezi about 40 kilometres below Tete. This was on the established trail of the seventeenth century linking Sena with Luanze, Dambarare and Masapa and in 1667 Manuel Barreto observed that a Portuguese named Manuel Pires de Pinho had a stronghold there. In later years the infamous Da Cruz family occupied Massangano as their headquarters. In 1891, an engraving appeared in *Relatorio da Guerra da Zambezi* published in Lisbon, illustrating the settlement as comprising a wooden stockade and dwellings on the banks of the Zambezi river (46). This gives us an insight into how the old *feiras* may have appeared — earthworks reinforced by a pallisade of wooden stakes.

The artillery pieces described earlier were not found but they could well have been removed by the Rozvi forces of the Changamire in 1693 and taken to Danangombe-Dlodlo in western Matabeleland. Two Portuguese cannon, one bronze breech-loader and one iron muzzle-loader with the Portuguese Coat of Arms, together with assorted Portuguese relics, were found there in the late 1890s by European prospectors. The cannon were subsequently removed to South Africa on the orders of Cecil John Rhodes and they are now displayed at Groote Schuur, the official residence of the South African State President in Cape Town .(47)

There are no signs of fortifications at the earthworks excavated by Garlake so António da Conceição's description about a Church within a fort may relate to another site altogether. There is a well-defined earthwork at map ref TR 763 674 which is defensively situated having clearly raised bastions still visible to this day. Almeida y Sousa says that the fort was a " stone's throw from the river" which although unidentified may well have been the Murowodzi which flows extremely close by. This earthwork is now occupied by farm employees who have built huts inside the perimeters.

The land has been extensively ploughed by hoe cultivation disturbing the foundations of a building. Considerable imported material is to be found scattered around the immediate area. During a visit to the site in 1986 the writer was handed a small bronze medallion similar to that found by Garlake in 1967 and this may provide yet another clue in retracing the footsteps of the Portuguese to Dambarare. The possible existence of another Church at this earthwork awaits further scientific investigation and the most promising reference point is the ruins of the old structure where hut dahka and imported porcelain shards abound.

For many years Dambarare was the front-line outpost in the Rivers and the focus of considerable mining and trading activity. Whilst recovery of gold by panning alluvial sands in the rivers around Dambarare was certainly taking place, the Portuguese may have engaged in their own geological exploration. The existence of ancient diggings at the Jumbo mine, including a horizontal tunnel about two metres wide with a square roof arch, are suggestive of this. More than thirty-five old workings, several with open stopes, deep shafts and large rubble heaps are recorded in the area (48) and some of these may have been the work of mining specialists like Videsy Albarado, the Spaniard, who visited the Rivers in the 1630s.

Angwa *Feiras*

The Portuguese settlements along the Angwa river were known collectively as *Ongoe* (49) which is a clear phonetic derivation of Angwa. They consist of at least six earthworks which extend for some eight kilometres on both banks of the Angwa river which is rich in alluvial gold. The largest is situated at map ref RM 155 118 on Two Tree Hill Farm in the Mhangura district of north-eastern Zimbabwe. In a brief account of the Rivers of Cuama by Father Filipe de Assunção, written after fourteen years residence in the region and obviously in the wake of the Changamire campaigns of the 1690s we are informed that the Angwa was three days journey from Dambarare. Francisco de Sousa, in his *Oriente Conquistado* of 13 December, 1697 describes the *Ongoe feira* as being four days from Dambarare. The feira was noted for its very good gold. There is no exact evidence of when the Angwa *feiras* were first occupied but in 1684 João de Sigueira was sent by Caetano de Melo de Castro to rebuild the *chumbos* against possible assault by the Changamire (50).

After 1693 most of the Portuguese withdrew but some hardy Indians remained including Domingos Carvalho who was a relative of Manuel Pires Saro, *capitão-mor* of the Portuguese garrisoned at the Mutapa's *dare* in the Zambezi valley in the post Changamire era. Domingos Carvalho developed successful trade with a local African Chief supplying him with cloth in exchange for silver (51).

The Africans were careful not to disclose the source of this precious metal but after some time a canny Portuguese Indian allegedly discovered the source of the silver lode. He secretly obtained samples of the ore which were sent to Jose da Fonseca Coutinho who was then Lieutenant-General of the Rivers. Part of this silver was melted down and reportedly wrought into a chalice for the Sena Cathedral (52). We cannot be certain about the veracity of this information by Father António da Conceição as the only evidence of ancient mining in the Angwa or Piriwiri region was for gold and copper. Most of the ancient workings which occur in this mining region were based on gold and copper but silver is present although extraction would have been difficult. There are no silver mines, per se, in this district. Although the modern day Alaska mine near the headwaters of the Angwa river is a major producer of silver, this is only a by-product of copper.

In 1919 some Chinese pottery shards, an iron spearhead and a gad (a primitive mining implement) were discovered at the Angwa claims. Within a few years, a brass cup of Indian origin was found Plate 6 in rubble 12 metres down old workings at the D Troop Mine and this

61

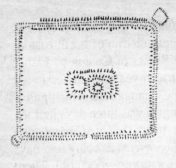

vessel is now on display at the Bulawayo Museum. No fewer than eleven ancient workings have been reported upon in the immediate area of the old Portuguese settlements. The Angwa river is close to the Mhangura and Shamrock copper deposits and semi-precious aquamarines occur in nearby hills. A fairly broad spectrum of gemstones is mined in the Miami district north of the Angwa river. One mine in particular, the St Anne's, produces good quality aquamarine, heliodor, golden beryl, blue topaz, tourmalines and garnets. During a field trip to the Angwa river

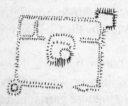

in 1988 the writer was offered gold dust and uncut aquamarines. After the 1693 exodus, *Canarins* or more correctly Marathi-Konkani Indians from Goa returned to this area and continued trading with the Africans. Goanese Indians with experience in mining manganese, iron ore and precious stones in India may have been able to

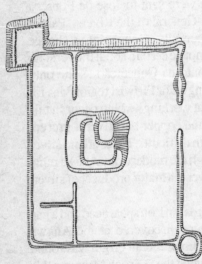

employ their skills. Old timbering found in the Crescent claims, which were opened up in the early twentieth century, may date back to the seventeenth or early eighteenth century. These timbers were never scientifically dated but were reported to be of considerable age when first discovered (53).

During 1941, H.B. Maufe, of the then Rhodesian Geological Survey Department visited the Angwa valley and reported the existence of the Portuguese earthworks. This prompted a field expedition to the region led by Elizabeth Goodhall of the Queen Victoria Museum in 1945. During her extensive survey, Goodhall visited and described in considerable detail four earthworks. (54)

The first of these is situated at map ref RM 147 092 and comprises a rectangle about 43 metres by 35 metres with a central mound likely to be the remains of a dwelling occupied by the Portuguese. The second earthwork is at map ref RM 132 116 and this measures approximately 57 metres by 47 metres with the northern and eastern walls about one metre in width and height. The central mound of this earthwork attracted Goodhall's attention because it had evidently been excavated by early prospectors. She was informed by her guides that the mound was the remains of a three-roomed house. Inspecting the site, Goodhall discovered that the structure was made from sun-dried oblong bricks similar to those employed at the Dambarare earthworks examined by Garlake.

Goodhall learned that in 1915-20 a mining family named Quarrie worked the Mum's Reef Mine a few kilometres distant. Old Mrs Quarrie was later interviewed by Goodhall and revealed that she had been attracted to the site by a large tree which was growing out of a curious shaped anthill. Suspecting this was no ordinary termite mound, Mrs Quarrie ordered a gang of labourers to dig into the hill where brick walling was encountered. The labourers destroyed much of the walling but were able to recover some fragments of blue and white porcelain and some arrow heads. These objects were removed by Mrs Quarrie but subsequently disappeared. A *stoep* or verandah was located adjacent to the broken walling. Mrs Quarrie described how she found a rectangular yard paved with sun-dried *kimberley* bricks which were so heavy they were almost impossible to lift. Goodhall concluded her examination of this site by determining that careful scientific work would be necessary to establish the full extent of this building. The only surface finds of any value comprised the rim of a fine-grained light brown glazed earthenware flask tentatively identified as being of Portuguese manufacture. Before leaving this site Goodhall was informed of the alleged existence of a " Portuguese fort " in nearby hills but was unable to visit it.

Goodhall then crossed the Angwa river to the east bank where she met an old prospector named Martin, who in 1945, was reputedly the oldest surviving European resident of the Angwa river

valley goldrush. He acted as her guide. Goodhall was shown the two earthworks originally found by Maufe in 1941 and the first of these is at map ref RM 159 145. It measures about 100 metres by 82 metres and is protected on all sides by earthen ramparts with parallel ditches about one metre deep. This earthwork is Monument No. 70

On the western side of the earthwork, running parallel to the nearby Angwa river is another outer wall beyond which the ground slopes down to the river banks. Modern trenching by prospectors has disturbed many features of the earthwork and the central foundations.

Close to the north-eastern boundary of Two Tree Hill Farm extension at map ref RM 161 154 the fourth earthwork was revealed. This extends some 62 metres by 50 metres and has clearly defined raised earth walls on all four sides. The north-west corner has a squared bastion, somewhat irregular in shape, measuring about 7 metres square. Three of the outer faces of the bastion were faced with stones. The south-eastern corner comprised an irregular round earth wall enclosing a raised platform well above the ground floor level of the inner enclosure. This earthwork also features a central foundation mound which measures 14 metres by 19 metres and in 1945, when inspected by Goodhall, showed signs of interference by prospectors. Goodhall noted that two rectangular stones were laid on the edge of the mound suggestive of steps about 90 centimetres by 51 centimetres. Martin informed Goodhall how prospectors had broken into this mound and found internal chambers.

The Angwa *feiras* were visited by the writer in 1986 when it was observed that large scale alluvial gold recovery was in progress along the river banks with consequent damage to the earthwork which has been declared National Monument No. 70. The surrounding countryside has been settled by peasant farmers who unfortunately, whilst engaged in the recovery of gold from the alluvial sands, are doing considerable damage to the fragile riverine ecology of the Angwa and many of its tributaries (55). The results of Goodhall's inspection of the Angwa *feiras* in 1945 still remains unsurpassed but more work is vital to determine the full extent of these settlements before the evidence is lost.

All four earthworks were large and well constructed with brick-built dwellings located inside. The type of masonry employed is similar to that described by Garlake at Dambarare and Maramuca. Clearly the Angwa *feiras* represent a complex of well established settlements which were probably occupied well into the eighteenth century by Portuguese traders. These *feiras* may yield important evidence of Portuguese activity and now await more serious archaeological examination. There is considerable urgency in this task for the increasing demographic pressures upon this hitherto largely uninhabited region of Zimbabwe now threatens the fragile physical remains of the *feiras*.

Feira of Maramuca

In 1667 Manoel Barreto (56) who was posted to the Rivers in 1664 wrote an account of Maramuca which he described as " the richest in gold known and that many thousand *pastas* could be obtained if the Kingdom were ours". (One Portuguese *pasta* was equal to one hundred *mithqals* with one *mithqal* being equal to about 4,5 grams of gold; hence one pasta was equal to about 450 grams of gold.) Manoel Barreto related how a respectable Portuguese trader named Gonçalvo João had secured tribute to Maramuca concessions from the King of *Mocaranga* according to proper procedure. Yet, António Roiz de Lima and a half caste or *Mwanamuzungo* named Simão Gomez, who were envious of João's possessions, conspired with a local African chieftain and mobilised an attack on Maramuca killing many of the residents including a number of *Mucoques* or *Canarins* (Portuguese Indians) and African troops in João's service. After plundering the settlement on the banks of the Suri Suri river, the two conspirators brought accusations against João to the Captain of Dambarare. They claimed that it was João who had fermented the local uprising, inimical to Portuguese interests in the region. João was found guilty and he lost his concessions to the two plotters. João later appealed against this judgement to the Viceroy at Goa. Clearly Manuel Barreto was sympathetic to João's cause because he recommended, in his text, that the lands be restored to the appellant (57).

In 1648 Father António Gomes reported that the territory of *Abatua* was located beyond a beautiful river (58) possibly the Mupfure or the Munyati, and the lands were rich in gold which its people came to trade for beads and *machira*. The lands of *Abatua* would have encompassed the modern goldfields of Kadoma, Golden Valley, Battlefields, Eiffel Flats, Kwekwe-Sebakwe and Gweru-Shurugwi.

Several sixteenth century maps of south-east Africa mentioned *Quitecuy, Quiticui* and yet others refer to *Quytege* or *Kitenge* in the lands of Monomotapa. Extreme caution must be exercised when trying to relate these Portuguese place names with the modern gold-producing centres, but in this case there is a vague orthographic reference to Kwekwe (originally named Que Que until its name was changed in the 1980s.) Other Portuguese place names are much more certain as in the case of Matafuna. During António Fernandes's travels through Zimbabwe he was evidently impressed by the amount of gold available in the country and his travels may well have taken him through the general Kwekwe-Sebakwe region. The Kwekwe district remains an important gold producing area and its numerous ancient workings and milling sites lend some credence to the Fernandes reports of the early sixteenth century.

An anonymous report of 1683 (59) mentions Maramuca as being in the heartland of *Mocaranga* and inhabited by people completely different from those elsewhere in the country. Maramuca had so much gold and of such fine quality that the local chief considered himself independent of the Mutapa. The same chief was said to carefully regulate trade between his people and the Portuguese, whom he described as being " thirsty for gold and therefore necessary to conceal the mines from them." Maramuca lay beyond Chitomborwizi in the lands of *Abatua* described by António da Conceição in his report of 1696 as *the mother of gold* so great was the legendary fecundity of this golden region. He lamented, however, that very little of this gold ever went to Portugal and that it only served to enrich India. The gold was mined in Africa only to be transported to India where it was reburied - a reference to the Hindu predilection for gold ornamentation and the custom of cremating the dead with all their jewellery.

For the Portuguese, the lands of *Abatua* must have seemed like the elusive *Eldorado* which they sought so assiduously. António Gomes , writing in 1620-30 said that:

> Blacks from Abatua bring a lot of gold in thick pieces weighing about three or four patacas being the best carats in all these lands.

Gomes also reported that Abatua produced copper and there are indeed several old copper deposits in the Kwekwe, Gweru, Sanyati, Hunters Road and Battlefields districts which all fall within the confines of the supposed regions of Abatua.

The same Abatua was famed for a medicinal and curative herbal balm made from a root to which the Portuguese ascribed the name *Abatua root* (60). In all likelihood the Abatua root was the *Trichodesma physaloides,* g*wiramwaka* in Shona, commonly known as the Bells of St. Mary. This perennial wild flower usually about 30 cm high, widespread at medium altitudes in open woodland and grasslands, is characterised by several stems clustered on top of a woody root (61).

The root contains a slimy substance with an astringent quality drying and healing wounds and sores quickly. Portuguese medicinal knowledge at that time was virtually nil and the few medications, if any, brought from Portugal or India were generally harmless if not completely useless. The universal treatment for fever was a phlebotomy and purging, often with fatal results. In all certainty, many Portuguese would have gratefully accepted treatment from African *n'angas* or traditional healers who treated their septic wounds, bouts of dysentery and other maladies of the day restoring them to relatively good health.

The evidence in support of the Portuguese reports about gold in the lands of Abatua is, to a slender extent, substantiated by the large number of gold workings around the *feira* of Maramuca and elsewhere in the modern day Midlands Province (on the eastern fringes of Abatua which lay further to the west corresponding to the Khame-Torwa State). These include the incredible Cam and Motor Mine at Eiffel Flats, the Golden Valley and Dalny mines at Chakari and the Globe and Phoenix and Gaika mines at Kwekwe which are all located on the site of ancient diggings discovered by European miners in the late 1890s during the gold rush. There are no less than twenty-four old workings including Dalny Mine in close proximity

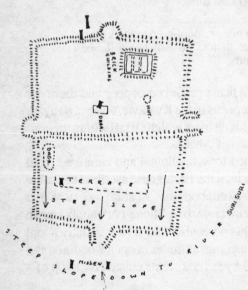

to Maramuca. Most of these claims have extremely rich ores and have been extensively worked during this century. To the east of Maramuca is the Gadzema mining area which is reputed for its extensive ancient workings including the Giant Mine where a nugget of weight 1,5 ounces was found in a large open–cast pit when the claims were first pegged early this century. The John Francis claims revealed a 12 metre deep reef paying up to 70 dwts. Surface outcrops of white quartz thickly studded or streaked with golden veins can still be found in the Gadzema-Chegutu district (62).

Located along the western banks of the upper Mupfure river are a series of ancient workings in an area known as Hartley Hills. Modern strikes of platinum and gold are associated with ancient workings in the district. Copper and gold was mined at the Reg M claims where an X–shaped copper ingot was found when the old claims were being developed (63).

The Golden Valley area has more than thirty old claims and yet others can be found in the Eiffel Flats and nearby Concession Hill districts. The entire region surrounding Maramuca is literally riddled with ancient workings and many of these are now being exploited by modern methods. With the mining and prospecting taking place around Maramuca in the early twentieth century it was only a matter of time before the remains of the old Portuguese settlement were discovered. In February, 1965, an old unsigned mining report dated 28 May, 1947 was found in the Kadoma Mining Commissioner's office and this described a "Portuguese fort near the Suri Suri river in the Golden Valley-Chakari districts" (64).

Garlake visited the site and established that the earthwork bore a close resemblance to Luanze with external walls measuring 60 metres by 70 metres and laid out in a north-facing direction. Bastions about 6 metres wide extend from the centre of each wall, and close to the western bastion the remains of a sun-dried brick structure can still be seen to this day. Garlake examined this building which he found to be 9 metres by 6 metres with an estimated height of 3 metres. Further identification was complicated by an encroaching ant-hill which has largely enveloped most of the old building. There is little doubt that this earthwork is identical to the Maramuca of the Portuguese texts. The positive identification of Mara-

muca is convincingly argued by Professor D.P. Abraham using African oral tradition and Portuguese text to locate this *feira* (65). The name Maramuca refers to *Rimuka* or the lands between the Mupfure and Umzwezwe rivers and this is exactly where the *feira* is located. A residential quarter of the modern town of Kadoma is named Rimuka. The discovery, in the 1930s, in the back-fill of ancient workings at the Bay Horse Mine on the western banks of the Mupfure river, of an ivory statuette depicting Our Lady of the Immaculate Conception - clearly an example of Indo-Portuguese craftsmanship of the late sixteenth and early seventeenth century - further substantiates the Portuguese presence in this area. Finds of imported ceramics at Maramuca are rare and restricted to shards of the ubiquitous grey-black Chinese stoneware jars.

Feira of Chitomborwizi

In his 1698 description of the Rivers of Cuama, Father Filipe de Assumção makes mention of yet another *feira* of the Rivers at a place known to the Portuguese as *Quitamboroizi*. António da Conceição claims that the *feira* of Chitomborwizi was located near the headwaters of the Angwa river (66) and this is evidently located in the vicinity of the modern day — Chitomborwizi district west of the Manyame river. The traditions of the Chirau people of the Zvimba district confirm the early presence in the area of Portuguese merchants as well as gold-mining activities at Zviringohwe hill (67), located at map ref SR 88 65. Chitomborwizi is also mentioned by António Bocarro in his Decada 13, Chapter 75, as a place frequented by traders from Masapa and raided in 1597 by an African chief (68). Zviringohwe is about twenty kilometres west of the Manhame river, but within the modern day district of Chitomborwizi

just north of the Zvimba Communal Lands. The Golden Kopje mines at Mara and Zviringohwe hills have been extensively worked during this century producing large quantities of gold. There are numerous ancient gold and copper workings in the vicinity comprising open stopes, pits and deep shafts. The Alaska copper mine to the north of Golden Kopje remains an important producer of both silver and gold as by- products from the copper refinery.

It has not been established whether the Portuguese ever built a settlement at Zviringohwe hill in the Chitomborwizi district and it is more likely that they visited for seasonal trade only. According to Portuguese records the *feira* of Chitomborwizi was three days march from Dambarare and it comprised a trading settlement with a few Indians (69). These conducted their business in great stealth so as not to alert the Changamire who lived in the lands of Abatua to the west.

Feira of Matafuna

In his 1698 report on the Rivers, Filipe de Assumção reports on the existence of *Matafuna* as a place where the Portuguese merchants pass through (70). Matafuna is readily identified by the existence of a hill of the same name close to the modern town of Shamva. The combined Shamva-Bindura geological area has over 49 recorded ancient workings with deep shafts, underground stopes and pillars. Some of the ore left behind in these rock supports has produced values of 40 dwt. Many of the ancient mines were obviously worked for some time and in some cases the narrow tunnels follow the reefs for considerable distances.

In common with many ancient mines the working depth was only restricted by the water table, below which mining was difficult because of constant flooding. The Big Slam mining claims feature small circular drives into extremely hard rock faces and are most uncharacteristic of traditional African mining methods (71). Evidence of early Iron Age human habitation around the Tafuna hill is available from the examination of sites at Oaksey Farm, Tafuna Hill, where " dolly holes " or milling sites were discovered in 1971 (72). These " dolly holes " were used to grind up gold ore before washing in nearby streams.

The importance of the *Matafuna feira* or region as a gold producer for the Portuguese is underlined on several seventeenth century Portuguese maps of the Rivers. On one particular map, Tafuna is marked as *tezouro de Rey* or the Royal Treasury, and on another Tafuna is identified with the legend *minas de ouro* or mines of gold. A number of rivers drain through the Shamva gold–field into the Mazowe river which flows in an easterly direction immediately to the north of the district. All of these systems and the Mazowe itself are extremely rich in alluvial gold and large scale panning by thousands of Africans continues to this day (73). According to Father Manuel Barretto's account of the Rivers:

> the principal places where gold is obtained in abundance are Dambarare, Ongoe, Mocanca and Maramuca.

He also reported on the presence of a Portuguese captain at *Chipiriviri* (the *Chipiriviri* district is associated with the Angwa river valley gold-fields.) Manuel Barretto's reference to *Macanca* or *Macana* and *Mocraz* as places where the best river gold of Mokaranga is produced are both readily identified as *Makaha* and *Mkaradzi* respectively and described earlier in the text.

Feiras of Manica

António da Conceição, writing in 1696, referring to events prior to the Changamire's rampages, described the *feiras* of Manica as being under Portuguese authority because they were rich gold producers (74). The most important of the Manica *feiras* was the complex of settlements located at *Macequece*. These consisted of timber and mud-walled houses, *chumbos* and *taipas* and a Dominican church (75). The garrison of *Macequece* was held by a mixed force of Portuguese and *Mwanamuzungos,* and African troops commanded by a *Capitão-mor.* Spiritual guidance, for Santiago and Eldorado went hand in hand, was the preserve of a resident Dominican priest. The Portuguese residents lived in peripheral settlements because they found it convenient to avoid the close scrutiny of the resident captaincy. There was fierce rivalry between

72

the Portuguese who clamoured to buy gold from the Manyika gold panners .(76) The general secrecy about the gold trade was noted in 1634 when Vides y Albarado and Francisco Figueiredo de Almeida visited Manica to survey known and suspected gold producing areas. (77)

As noted above, the principal *feira* was Macequece (Masekesa in Shona) but the place was more commonly referred to by its Manyika name of Chipangura. (78) Today, the central feature of this extensive trading complex is a stone-wall and earth-bank fort adjacent to the Mazi river at map ref VQ 8706. The architecture of this fort is interesting because of five defensive bastions with loophole gun emplacements. The fort was examined by the author in 1990 and it is clearly of nineteenth century construction. The fort is built with stone blocks on high land and commands a good defensive view of the surrounding countryside and the Revue valley. (79) This is the general area of *Velha Macequece* and the late nineteenth century fortifications were built here. During an investigation of the old ruins conducted by Engineer Pires de Carvalho in 1946 it was established that the modern fort had been constructed on a much older site. Closer examination of these remains revealed pieces of Portuguese faience ware and other imported ceramics (80). In 1634, Macequece was governed by a *Capitao-mor* named António Coloco (81) and this suggests that an official *regimento* declaring *feira* status on Macequece had been issued by the Portuguese authorities. Itinerant Portuguese, *mwanamuzungo* or *vashambadzi* population at Macequece fluctuated according to the seasons, but peaked during April and May when the summer rains had abated and gold recovery was at its height. But at most times of the year Macequece served as a focus for the Manyika people who came on a regular basis to trade with the Muzungos.

The Manyika brought agricultural produce, metal work, gold-dust and other goods for exchange. The Portuguese *feira* concept became firmly entrenched in Manyika tradition and endured long after the departure of the Portuguese (82). Father António Gomes visited the Manica area in 1648 noting that the region was frequented by traders from Sofala and Sena. Gomes also remarked upon the medical properties of the local African herbal remedy which the Portuguese described as the Manica Root; possibly identical to the Bells of St. Mary *Trichodesma physaloides*. This wild flower occurs throughout the lowland slopes of the Eastern districts mountains. It can also be found growing in proximity to old stone wall ruins of the Ziva culture in the Nyanga District. The *Ximenia caffra* or Sour Plum which also grows in the Manicaland province is another alternative as this is extensively used for the treatment of sores and wounds.

Feira of Matuca

The Vicar of the Rivers of Manica, Father Gaspar de Macedo visited the *feira* of Matuca in 1633 (83). The present-day whereabouts of this *feira* have not yet been ascertained, but according to Portuguese documents it was located in the *Mukahanana* hills in the Odzi District. Here he preached at the Chapel of Saint Dominic (84). *Mukahanana* may be a corruption of *Nyamkwarara,* a river which rises in Mozambique near boundary beacon No. 13 and flows eastwards for about eight kilometres before turning north-east where it enters a flat stretch of alluvium which extends for approximately two kilometres to the Zimbabwe border. The river continues through precipitous country and is joined by the Tsanga, the Chisanza and Nyamakwadobi before widening and flowing back into Mozambique. During the early twentieth century the river alluviums were extensively mined by Europeans who reported the existence of extensive terraces, craters and gravel dumps. This was said to be the work of African miners who washed the alluvial gravels during pre-colonial times (85). The writer has visited gold sluicing sites at the old Mimosa claims above the Nyamkwarara (also written *Inhamucarara* in Portuguese orthography) river valley in the Manica mountains adjacent to the Zimbabwean border and observed large numbers of Africans engaged in gold mining. The priest described the gold fields of Matuca as being so rich in gold that the Africans could readily afford to buy many *bares* of cloth from Portuguese traders (86). Extensive gold panning took place in the rivers which drain the Odzi gold belt, including the Mtanda range and the Dzungarara hills. The Mutari river, which in the local Manyika dialect means River of Metals, is noted for the alluvial gold in the river gravels.

The afore-mentioned river drains the Mutare gold belt flowing in a westerly direction to its confluence with the Mbeza and the Odzi (87). The Odzi gold belt is a geological formation approximately 5 kilometres wide on average giving rise to a persistent range of hills running in a south-westerly direction. In addition to gold and some silver, tungsten, tin, tantalum, lithium, lead and copper also occur (88). Gaspar de Macedo continues his account of the Matuca region describing the presence of crystal or clear quartz deposits in the Mukahanana hills (also possibly a corruption of Dzungarara) which were exploited by the Africans to manufacture gold weights (89). The quartz deposits could be seen from some distance away by the reflection of the sun on the glistening outcrops (90). Quartz occurs in considerable quantity on the western side of the Murapa hills in the Mtanda range where it is associated with tantalite (91).

In 1535-36, João da Costa (92) was the chief Portuguese trader at Matuca when the geologist Vides y Albarado visited the Tambarira silver mine and recovered some seven and a half *árrateis* of the precious metal (93) (one *arratel* is equal to one pound weight i.e. 16 ounces.) The Portuguese experts conducted a survey of the Muramba mine in the Murapa hills but were disappointed with the results and they recommended that the most profitable way to recover gold was to sluice and pan the rivers in the same manner as the Africans (94).

The Tsungwizi river which flows through the Mtanda range near the Muramba mine is extremely rich in alluvial gold and during a visit to the region in June, 1990, a local miner demonstrated the recovery of tiny nuggets from the sands for the author (95). There are numerous ancient workings in the Mutare, Penhalonga and Odzi mining districts of Manicaland and whilst most of the mines produce gold there are some rich in silver but not in pure form (96).

The Penhalonga reef extends into Mozambique and mining takes place on both sides of the international boundary. There are extremely rich alluvial deposits in the Revue river valley of Mozambique (97). Virtually all the modern mines of the district owe their existence to the old workings which were revealed to late nineteenth century and early twentieth century prospectors. Some interesting artifacts including a copper coin of Antonius Pius found at Odzi and a silver Sixpence of Elizabeth I (1572) found at Quagga Mine have been recovered.

Although the exact site of Matuca has not been established it is clearly within the confines of the Mutare and Odzi goldbelts. The word *matuca* may be a dialectic corruption of the Shona word for *dhaka* or *mutaka* being the contemporary Portuguese word for the gold bearing mud. The Mutare river, with its alluvial sands, may well be the general region of *Matuca*. Portuguese accounts state that the countryside surrounding Matuca was found to be most suitable for human habitation with the cold winter months followed by relatively cool highland summers which were compared favourably with European climatic conditions (98).

This corresponds exactly with the prevailing climatic conditions of this picturesque region of the Eastern Highlands. Macedo observed many exotic fruits growing in this region included figs, pineapples, guavas, papaya, oranges, limes and lemons. He also remarked that local water-melons were excellent and as good as those from his native Ribatejo village in Portugal. In Matuca and Manica the months of June and July were especially cold and water froze at night and fields were covered in frost.

On 28 June 1684, the Captain of the Rivers garrisoned at Sena, Caetano de Melo de Castro, appointed Belchior de Castro Soares to the sub-captaincy of Manica – a task which the incumbent does not appear to have relished in view of the threatening Rozvi invasions. Soares is subsequently reported in *Livro das Monções* (Vol. 49,) to have abandoned his command returning to Tete where he was arrested and charged with cowardice. This official action did little to stem ebbing Portuguese morale in the Manica *feiras* and inevitably the settlements fell to the advancing Changamire. By the beginning of the eighteenth century, all the Portuguese stations of Macequece, Vumba, Matuca and Bamba (possibly named after the Mbama peak in the Mtanda range, Odzi district) were deserted.

Feira and Zumbo

After their expulsion from the Rivers in the 1690s the Portuguese settlements near the confluence of the Zambezi and Luangwa rivers (on the borders of Zambia, Mozambique and Zimbabwe) started to assume greater importance, particularly in the ivory trade. Early evidence of Portuguese settlement of this region can be found on the 1655 publication of a map by Nicholas Sanson (1600-67) famed for his Atlas *Cartes Generales de Toutes Les Parties du Monde*, which marks the position of Chicova (99) and the suspected location of the legendary silver mines. The map defines the correct geographic flow of the Zambezi and thereby supports the contention that the Portuguese were already established on the upper Zambezi prior to publication of the map.

Some time around 1720 (100) a settlement was in existence on an island known as Chitakatira near the confluence of the Zambezi and the Luangwa but this was abandoned in favour of the slightly healthier north bank of the Zambezi where the little town of Zumbo was built. Zumbo was only granted official status in 1788 (101).

In 1754, Father Pedro da Trinidade, O.P., was granted title to a section of land by Chief Mburuma, an important African potentate, and a Chapel and living quarters were built here (102). Pedro da Trinidade died in 1751 after a long and fascinating life. Professor Charles Boxer, in his epic *Portuguese Seaborne Empire* states that contrary to Portuguese sexual proclivity in the tropics, Father Trinidade remained celibate until his death (103). The Priest was held in high esteem by the local people whom he taught various skills including the use of European agricultural implements and farming techniques and his memory was revered long after his death (104). To this day Trinidade's name is well remembered in local oral traditions because he has become a *mudzimu* or ancestoral spirit and as late as 1862 there was a local medium or *svikiro* claiming to host Trinidade's spirit (106a). His ecclesiastical status notwithstanding the good Father traded on an extensive scale in gold, copper and slaves (105) and Zumbo and the surrounding district were his private fiefdom.

This industrious Dominican Friar is also attributed with the creation of gardens laid out along the fertile flood plains of the Zambezi with orchards of mangoes *(Manifera indica)*, limes *(Citrus aurantifolia)*, bananas, papaya and other food crops (106). As in the case of his Dominican colleague, Father João de Meneses, O.P., the virtual Lord and Master of the Querimba islands of northern Mozambique, Trinidade certainly did not exemplify the ideals of a Christian missionary. Still, both Trinidade and Meneses kept the Portuguese flag flying and did more for Portuguese interests than the dissipated administration. An intriguing stone cross on the Hill complex at Kame may have been the work of Pedro da Trinidade or another Dominican priest who visited the old Torwa state during the eighteenth century but there is no supporting evidence for this contention. This Christian symbol was constructed from dressed stones in the shape of the Maltese Cross and laid out on a large rock on the top of a walled hut platform. It was restored in 1938 and is clearly visible to this day.

In the late 1750s a second settlement was built on the west bank of the Luangwa, on high ground overlooking the Zambezi, and this subsequently became known simply as *feira* (107).

The economic development of Zumbo and Feira was never as dependent upon the eastern highveld gold as the *feiras* of the Rivers had been during the sixteenth and seventeenth centuries. The settlements traded up the Zambezi river and had commerce with the Rozvi. There is a strong association between Zumbo and the Rozvi although their commerce was supervised largely by *vashambadzi*. The extent of this relationship is best illustrated in Rozvi willingness to provide Zumbo with military assistance against the Mutapa in 1743, 1772 and 1781 (107a). The Rozvi were also willing to ally the Portuguese at Manica during the 1780s. This military support for the Portuguese at Zumbo underlines the prevailing Rozvi superiority on the highveld. This trade was likely to have persisted until the 1830s when Rozvi cohesion was shattered by the Nguni invaders from the south.

The Zumbo *vashambadzi* carried with them great inventories of beads, Chinese porcelain and cloth receiving in exchange gold and ivory. Muzzle-loaders, lead and gunpowder were also in demand.

Kame, the first Torwa-Rozvi settlement was replaced before 1700 by Dlodlo or Danangombe which continued to be the centre until 1866 when the Rozvi finally yielded to the Ndebele. Rozvi clans scattered to new locations in central Zimbabwe where they survive to this day. In some cases, the old *vashambadzi* units of measure for cloth have survived in local Rozvi dialects (107b).

There may also have been trade with the eastern Shona around the old feiras. A new trade started to develop between 1730 (108)

78

and the early 1800s. This was directed at the Kafue pedicle (109) and the rich Katanga province of Zaire which produced ivory, copper and malachite, a greenish coloured, semi-precious stone. The trade in malachite must have reached substantial proportions as artifacts fashioned from the attractive green marbled stone is much in evidence in homes of older Goanese families around Panjim and Calangute in the Indian state of Goa (110). In 1766 António Pinto de Miranda published a report on Zumbo and its inhabitants described as *zumbeiros*. All of them were apparently Goanese whose leader was Manuel da Costa who owned some 1000 slaves. The christian ecclesiastical needs were served by a pole and mud under thatch church administered by Dominican Brothers. This visit must have taken place during the tenure of Father Pedro da Trinidade.

Cloth, glass beads, and possibly *ndoro* and some ceramics were the mainstay of Portuguese currency until the settlements of Feira and Zumbo were destroyed by Mburuma's forces around 1836. When David Livingstone visited Zumbo and Feira in 1856 the old settlements were in ruins (111). The Portuguese took the initiative and tried to regain their upper Zambezi settlements in 1861 when Captain-Major Albino Manoel Pacheco was despatched to rebuild Zumbo. Unfortunately Pacheco proved unpopular with his men who mutinied and threw him into a dungeon where, but for the assistance of an African concubine who helped him to escape, he might have perished (112). In August of 1888, Frederick Courtney Selous visited Zumbo where he was shown the ruins of the old town by the resident Portuguese, Senhor Gourinho (Goudinho). Only the ruins of the two hundred year-old church with solid white walls were still standing.

In 1892, the Dominican tenure on Zumbo having ended, Jesuit Priests built the magnificent church of Saint Pedro Claver at their Miruro mission station on high ground some 36 kilometres from Zumbo between the Chossavo and Lualadesi rivers, tributaries of the Luangwa. In the early 1970s the mission comprised extensive farm lands, orchards of tropical and European trees and an agricultural training school. Father Pedro da Trinidade would definitely have approved.

So pervasive was the Portuguese word *feira* that it became the *de facto* place-name and its use continued long after the Portuguese were gone. This sleepy administrative hollow of Feira was recently re-named Luangwa by the Zambian government. Although Zumbo was later re-occupied by the Portuguese in the 1860s the village of Feira was completely deserted until, later in the nineteenth century, British colonial administrators built a *Boma* or District Commissioner's office there. In 1901 the British used stonework from the old Portuguese fortifications to construct Government offices. The site of the old Portuguese *feiras* was examined in 1960 by J. Desmond-Clark who discovered stone walling laid out in a defensive configuration on a hill-top above the Zambezi river just west of the Luangwa confluence. On the north slope of this high ground the ruins of a substantial dwelling, laid out in an H shape, were detected. This, according to Clark was reminiscent of architectural styles popular with the Portuguese in Mozambique and Angola during the seventeenth and eighteenth centuries. A cursory examination of a midden, exposed by erosion, on the southern slope of the hill facing the Zambezi river revealed potsherds of Chinese blue and white porcelain and one fragment of porcelain with a yellow line round the rim (possibly a piece of Portuguese faience ware), various glass beads and pieces of glass-case bottles (113). Clark also noted that most of the indigenous African earthenware pottery found in association with this site consisted of shallow bowls with a flat pedestal base and decorations on the inside. These bowls resemble those still being manufactured by the Chewa-Nsenga and Gowa potters of the upper Gwembe valley, the Tonga name for the Zambezi river. Clark contends that these pottery traditions may have been influenced by the large volume of imported Chinese and Portuguese wares brought into this region during the heyday of the Portuguese.

It might be tempting to make similar assumptions in the case of African pottery found at the Zimbabwean feiras and particularly so in the case of shards of graphite-burnished wares which occur at Masapa. Argument could be advanced that the large storage vessel known as *gate* in Shona was influenced by the imported Chinese stoneware jars but this is unlikely. During Gonçalvo da Silveira's mission to the Monomotapa in 1560 which took him to the Dande by way of Tete, Luanze, Bocuto and Masapa he was faced with a dilemma when attempting to cross the flooded Mazowe river. Silveira left Tete on 18 September 1560 and he would have reached the Mazowe area during the rains. Luis Fróis S.J., reported that Silveira had to endure the indignity of huddling inside a large earthenware pot which was pushed across the river by African companions. A similar large pot was used to ferry the priest's regalia and both of these vessels are undoubtably identical to the *gate*, (a large earthenware pot for brewing millet beer.)

Although the Portuguese were restricted from entering the Rozvi lands they did penetrate for a considerable distance up the Zambezi and may well have pre-dated David Livingstone's famous claim to have been the first European to have gazed upon the Victoria Falls. There is unconfirmed speculation that the stone cross at Kame was built by a Portuguese priest. (In May, 1990 a clearly defined stone cross laid out on a large stone boulder was still intact.) There are similar, unsubstantiated reports that the curious ramparts or battlement configuration on the decorated western wall of Nhandare ruin may be the work of Portuguese captured by the Rozvi in the 1690s. During the late eighteenth and the early nineteenth century, Portuguese traders in search of ivory and slaves ranged up the Zambezi and traded extensively with the Tonga supplying them with beads, cloth and ceramic *ndoro*. Examples of these beads and ceramic ndoros may still be found amongst the African people of the Gwembe valley, the Tonga name for the Zambezi (114). During the mid-nineteenth century the Portuguese and their *Chikunda* vassals operated an important trading entrepôt at Kasoko (115), some 6 kilometres upstream from the present day Chirundu border post.

The economy of this settlement was based upon gold, ivory and slaves which were exchanged for glass beads, cloth, ndoros and cowries. The slave trade in Mozambique reached real commercial proportions around 1750, and when the sale of firearms was legitimised in 1787 (116), it gave further impetus to this iniquitous traffic. Although the bulk of the trade was restricted to northern Mozambique and the Zambezi *prazos* slaves did move through Feira and Zumbo. The Portuguese also traded up the Luangwa valley during the nineteenth century where they had four major settlements at Mosiko, Kalunga, Kakengi and Nyakatoro (117). A settlement was allegedly built at Macambo in 1827 close to the confluence of the Rukusuzi river and the upper Luangwa in Zambia's north eastern province (117a).

There are a number of ruined stone houses on the high ground of the Zimbabwean bank of the Zambezi overlooking the confluence and these date back to the nineteenth century. Middens associated with these dwellings all yield typical nineteenth century wine jars — particularly popular are stoneware bottles marked *vinho verde* — amongst other detritus of human occupation (118).

Portuguese cartography of this period indicates an extensive geographic knowledge of the Zimbabwean highveld. Most of the *feiras* are clearly marked on the old maps but not all of them have been positively located or properly examined, specifically Chitomborwizi, Matuca, Maungwe, Bocuto and Masapa. Recent work at Mount Darwin now points to the existence of Masapa as a complex of settlements over an area of about four square kilometres (119). The physical remains of the earthworks at the known *feiras* are fragile and the encroaching bush, the passage of time and the ravages of human activity pose a serious threat. Given suitable financial and human resources more archaeological work at the *feiras* would undoubtably contribute much to a better understanding of African-Portuguese activity on the highveld. Garlake's pioneering work at Dambarare has shown us that many secrets remain buried. Urgent scientific work is indicated. The debris left behind at the *feiras* together with other physical evidence of Portuguese-related finds will be examined in the next chapter. This provides an intriguing and different Luso-Zimbabwean perspective on the Portuguese expansion during the Age of the Discoveries.

REFERENCES

1. *Documents*, Vol. VIII, p. 271. See also Theal's *Records* Vol III, p. 468.
2. There are three seasons in Zimbabwe; a dry winter from April-August with morning frost, a hot season from October to mid–November and the third when the rains start and continue until March — Cloudy weather moderates the temperature during the rains. The climate on the highveld, which includes the principal goldbelts is generally moderate and healthy compared to the lowveld. See also Theal's *Records* Vol III p. 482.
3. *Documents.* Vol VIII, p 269.
4. Personal communication W. Atkinson to H. Ellert, 1986. Atkinson was the manager of the G & P mine when the bullion was found.
5. ditto
6. *Documents.* Vol VIII p. 271-273
7. Summers R, *Ancient Mining in Rhodesia*, 1969 p. ???
8. Personal observations when interviewing gold panners at Mount Darwin, Mazowe and Ruenya. H. Ellert, 1988-89-90.
9. *Documents.* Vol VIII p. 271-273, Documents Vol IX p. 125,127.
10. *RSEA* Vol II p. 416-417.
11. Drummond & Coates Palgrave, *Common Trees of the Highveld,* Longmans, 1973, p. 7 and others.
12. *RSEA* Vol II p. 416-417
13. *Vlei,* Afrikaans expression, adopted into Zimbabwean English usage meaning an open grassy valley - a catchment area or headwater.
14. Frei Gaspar de Macedo, *Monções*, Vol 41, Beach/Noronha translations, 1980.
15. Zimbabwe-Monomotapa culture in SE Africa, Menasha, WISC. USA, 1941, p. 57-64. Summers R. *Ancient Ruins of Rhodesia,* 1971, p. 27.
16. Garlake P.S., 17th Century Port. Earthworks in Rhod. *Arch.Bull.* Vol XXI No. 81-84, 1966 p. 157-170.
17. D.P. Abraham to J.A.N.Whitty 1-8-61 QVM., details of a stone-lined well buried by overburden of river sand in the Nyadota river.
18. Summers R. *Ancient mining in Rhod.*, 1969. see The Geology of the Makaha Goldbelt, *Bull.*, 1935.
19. *The Monuments of SR.*, 1953, Edited by R.J. Fothergill, Comm. Preservation of Nat. & Historical Monuments.
20. ditto.
21. Personal communication M. Igoe to H. Ellert, 1989.
22. QVM ref. 1631 DD4, DD7, DD 18, Macguire.
23. *Documents* Vol IX p. 127
24. QVM ref 1632 DA1 Macguire.
25. QVM ref 1631 D4 Macguire.
26. QVM ref 1632 DA2, 1631 D1 Calder.
27. QVM ref 1632 DB1 J. Sutton, 1972.
28. Fransisco de Sousa, *Oriente Conquistado,* 1696, description of Rivers-Beach/Noronha translation, 1980.
29. Mudenge S. op. cit. p. 265.
30. Beach D.N. op. cit. p. 232.
31. *Documents* Vol VIII p 273
32. O. Mather, Umtali Museum, report, Mount Darwin District. Sites of Archaeological Interest, 1960.

33. QVM, 1932 report by R.L. Hobson.
34. Geology of Mount Darwin district. *Bulletin* Nr. 73, 1974.
35. Garlake P.S. 17th Century Port. Earthworks
36. ditto
37. ditto
38. Personal observations at the site, see also Axelson E., *Port. 1600-1700*, p. 179.
39. Fr. Filipe de Assumpção, 1698, *Ajuda* 51 VIII 40, 270/2 Beach/Noronha translations, 1980.
40. Axelson E. *Port. 1600-1700*, p. 182-83
41. *Citris limon*, wild lemons grow along the banks of the Marowodzi river immediately below one of the earthworks, personal observations H. Ellert, 1989-90.
42. D.P. Abraham to Cooke QVM 31-12-60 advising location of Dambarare - mention of Dambararwa hill near the Maruwodzi river.
43. Garlake P.S.
44. Gold panning still occurs along the banks of the Marowodzi river, observations by H. Ellert, 1991.
45. Garlake P.S. Some Early Port. Relics from Dambarare. *Rhod Scientic News* Vol II, No. 12, 1968 p. 260-261 for details.
46. Newitt M.D.D. and Garlake P.S., The Aringa at Massangano, *Journal of African History*, Vol VIII, 1967, p. 133-156.
47. Cooke C.K. Dhlo Dhlo Ruins, The Missing Relics, *Rhodesiana* No., 22, 1970, p. 45-52 in which Cooke has traced the present whereabouts of artifacts removed from this site in the late 1890s.
48. Summers R. *Ancient Gold Mining in Rhod.*, 1969.
49. Fr. António da Conceição & others.
50. João de Sigueira - Angwa in 1684.
51. Axelson E. *Port.*, 1600-1700, p. 184.
52. Fransisco de Sousa, *Oriente Conquistado*, 1696, Beach/Noronha translations, 1980.
53. Summers R. *Ancient Mining in Rhod.*, 1969.
54. Preliminary Report on Portuguese Earthworks in Angwa Valley, 1945 by Elizabeth Goodhall, QVM.
55. H. Ellert, visit in 1986, personal observations.
56. Manuel Barreto SJ., wrote prodigiously about his experiences and observations in the Rivers. Abrahams D.P. Portuguese Records and Oral Traditions, *JAH* Vol II, 1961, p. 218-219.
57. ditto.
58. António Gomes, 1648
59. Abrahams D.P. op. cit., p 220.
60. António da Conceição
61. *Trichodesma physaloides*, see Margaret H. Tredgold and H.M. Biegel, *Rhodesian Wild Flowers*, Museums and Monuments of Rhod., Thomas Meikle Series No. 4, 1979, p. 45.
62. Summers R. *Ancient Mining in Rhod.*, 1969.
63. Summers R., op. cit.
64. Garlake P.S. 17th c. Portuguese Earthworks, *Arch., Bull.* Vol XXI, No. 81-84, 1966, p. 165-170. see also O. Mather to C. Cooke 23-2-62 with report from local farmer Mr. Eric Wilson on Suri Suri earthworks.
65. Abrahams D.P. op. cit. p. 220
66. Filipe de Assumpção, 1690, Beach/Noronha translations 1980.
67. Abraham D.P. op. cit. p. 221.
68. ditto
69. Mudenge S. *Pol. History of Munhumutapa*, ZPH., p. 290.

Plate 22B

Plate 23

Plate 25

Plate 24

Plate 26

late 27

Plate 28A

Plate 28B

Plate 29

Plate 30

Nine Slides of Shards

Nine Slides of Shards (continued)

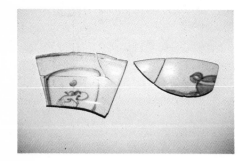

Plate 31

Plate 32

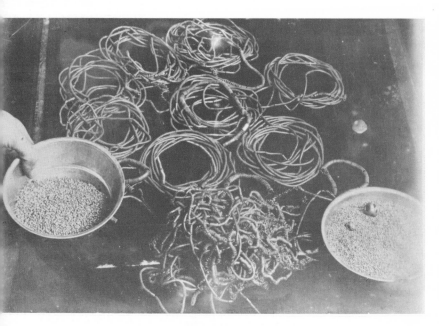

Plate 33

Plate 34

Plate 35

70. Assumpção, 1698. Note that Matafuna features on most 17th and 18th Century maps of the Monomotapa Empire evidencing the importance of gold from this area - Shamva valley, Mazowe valley.

71. Summers R. op. cit.

72. Garlake P.S. *SA Arch Bull.* No. 26, 1971, report on Tafuna Hill iron age sites.

73. Personal observations by H.Ellert in 1991 along the Mazowe river and tributories. A visit to the Nyagui river confluence with the Mazowe and indications by Steven Kasingasenge, P.O. Box 17, Chiwore School, Shamva, of extensive gold panning near the confluence with work being done by women chipping away at tiny rock crevices to expose heavier gold concentrates trapped below.

74. António da Conceição,

75. Bhila H.H.K. *Trade & Politics in a Shona Kingdom*, Longmans, 1982, p. 79. In 1790, Manuel Galvão da Silva reported that the garrison consisted of a square stone and clay construction. The only function of the fortification was to provide an enclosure for the church built also from stone and mud under a thatch roof. Bhila., op. cit. p. 122. This description of Macequece appears consistent with the prevailing state of Portuguese settlement in the region.

76. Bhila., op. cit. p. 79

77. Fr. Gaspar de Macedo, *Monções,* Vol. 41, 17-19v. Beach/Noronha trans., 1980. p. 12.

78. Bhila., op. cit. p 79

79. H. Ellert, visit to Vila Manica district, Mozambique, 1990, The 19th century stone-walled fort is located on a farm belonging to the District Administrator of Vila Manica. The site was indicated by Mr. Pedro Américo from Museu Geológico, Delegação Provincial de Recursos Minerais, Manica, Mozambique, 27-10-90.

80. Pires de Carvalho, Velha Macequece, Moçambique, 1946.

81. Bhila, op. cit. p. 79

82. ditto p. 280

83. Fr. Gaspar de Macedo, Monções, vol 41, Beach/Noronha trans., 1980., p. 13

84. Bhila., op. cit. p. 80

85. The Geology of the Odzi Gold Belt., *S.R. Geological Bull.* No. 45, 1956.

86. Gaspar de Macedo, op. cit. p. 13.

87. The Geology of the Umtali Gold Belt, *S.R. Geological Survey Bull.*, Nr. 32, 1937-1964, p. 74-81., details of the alluvial gold.

88. ditto, and visit by H. Ellert to Nyamkwarara valley 27-10-90.

89. Gaspar de Macedo, op. cit. p. 15

90. Gaspar de Macedo, op. cit. p. 15

91. M. de Klerk to H. Ellert, 15-6-1990, report on quartz deposits at the mine.

92. Theal G. *R.S.E.A,* Vol II, p. 412.

93. Bhila H.H.K. op. cit. p. 80

94. ditto p. 280

95. De Klerk to H. Ellert, 1990, visit to Tsungwizi river and examination of the alluviums.

96. The Geology of the Umtali Gold Belt, The Geology of the Odzi Gold Belt.

97. D. Sheeran to H. Ellert 13-8-90. Mr. Sheeran is a geologist working for Lonrho at the Alluviões de Manica Lda. engaged in the exploitation of the alluvial gravels in the Revue, Chua and Inhamcarara valleys of the Vila Manica district.

98. Gaspar de Macedo, op. cit. p. 15

99. Desmond-Clark J., The Portuguese Settlement at Feira, *N.R. Journal,* 1965, p. 276.

100. Desmond-Clark, op. cit. p. 276, mention of a small party of Portuguese from Goa settling on the island.

101. D. N. Beach to H Ellert, 1991.

102. Desmond-Clark, op. cit. p. 277-279.

103. Boxer C.R. *Port. Seaborne Empire 1415-1825,* 1969, p. 145.

104. Boxer C.R. op. cit. p. 145

105. Boxer C.R. op. cit. p. 145
106. Desmond-Clark J. op. cit., p. 279, quoting Pacheco on the extent of the gardens at Zumbo.
106a. Beach D.N., *Rhodesiana*, No. 36, 1977 p. 100
107. Desmond-Clark, op. cit. p. 280-281.
107a. Beach D.N., *The Shona and Zimbabwe,* Mambo, 1980. p 221-222,243-244.
107b. S. Mudenge to H. Ellert, personal communication, 17-1-1992.
108. ditto p. 280
109. ditto p. 280
110. H. Ellert, visit to Goa, Panjim, Calangute, 1990, personal observations in several private homes.
111. Livingstone D. *Travels*, 1860, p 532.
112. Desmond-Clark J., op. cit. p. 286
113. ditto p. 286-287.
114. Reynolds B., *The Material Culture of the People of the Gwembe Valley*, Manchester, National Museum of Zambia, 1968.
115. *Zambia Museum Journal*, Vol 3, 1972.
116. Boxer C.R., An African Eldorado-Monomotapa and Mocambique, *CAHA*, 1960, p. 10-11. Alpers E.A., The East African Slave Trade., Hist. Assoc. of Tanzanian, 1967, p. 6-7.
117. Baxter T.W. *Zambia/N.R. Journal,* Vol VI, 1965,p. 167.
117a. Flemming, C.J.W., In Search of Macambo in *Rhodesiana,* 25, 1971, p.53. In 1824, the governor of Sena, Col. Jose Francisco Alves Barbosa recommended the place as being suitable for an ivory trading post.
118. H. Ellert, visit, 1988.
119. H. Ellert, Feira of Masapa : Portuguese Settlement in Zimbabwe during 16th and 17th c enturies, Mount Darwin district, *Zim. Science News,* Vol 22 , No. 5-6, 1988, p 62., and UZ., Dept. of Archaeology, field investigation and test pits in same general area. Evidence of imported Chinese ceramic shards and other material. Report yet to be published.

CHAPTER 3

Finds

Description of the imported artifacts and their impact upon African society

The association of imported Chinese ceramics with historical sites in Zimbabwe seems most unlikely, but this is indeed the case. Porcelain shards and other artifacts provide us with tactile proof of Portuguese enterprise in north-eastern Zimbabwe during the sixteenth and seventeenth centuries. Exotic finds of Chinese blue and white porcelain, Dutch Gin or case bottles, Portuguese and Persian faience wares, ornaments, religious artifacts, weapons and a whole miscellany of objects associated with the Portuguese are absorbing reminders of a little-known period in Zimbabwe's pre-colonial history. Most of these articles were for domestic use, as the Portuguese had quickly discovered that African tastes had been conditioned by centuries of Swahili trading involving the exchange of gold, ivory and slaves for beads and cloth. This routine endured throughout the sixteenth and seventeenth centuries and long after the ejection of the Portuguese from the Rivers, Portuguese traders, principally Goan *prazeiros* and Banyans from Portuguese India, based at Mozambique Island, sold muzzle-loaders, beads, shells and cloth. For these, strong demand persisted until the early nineteenth century when British commercial interests were asserted. The Portuguese also sought semi-precious stones, copper and silver. Cotton and to a certain extent silk, were much in demand as the indigenous cotton growing and weaving industry was unable to cope. Cloth was known to the Shona speaking people as *machira* and the Portuguese dutifully recorded this in their contemporary records. The Portuguese term *retso* for silken cloth has also survived particularly in Njanja cultural traditions. Small yellow, red, green and blue glass beads were highly prized in trade and many of these have been recovered from the *feiras*.

The Portuguese may also have been responsible for the introduction of exotic flora and fauna to the Zimbabwean highveld and the evidence for this will be reviewed in greater detail. All these imports verify the presence and activities of the Portuguese during their 150 year tenure of the Rivers. Each has a fascinating account of a provenance in distant lands, a long and arduous voyage by sea before the overland journey to the Rivers of Cuama (1).

Chinese Ceramics

The story of Chinese ceramics in Zimbabwe is not restricted to the Portuguese phase but dates much earlier. In 1902, a vast hoard of objects, ascribed to the Royal Treasury of Great Zimbabwe, was uncovered by fortune hunters in the valley below the Hill Ruins of Great Zimbabwe, near Masvingo, Zimbabwe. Included in the inventory of imported artifacts were a number of thirteenth century glazed Chinese Celadon *Lung Ch'uan* dishes in pale green and blue hues dating to 1300-1500, a blue and gold inscribed Persian faience bowl from the fourteenth century and a small assortment of Far-Eastern glazed stoneware (2).

Shards of green Celadon have also been found at other *Zimbabwe* sites concurrent in archaeological terms with this great central African society (1100-1450) characterised by its unique stone masonry and decorative walled enclosures. These discoveries merely confirm the widespread order of trade down the east coast of Africa from around 900 which was dominated by Arab, Persian and Indian merchants who brought Islamic and Chinese wares and other trade goods. From 1300 onwards Chinese porcelains, including Celadon, became fashionable at coastal settlements from Lamu on the Kenya coast (3) possibly as far south as Sofala and Manyikeni from whence such material was traded with inland communities such as Great Zimbabwe (4).

These Chinese wares, bowls and dishes, were favoured as decorations in mosques and graves at Swahili coastal sites. Chinese ceramics were often set into elaborate headstones. Fine examples of these may be found on the Tanzanian and Kenyan coastline - specifically noteworthy is a tomb at Kunduchi, twenty kilometres north of Dar es Salaam, Tanzania, where it stands in the midst of other early Swahili ruins.

In the 1300s and 1400s Celadon was a famous export ware from China with its plain glazes ranging from shades of green, grey and blue. Pieces similar to those retrieved in Zimbabwe have also been found at Ishikani, Ungwana and Gedi along the East African coast (5).

There is also hearsay evidence that Chinese ocean-going junks visited Malindi on the Kenya coast between 1417 and 1422 (6). Although their furthest ports of call were usually in India and Malacca it is not known for certain exactly how far west *Cheng-Ho,* the great Chinese navigator of this era, sailed.

The arrival of the Portuguese in the Indian Ocean established them as the dominant maritime power of the region until their superiority was successfully disputed by the Dutch around the turn of the seventeenth century. The landfall of Jorge Álvares in China and the founding of Macau in 1513-14 were important milestones in commercial expansion and the introduction of Chinese porcelain to the European market. In 1603, a Dutch naval force, commanded by Jacob Van Heemskerck, seized the Portuguese Carrack *Santa Catarina* whilst at anchor in the Johor river, Patani. The prize, near to thirty lasts, comprised a rich cargo of porcelains, lac, silk and other exotic goods from Macau. When the plates, dishes and bowls, decorated in blue and white, were first sold in Amsterdam the following year they caused tremendous excitement (7). As the Santa Catarina put into the river Eems the crew had already started to illicitly sell porcelain at Embden before the rights to the cargo were finally agreed upon. From this vessel and others seized by the Dutch during their global struggle against the Portuguese the name *Kraak porselein* has endured becoming the generic name for porcelain of this type and period. After establishing a foothold in China the Portuguese quickly controlled the carrying trade in Monsoon Asia, carrying goods from Nagasaki in Japan throughout south-east Asia to Goa, Africa and Lisbon.

Homeward-bound Indiamen of the *Carreira da India* carried immense cargoes of Chinese blue and white porcelain from Macau to Goa and Lisbon. The porcelain proved exceptionally popular and found its way into daily domestic use in the Lusophone world. Some of these wares from the *Wan-li* (1573-1619) period of Ming, the transition (1620-1683) and early Ching found their way into Zimbabwe. Wan-li was the last great Ming emperor of any importance and by the end of his reign the imperial Chinese government was dominated by palace eunuchs while the country-side was torn by civil strife as warring Mandarins struggled for territorial gain.

Even from the start of his reign, Wan-li ruled in name only as the *de facto* power rested in the hands of Zhang Zuzheng, the Grand Secretary. Zhang Zuzheng was a man of extraordinary ability who imposed economic reforms and was responsible for a period of economic prosperity in China when exotic food crops like maize and groundnuts were introduced. Unfortunately his measures were not sufficient to prevent dynastic decline and when the dissipated and corrupt Wan-li died, power fell completely into the hands of the eunuchs who continued to rule until 1620 (8).

Not surprisingly, it was during the final years of Wan-li that considerations of quality gave preference to quantity as the potters of the Imperial kilns at Jingdezhen, the porcelain capital, laboured to produce ever increasing amounts of porcelain to satisfy the demands of the eunuchs (9). With the incipient corruption and mal-administration of the imperial bureaucracy a critical change in the ceramic industry occurred as the potters, frustrated by Imperial demands and indecision found it more profitable to make and sell porcelain on private account. The Imperial kilns were largely forsaken by the potters who started to produce wares in private kilns beyond imperial control. The ceramics of this period (1620-1683) are generally known as transitional wares for this was a time when neither the dying Ming nor the succeeding Ching dynasty were able to exert control over the Jingdezhen production. The kilns were once again brought under official jurisdiction during the reign of *Kangxi* (1662-1722) in the Ching dynasty (10).

In appraising blue and white porcelains exported via Macau by the Portuguese during the sixteenth and seventeenth century, it is essential to discriminate between wares made specifically for export to south-east Asia and those for Europe. During the reign of Zhengde (1506-21) a variety of pieces were requested for King Manuel I of Portugal and these pieces bear the armorial sphere of Manuel and the relative Chinese reign marks on the base. This specially commissioned ware pre-dates the later *Chine de Commande* which evolved into a predominant industry controlled initially by the Portuguese but later by the Dutch and successive European nations who all kept trading stations or *Hongs* at Canton in the eighteenth and nineteenth centuries. But it was first in 1517 that Fernando Perez de Andrade anchored off St John's Island, nearly one hundred kilometres south-east of Macau, before reaching Canton where he was the first European granted authorization to trade (11).

Our interest spotlights the more mundane wares of the type commonly referred to as Chinese *export wares*. Porcelains in this category had traditionally been made in China for sale to south-east Asia including Japan, the Philippines, Borneo, Java, Sumatra, Siam, Malacca, Burma, India, the Persian Gulf and the east coast of Africa (12). The Portuguese, as already noted, became involved in

90

the carrying trade and before long many of these pieces found their way to Goa, Damao, Diu, Mombasa, Mozambique Island, Angoche, Sofala and ultimately to the *feiras* of the Rivers.

Export wares were made at many provincial kilns including those at Guandong in southern China (13) where there was easy access to the sea. Such wares were normally of second-rate quality but stoutly potted all the same in anticipation of the rough handling during export transport. A well known export-ware made during Wan-li and the transitional period is *Swatow* and this can be identified by the comparatively poor glaze and the presence of sand and grit on the footrims (14).

Early in the seventeenth century, during the reign of *Tianqui* (1621-27) but still within the transitional period, a somewhat rough and ready blue and white porcelain was produced mainly for export to Japan. Known as *Ko-sometsuke* ware (15) these pieces can be distinguished by the presence of a rather thick glaze which in some cases is more grey than white. The blue decorative underglaze varies in quality depending on the degree of refinement of the cobalt used. It was not uncommon for the glaze to shrink from the rim during firing. This problem was eliminated by the application of a brown dressing to the rims and this practice was common during *Chongzhen* (1628-43). As the Portuguese were then trading with Nagasaki it is possible that examples of the *Ko-sometsuke* ware made its way to Goa and Africa.

The rights to the annual sailing from Goa to Macau and Nagasaki were granted by the Viceroy in return for favour or profit - not surprisingly the Goanese court was regularly petitioned by *fidalgos, fidalgotes, agiotas e vigaristas* (16) (aristocrats, squires, speculators and swindlers) all in search of fame and fortune, fair or foul. The financiers and captains of the great Carrack or Black Ship, known in Japanese as *Kurofune* (17) which returned to Goa after a successful return voyage earned a fortune.

A royal decree of 1609 ordered that 30 barrels of wine and olive oil be sent to the Rivers for the conquest expeditions of Nuno Álvares Pereira as rations for the soldiers (18). The wine was reputed to have therapeutic value against tropical diseases (19) but when it finally arrived in Sena, the factor Adrião Preto, reported that most casks had short measure and the little that remained had been watered. It was finally sold by public auction to a trader Pero Nunes Salgado who paid 445 *meticals* in gold dust (20). Profits on this type of trade were enormous.

Vessels standing out to sea from Goa and bound for Macau – the so called *Grande Navio de Macau* – regularly carried in excess of 200 000 *cruzados* in gold and silver coin and bar (the silver specie was chiefly destined for the Chinese market which had an insatiable appetite for the white metal), ivory tusks, Spanish velvet, barrels of wine, olives and capers (21). Ivory landed in Macau was graded by colour and sold at the rate of 50 *taeis* (silver *tael*, a Chinese coin) for approximately 50 kilos by weight of ivory (22). Olives must have landed at Mombasa for the Swahili word *zeituni* for *Azeitona* is a cogent reminder.

The gold (23) embarked on these China ships was said to be worth a million or more (unfortunately there are no specific details) and much of this was used to purchase pepper and other spices at Malabar and Banda. Return cargo manifests listed thousands of bolts of silks in varying quality, brass ingots, musk, mercury, vermilion, bracelets, camphor and huge quantities of blue and white porcelains stuffed into every nook and cranny on board the creaking vessels (24). The ships – some of the great Carracks and Galleons had a displacement weight of 2 000 tonnes – also carried large numbers of the ubiquitous Chinese stoneware storage jars useful for oil, wine, grain and spices. Most of the fine quality porcelain was sent to Lisbon but some was disposed of in India for domestic household use and regional trade. Around the turn of the seventeen century porcelains available for sale at Canton were categorised into three qualities and prices. Average quality porcelain including dishes and plates cost one and a half *maz* (a Chinese silver coin), ordinary grade plates and dishes were available for one *Real* whilst the fine quality blue and white *palace wares* from Nankin were the most expensive (25). Porcelain subscribing to these descriptions has been found at the old *feiras* as shall be revealed.

Approaching the west coast of India the richly laden Carracks or Galleons from the Far East would sail up the Mandovi after saluting Fort Aguarda which commands the mouth of the river which is the very heart of Goa (now *Velha Goa* for in more recent times the capital moved to Panjim after a great plague struck down the denizens of this bustling Portuguese entrepôt.) In the golden sixteenth and seventeenth centuries, merchants and adventurers from every part of the known world converged on the streets of Goa offering silks and jewellery, porcelains and spices, cotton cloth, ivory, coral and wooden carvings. Customers and traders bargained in a myriad of tongues although Portuguese was the universal *lingua franca*. Magnificent Persian and Arabian horses (26) came ashore destined for the fabulous court of Krishna Deva Raya at

Vijayanagar, the old hereditary ruler of pre-Portuguese Goa, and so did velvet and fine crystal glass from Europe and, of course, gold, ivory and slaves from Africa.

The gold-producing territory of Monomotapa was embodied in the *Estado da India* and subject to the authority of the Viceroy in Goa through a chain of command reaching to Mozambique Island, Sofala, Sena, Tete and finally the Rivers. Successive campaigns and private initiatives into the district enlarged into a steady stream between Goa and Zimbabwe. Vessels from India with passengers and cargo bound for the Rivers would typically embark with the early monsoons which begin on the northern coast of western India around November and December and blow until March the following year. Vessels bound for India would sail from Mozambique around September taking advantage of the best winds.

In the early 1620s, Father António Gomes (27), a Jesuit priest, boarded a vessel which left Goa in the middle of March - extremely late in the season but not unusual as most Portuguese sailings were late. The passage lasted many months as the ship was blown off course by unfavourable winds and adverse weather. In the Maldives, two large porcelain bowls and some rice were traded with the islanders. Before finally reaching Mozambique Island the journey took them south to São Lourenço as Madagascar was then known. After a short respite on Mozambique, António Gomes recommenced his journey to Quelimane via Angoche. Men and cargo were disembarked at Quelimane for the overland trip to Luabo on the Zambezi which was navigable to Sena using small boats and canoes with hoisted sail.

The destination was Sena, which in the sixteenth century was the administrative centre of the Rivers boasting a Fort, Cathedral, hospital, Dominican and Jesuit churches, private dwellings and a school where illegitimate children of the Empire were taught. During his trip along the river Gomes heard complaints about the shortage of marriageable Portuguese women. In the absence of such female companionship, Gomes noted the effects on the men of local African women who were said to be lethal to white men with whom they had sex as their (the Portuguese) blood became infected within a few hours and many would die as a result of the disease known as *antaca*. (A possible reference to a condition known in Shona as *rukau* or *runyoka* (28) which also includes a form of venereal disease.) The incidence of venereal diseases in the Rivers is not generally discussed in Portuguese documents of the time but is likely to have been present given the continuous human traffic and cross-fertilization of people and cultures. Albino Manuel Pacheco discovered that syphilis and diarrhoea were common complaints in the Chedima district (adjacent to north-eastern Zimbabwe) during his 1861 travels from Tete to Zumbo and in 1872 Karl Gotlieb Mauch visited Sena where he reported on the pathetic state of a Goan *mwanamuzungu* laid up with the venereal disease.

In return for all the human miseries visited upon the Amerindians of central America and the Aztecs of New Spain in particular, the Spaniards received syphilis. Hernando Cortes, the *Conquistador*, contracted and suffered from this disease until his death (28a). As Lisbon was a regular port of call for the transatlantic crossings the disease is likely to have become established in the Portuguese capital. Natural sexual propensity accounted for its subsequent spread throughout the Portuguese dominions including the Rivers. The disease was recognised and treated by African folk medicine and at least nineteen different plants are employed in its treatment. These include *Trichodesma physaloides* and *Ricinus communis* (28b), the castor-oil plant indispensable as a binding agent for medicinal preparations.

The trail into the Rivers of Gold now continued westwards up the Zambezi to the junction of the Mazowe-Luenha rivers where a settlement or *aringa* (a Portuguese term describing a stockade made of wooden stakes which surrounds an entire settlement of a great many huts) was built at Massangano. It is about 40 kilometres from Tete and about five kilometres from the confluence of the Zambezi and the Luenha.

In 1667 Manuel Barreto noted that a Portuguese trader Manuel Pires de Pinho had a stronghold here. The site was investigated in 1967 by M.D.D. Newitt and Peter Garlake who excavated finds of seventeenth century Chinese porcelain. Massangano was part of the great highway to the *feiras* during the seventeenth century.

The place was continually occupied until the late 1880s when the last of the great Da Cruz *prazeiros* known as *Bonga* was defeated.

Beyond Massangano, the Portuguese took well-trodden African footpaths and a journey from Sena and Massangano might have taken several weeks. Father Filipe de Assumpção's description of the Rivers of Cuama indicates that the journey from Tete to Masapa lasted between 12 and 14 days overland (29). The accepted routine was to march during the early hours of the morning until midday when the party halted and arrangements made for meals and the gathering of thorn scrub for camp security at night.

The footpaths which connect rural communities follow a winding configuration, twisting and turning to avoid physical obstructions such as hills and kopjes (30). In some cases the paths traced major watercourses like the Mazowe. In the dry season the lowveld countryside, comprising *Mopani* scrubland, was most inhospitable, dry and arid with temperatures reaching forty degrees Celsius. During the rains the extremes of climate were aggravated by the oppressive humidity, biting insects and mosquitoes. Wild animals were a constant danger. All the Royal merchandise, private trade goods, possessions, armaments and foodstuffs were physically manhandled by porters to their destination. It was in this manner that the Chinese porcelains and trade goods were delivered to the Rivers. Some Portuguese were carried in *manxilas* or american hammocks if they were unable to make the tiresome journey on foot.

Diogo do Couto, the soldier-chronicler writing in his *Décadas* (31) gives us a glimpse of these trading caravans marching from Tete to the trading-fairs of the interior:

> there are some merchants who have a hundred or even two hundred captive Blacks of their own whom they order to go trading for them...each of these Blacks carries on his head a small, oblong, well-tied bundle, which they call *mutoro* which bears two *corjas,* that is forty blue cloths, cheap material about seven or eight *corvados* (four to five metres in length) and a little over one *corvado* in breadth... striped cloths...greatly prized by the Blacks and they part them into pieces, in which they wrap themselves, this being the finest apparel in the world for them. The traders also carry small beads made of clay, some green blue and yellow, these making up the necklaces that the Blacks wear around their necks...

The Portuguese *corja* appears to have its origins in the French *corde du roi*, a coarse, thick–ribbed cotton material which gave origin to the English *corduroy*. This is known in Shona as *kodhoro*. There may be some transposition of the two words, *curva* and *corja* as they both refer to bolts of cloth and tribute paid in kind, viz cloth. *Mutoro* is the standard Shona word for a load and presents no speculation. The *corvado* was a standard sixteenth and seventeenth Portuguese unit of measure representing three quarters of an English yard. It was also used extensively by the Chinese in their Portuguese trade. The Portuguese marketing mix changed little and in 1831 Joao Juliao da Silva listed his inventory of trade goods earmarked for the

Bandire *feira* (to the west of the Chimanimani mountains and in the valley between the Musapa and Rebvuwe rivers). This included :

zuartes	blue Nankin cloth
dotins	white cotton cloth
chales	rough calico
capotim	two lengths of cloth
missangas	beads
chadares	cloth sheets
aguardente	a fiery alcoholic spirit
cabaia	wide–sleeved tunic of red fabric
lencois	kerchiefs from Diu, red or striped
roupas	clothes
calaim	oriental tin

The known historical context assists us in dating most of these imported items of which the most striking are the Chinese ceramics. Before advancing to a more detailed appraisal and catalogue of the various ceramics a brief depiction of porcelain and stoneware and the process of manufacture which makes it so different from African and European earthenware and faience wares of the time will be useful. Porcelain is created from two basic clay materials, Kaolin and Petuntze, the finest of which were obtained from the hills surrounding Jingdezhen (the largest porcelain producing centre in China).

These two substances were blended together through an elaborate and painstaking process to make the porcelain paste which was then pounded and kneaded before being left to mature for a number of years in brick form. After curing, the porcelain was reworked into the required shape and then stored for a predetermined period. Powdered flint and other ingredients were often added depending upon the experience of the potters. Finally the characteristic blue decoration, using a fine quality imported cobalt (mainly imported from the Middle East although domestic deposits were also used) was applied as an underglaze and these designs were then covered by a piping or dip of opaque glaze (32).

During the firing, around 1300 degrees Celsius, the overglaze turns transparent in the heat of kiln allowing the spectacular blue and white effect to emerge. It should be noted that porcelain is in fact a stoneware in which the glaze and the body fuse perfectly to produce an absolute blend of the two elements. A final requisite of fine porcelain is that it must be translucent and give a resonant ring when struck. Stoneware jars and vases were also produced at the great Jingdezhen kilns of Jau-Chou prefecture but it is thought that most of the export jars were manufactured at lesser provincial kilns including those at Te-Hua in the Fukien province and in Swatow in northern Kuang-tung (33). The common stoneware jars were also manufactured elsewhere in S E Asia and an important kiln site at Bang Rachan, Singburi Province, Thailand was surveyed in 1988 (34). The manufacture of stoneware is a tradition which continues to the present day remaining concentrated in the same regions. Stoneware is generally defined as a ceramic substance of varying colours and textures fired at temperatures between 1200 and 1280 degrees Celsius and usually glazed in the final form.

When considering the various known ceramic forms and shapes the following types can be clearly identified from shards recovered at the *feiras* in Zimbabwe.

Dishes

Many of the dishes or plates found at the *feiras* have grit and sand adhering to the footrims and have a flattened edge similar to the types produced during the latter half of the sixteenth century, during Wan-li. Several of the shards found in Zimbabwe come from plates

or dishes with divided panels typical of the style often associated with *kraak porcelain*. Depicted in the centre of one shard, found at Masapa *feira*, is a water landscape with geese among rocks and lotus plants. Ducks and geese were symbolic of marital bliss as these birds are known to pair

Plate 7

97

for life. Aquatic birds often formed part of the decorative motifs of fourteenth and early fifteenth century wares and are much less common on later porcelains unless there was a deliberate attempt to copy decorations of the earlier period. This particular shard would appear to belong to the transitional period produced for export as it lacks fine quality. Other shards found at the *feiras* feature deer surrounded by the *three friends*, the pine, prunus and bamboo. A fine shard depicting this classic theme has been found during archaeological digs at Kame ruins in western Zimbabwe and is now Plat on display at the site museum .

The three friends all thrive in winter and are also known to the Chinese as the "three cold weather friends". Deer were often depicted on dishes and plates made during Wan-li and the transitional period and for the Chinese they symbolise longevity. This is because deer are thought to be the only animals capable of finding the sacred fungus of longevity known as *lingzhi*. In the 1600s this style of plate, which has a central theme or scene with a wide rim divided into panels, usually eight in number, became the vogue (35). The subject varied from land – and waterscapes with deer, birds, insects and fruit. These styles are a common feature of blue and white *kraak porcelain* and shards of this fine quality ware have been found at Luanze, Masapa and Dambarare.

Bowls – Lianzu

Shards of blue and white bowls have been found at Luanze, Dambarare, Masapa and the Angwa. Most of the shards belong to the standard export-ware category although some shards of *kraak* quality wares are also present at the same sites. At Dambarare and Masapa shards of blue and white inside and light chocolate or *café au lait* glaze on the outside have been recorded. Fragments of various bowls, plain, everted or with foliated rims have been recovered from the same *feiras* yet the largest concentration of shards clearly belongs to the export-ware classification with sand and grit on the footrims and nearly all without any evidence of reign or hallmarks. Only one bowl, bears a mark which is rather indistinct but could possibly be a cyclical mark. (The Chinese calender is measured in sixty year cycles and these marks indicate in which century a particular piece was produced.) This bowl has been reconstructed from shards recovered in the late 1890s at Danangombe (Dlo Dlo) ruins and is now on display in the Bulawayo Museum. This bowl appears to be an example of typical south-east Asian export-ware but could possibly be a piece of *ko-sometsuke* ware because of the presence of the brown rim glaze.

Plate 9, 10 11, 1

A fine shard of Imperial blue and white ware was recovered from the Sofala shoals (the site of the Portuguese settlement which has now largely disappeared) on the coast of Mozambique (36). It bears four- character reign marks consistent with *Chongzhen* (1628-43) the last Ming emperor. The inside of the bowl is decorated with a classic lotus spray design. Pieces of this quality have not been found in Zimbabwe. An interesting religious symbol or mark appears on a second bowl shard found at Sofala. This depicts the open lozenge or one of the Eight Precious Things *(Ba-bao)*. These markings were often used as part of general decoration or, as in this case, individually as a mark on the base of the bowl. A single floral display appears on the inside of the same bowl. Among the shards found at Luanze feira (37) is a clearly recognizable piece of eight panel Wan-li blue and white together with a bowl fragment bearing eight character Wan-li reign marks or *Nian hao* on the inside.

Plat 13,

During a field survey on farm No. 7 Chesa, in April 1990, the writer found a bowl shard decorated in characteristic green *famille verte* enamels. Polychrome porcelains of this type were generated for export during the late seventeenth century and ever increasingly thereafter. This find might, therefore, point to later occupation of Masapa and at some time during the eighteenth century.

Jars — Kuan

Stoneware storage jars or *Guan* were imported in considerable numbers to East Africa during Portuguese suzerainty of the coast and many complete jars can be found in private ownership along the Kenya coast particularly at Lamu. Known as *jarras* in Portuguese, these large vessels were often used to store gunpowder and a report in *Monçõs, Vol. 29-30* by D. Manuel Mascarenhas of 16 March 1665 confirms this application at the powder stores of São Sebastião on Mozambique Island. The large number of jar shards recovered at the feiras in Zimbabwe indicates that significant numbers were brought into the country. This was no mean feat considering the sheer mass and volume of these vessels. The largest stood 1,2 metres high with a body about 61 centimetres wide and a gross weight of about 20 kilos. This type generally had a row of studs on

Pl 15 17

the shoulder and was finished with a glossy black glaze. It represents the largest of the jars imported to the Rivers and a number of these shards have been found at Masapa (38). The jar has four cord handles used in securing the contents.

The most popular type was a medium sized vessel ranging from 53 centimetres high to 25 centimetres. These generally have a black, yellow-brown or brown glaze, a projecting lip, grooved on the top and with a series of four cord handles on the shoulders to fasten the stopper. Included in the medium size group is a vessel with a green under-glaze sprigged with floral acanthus leaves and a *jui* border in yellow and orange glaze. Shards of this type have been found at Luanze, Dambarare, Masapa and the Angwa (39). The jars also have cord handles but are different from the others because of a slightly raised or elongated neck and everted lip rim. This type of jar is a late Ming or transitional period copy of a jar (40) originally manufactured during the Tang dynasty (618-907.)

Evidently a few Dragon jars were imported to Zimbabwe for a number of shards have been found at Masapa. This type of jar stands about 65 centimetres with a width of 44 centimetres. The glazing is grey-black and the body is sprigged with a Dragon motif (41). The neck is slightly elongated similar to the polychrome jar described above.

A shard about 60 x 40 mm in size and about 12 mm thick weighing 50 grams was recovered at Masapa. There is a thick, black glaze on both sides and the outside has two buttons or studs with lighter colour glaze. A section of other applied decoration is apparent. This shard is from the upper part of a medium to large jar and judging from the curvature, its thickness and placement of decorative studs the diameter of the vessel would have been about 800 mm. The shard has been given a Burmese provenance although the kiln cannot be pinpointed at this time. Modern jars of this type are made at Twante and Shwebo, Burma, and there is a strong possibility that these jars were made at other sites, including Martaban, Burma, in historical times. Remnants of these jars have been found in surface collections at old sites but none have been found in controlled excavations and whilst no dating has been conducted, this particular Masapa shard appears to have been produced in the sixteenth century (42).

Jars of this type are still in common use as water containers in the Burmese countryside. They measure about a metre high and wide but smaller versions in various shapes occur. These jars are described and illustrated in several references but that of Sumarah

Adhyatman on Burmese Ceramics is probably the best. The Portuguese were masters of south–east Asian trade during these historical times and Burmese ports of call were included on their itineraries.

From the early sixteenth century the Portuguese were trading with the Kingdom of Ayutthaya, Thailand (43) and this commerce is likely to have included consignments of these ubiquitous stoneware jars. Jars of this type are characterised by a rolled neck with lug handles on the shoulders. Some of the jars were unglazed whilst others were glazed in various hues. Jars of this type have been recovered from shipwrecks including the São João (1552) and the São Bento (1554) off the coast of South East Africa (44) giving further proof that these jars were in general use by the Portuguese and were certainly transported for the Rivers' trade.

Jars — Mei Ping

Shards of Mei Ping, or Plum Blossom jars, in a sturdy blue and white Plate 21 stoneware have been recorded at Dambarare. These are 7 mm thick and are glazed internally and externally. The exterior is decorated with the classic lotus scrolls popular on jars and temple vases during the period under review.

The Chinese wares imported to Zimbabwe are similar to those Plate 22 found in sixteenth and seventeenth century levels during excavations at Fort Jesus, Mombasa, Kenya in the early 1960s (45). Similar wares have been recorded at Angoche and Sofala in Mozambique (46). As noted above, the vast majority of the wares found in Zimbabwe belong to the standard export-ware classification and this forms an interesting branch of Chinese ceramic study. Very little attention has been paid to this field by conventional scholarship which has generally focused on the finer *kraak* wares or *Chine de Commande* which became so popular and had such a profound impact on western ceramic convention from the seventeenth century to the present day. This brief scan of Chinese ceramics, imported to Zimbabwe, should be seen not only as an integral component of this research into the Rivers but also as a modest contribution towards a better understanding of this rather neglected aspect of Chinese ceramic study.

Portuguese faience wares

Portugal was the first country in Europe to initiate the purchase of Pla Chinese porcelain by special order in the mid-sixteenth century. Chinese artists painted various pieces with specific Portuguese designs. Portugal, as the leading European maritime trading nation of the day distributed the imported Chinese porcelain throughout Europe, supplying in the main, principal Courts and rich merchants of the major cities. The trade in imported ceramics motivated potteries in Lisbon to start producing similar items but at much lower prices. By 1582, wares of an acceptable quality were being manufactured and pieces were offered to King Filipe II of Spain Filipe I of Portugal) who subsequently wrote enthusiastically to his daughters proclaiming the merits of the imitation China. Faience ware, inspired as much in form, shape, design and colour by the original blue and white, was now being produced in Europe for the first time. (47)

Portuguese commercial activities of the sixteenth and seventeenth centuries made it possible for the spread of this faience or decorated earthenware into the broader European markets of the day. In 1620 there were a total of 28 kilns producing faience ware in Lisbon, employing 76 artists and 46 designers. This represented the largest producing centre in seventeenth century Europe. Another factor which contributed to the popularity of porcelain was the growing trend away from traditional pewter to ceramic and the desire to eat from individual plates rather than from a communal bowl. Faience became extremely popular in Europe and by the beginning of the seventeenth century a large portion of the important Italian market was taken by Lisbon.

Also relevant to the flowering of Portuguese faience ware was the emergence of Dutch seaborne trade in the seventeenth century and the development of Amsterdam as the major centre for the importation and distribution of Chinese blue and white *kraakware*. Having pioneered the introduction of Chinese porcelain to Europe the Portuguese again took the commercial lead by being the first to start manufacture in Lisbon and successfully distribute in Europe and overseas. (48)

Recent archaeological work has yielded finds of Portuguese faience of the late sixteenth and early seventeenth century in

England (distributed around London, Southampton, Exeter and Bristol) Oslo in Norway, Germany, Denmark, Gothenburg in Sweden and Poland. Finds of Portuguese faience have also been made in North, Central and South America and it has been ascertained that virtually all regions within the Portuguese or Spanish sphere of influence took supplies of Portuguese faience. Spanish Armadas victualled in Lisbon before embarkation to the Americas and evidently took on board the decorated earthenware now found at sites of former Spanish colonies. An archaeological survey in 1986-87 has revealed Portuguese wares in a fort on the Caribbean island of São Mauricio which was occupied by the Spanish in 1633-1648. Excavations at the site of a *Samurai* dwelling in Tokyo, Japan, has identified a bowl as being Portuguese decorated earthenware from the earliest period of export dating around 1600-1625 —the Portuguese were also established at Nagasaki, southern Japan by 1555 (49).

The wreck of a Portuguese frigate, the Santo António de Tanna, which sank in front of Fort Jesus, Mombasa in 1697, was found by divers in 1963. During this and later excavations, artifacts of the seventeenth century were brought to the surface. These included a large Siamese (Thai) stoneware jar, a bronze breech-loading cannon, case bottles and fine examples of Portuguese faience wares including a fine plate and water jug both lavishly decorated in the classic blue and white style of the time.

Seventeenth century faienceware shards have been found in Plate 24 Zimbabwe at the *feiras* of Dambarare and Luanze. The low incidence of decorated earthenware at the *feiras* suggests that imports of these wares was not common (50).

A much greater proportion of plain undecorated terracotta wares Plate 25 have been found at Dambarare and Masapa (51). These comprise glazed earthenwares produced in Portugal during the sixteenth and seventeenth centuries and designed for daily household use. Shards of yellow-green, olive and brown glazed earthenware vessels are similar to those found at Fort Jesus in Mombasa (52).

From these shards it is possible to make tentative identifications of the different types of vessels and these may have included jars, basins and bowls. Because of the strictly utilitarian nature of these domestic wares, unprepossessing in appearance and without any particular design or decoration, little heed was ever paid to the preservation of these vessels. Interesting comparisons can be made with wares recently unearthed during building operations in metropolitan Lisbon and now displayed at Museu da Cidade, Lisbon (53). Most of these wares date from the late fourteenth century but the styles are likely to have endured and influenced successive traditions. Most of the terracotta Portuguese earthenware was made from *barro vermelho* or red clays which have inclusions of mica (54) and are extremely characteristic of Portuguese wares of the sixteenth and seventeenth centuries. Shards found in Zimbabwe appear to correspond to this type.

Persian ceramics

Shards of suspected Persian ceramics have been found at Dambarare Plate *feira* and these appear to come from jars and bowls. They consist of a rather thick earthenware or stoneware with a turquoise or light green glaze. During 1967 excavations at Dambarare it was determined that of the total number of shards recovered 79% were of Chinese origin, 15% of Portuguese and 6% of Persian or unidentified Islamic origin (55).

Glass

The imported glass found in Zimbabwe consists of European case bottles made from a smoky black or dark green glass. Broken pieces

have been found at most of the *feiras* suggesting a general pattern of importation and use by the Portuguese. The case bottles found in Zimbabwe corresponded to those located at Fort Jesus (56). A bottle has been completely restored from fragments found at the Rozvi settlement of Dlodlo — Danangombe in 1895 and this is now on display in the Bulawayo Museum, Zimbabwe. Similar case bottles were found on the wreck of the Santo António, described above. Some were fitted with pewter screw tops and others were found separately. Evidently, the case bottles contained wine rations which were drunk on empty stomachs by the Portuguese sailors on 16 September 1697. The Portuguese became drunk and unable to carry out their duties effectively as Arab guns engaged them. Case bottles were normally supplied in sets of 6, 9 or 12 bottles and those imported from Holland in the seventeenth century containing *geneva* (Dutch gin flavoured with juniper berries) or brandy, were kept in specially made wooden boxes, called *keldertje* in Dutch.

Beads

Typical beads encountered at the *feiras* are the *Contas miúdas* or small glass beads also known as *contas de Cambaya* — Cambay or Indian beads. Trade in this type of bead, known in Shona as *chuma* was a well established tradition before the advent of the Portuguese who merely continued this lucrative business. Thousands of beads have been recovered from the excavation of burials at Dambarare *feira* in 1967 (57). Similar green, yellow, blue and red beads may be found scattered over a wide area of the Masapa feira in the vicinity of Farms No. 3, 4 and 7, near Mount Darwin (58). Red, yellow and green glass beads feature prominently in Zimbabwean material culture and a cursory study of beads in the context of Njanja ethnic traditions is illustrative of this contention. The Njanja people live predominantly around the banded ironstone Wedza mountain with its twin peaks of Gandamasunga and Chipangura under the chieftainship of Neshangwe, Makumbe and Chitsunge. The Njanja territory also extends to the Nyazvidzi but it was only the northern Njanja around Wedza mountain who really excelled at ironwork particularly during their nineteenth century heydays. Although there is very little *prima facie* evidence linking the Njanja with the Portuguese of the sixteenth and seventeenth century it is likely that they either traded directly or indirectly through the *vashambadzi* system of intermediaries.

At some stage, one of the Njanja clans adopted *Sinyoro*, a corruption of the Portuguese word *Senhor* (lord or master) as their *chidau*. They acquired their *mutupo* of *Moyo* in the early eighteenth century linking them with the Rozvi people during the post-Torwa state period. This coincided with the ascendancy of the Changamire when the Rozvi nucleus expanded into the centre of Zimbabwe from their old western strongholds.

There are conflicting accounts about the origins of the Njanja but fact is that they were known for incredible skill in iron smelting and smithing which reached a high point in the mid- eighteenth century (59). The iron was extracted from mines on Wedza mountain and wrought into weapons, tools and implements of which the most important was the *mapadza* or hoe blades. The Portuguese recognised the importance of the hoe in the traditional African economy for they incorporated it in a fanciful coat-of-arms which they prepared for the vassal Mutapa. The *mapadza* was the universal unit of account when calculating bride-price or *roora*. A legend recounted by some Njanja traditionalists, on the origins of the Njanja, tells of a man named Muroro, one of a group of *Mwana-muzungo* or *vashambadzi* visiting Wedza from Sena.

Muroro fell ill and was unable to return with the caravan to Mozambique. After being nursed back to health he was assimilated into local society and married a daughter of a local chief named Chirwa, a Shiri clansman. Muroro's offspring are said to be the progenitors of the modern Njanja (60).

There is no suggestion that Njanja prowess in iron smelting and smithing was acquired from the Portuguese but they must have influenced Njanja society because several of their ancestral spirits or *shave* are associated with superior weapons, special skills, groundnuts and donkeys which are all closely identified with the Portuguese or *muzungos*. One of these spirits is known as *Shave chidona* (61) — a likely reference to the spirit of the Lady — Dona means Lady in Portuguese. During ceremonies to summon the ancestral spirits music is an important element. When *Zungo* spirits are summoned a special *mbira dzemuzungo* or *njari mbira*, which can be traced to the lower Zambezi valley in Portuguese-speaking territory, is employed (62). These special Mbira or hand pianos are played to the accompaniment of singing, hand clapping, and dancing. The *Svikiro* or spirit medium wears beads or other paraphenalia which belonged to the ancestor.

There are a number of *svikiro* or mediums of *Zungo* or Portuguese –associated ancestral spirits among the Njanja. These spirits, *vadzimu* or *shave* demand that their mediums must wear special red, yellow and green beads during the possession ceremony before manifestation (63). The spirit may also demand other Portuguese-related items such as a symbolic muzzle-loader or a piece of fabric known as *maretso* — this cloth was generally worn round the waist and was procured in Mozambique (64). *Bertangil vermelho* or red cotton cloth was commonly exported to Mozambique for coastal and Rivers trade. A string of red beads symbolises hunting and blood and is commonly associated with *Zungo* spirits. During Captain J.C. Paiva de Andrade's tour of the highveld in the 1890s he allegedly met several African chiefs who declared themselves Portuguese subjects and pointed out Portuguese trees planted during ancient times as well as the ruins of Portuguese houses and fortresses. The reliability of this report may be suspect given Portugal's territorial ambitions of that time but it does make specific mention of a Njanja chief flying the Portuguese flag.

Chuma, as beads are generically known in Shona, featured prominently in the accoutrement of the African traditional healer or *n'anga*. Beads may be worn as a necklace or in the case of the *n'anga* possessed by a *shave* spirit, they are worn around the wrist as bracelets. A *shave* spirit is one with decided healing powers and need not be related to the same family as the medium, whereas a *mudzimu* spirit is directly connected by family lineage and is not necessarily endowed with healing abilities. Nearly all *n'anga* favour red beads followed by orange, black, white and blue. Central to the herbalist's equipment is the *gona* which is a special medicine container made from animal horn or a calabash. The *makona* (pl) are held in such awe that none but the *n'anga* may look into it for fear of dire consequence.

In the case of witches or wizards, known as *varoyi,* the *makona* (pl) contain evil or deadly potions. Fortunately the vast majority of *n'anga* are benevolent and their *makona,* often richly decorated with orange, red and blue beads, are used for the power of good and healing (65). During the Francisco Barretc expedition, Monclaro recorded the death of a *n'anga* who had been observed spreading *mushonga* or *muti* to protect the Mutapa's forces against the bullets

107

of the Portuguese. War medicine which provides immortality to warriors and is especially effective against bullets is known as *ndudzo* in Shona. The Shona word *manhedzwa* (from *kutedza*, meaning to slip off, e.g. a bullet) also applies in some cases. The *n'anga* was killed and the gourd or *gona* containing the evil spells was smashed by shot — apparently the *muti* in this case simply wasn't strong enough !

The earliest record of Portuguese import and distribution of beads is in October 1505 when Pêro de Andaia, the Captain of Sofala, ordered the disposal of crystal beads (66). A further 100 000 glass beads and assorted goods including brass bangles were sold on 29 December, 1505 by the factor Manuel Fernandes (67). In all likelihood some of these beads would have found their way inland to the goldfields of Manica.

Coloured glass beads have long been cherished in Zimbabwean society where they were worn as broad bands on the head as in the case of women in the Pfungwe district of north-east Zimbabwe who, as late as the 1930s still wore these multi-coloured string bands known locally as *chipondo*. Strings of red and white and red and black beads were also worn around the neck. The same Pfungwe women favoured distinctive locally dyed black calico with a white waist band or *mucheka* (68). Beads retain their powerful links with traditional African society and are still commonly worn by many people as personal jewellery or as some form of charm.

During the mid-sixteenth century Portuguese traders at Sena and Tete despatched their intermediaries or *vashambadzi* to the principal *feiras* of Luanze, Bocuto and Masapa. The agents walked alongside bearers who carried bundles of small green, blue and yellow beads which were strung on *macuti* threads known as *miti* after a measure of weight common in the sixteenth century. Ten *miti* were equal to a *motava* in local African terms and to a Portuguese *cruzado* (69). This Shona term has survived and occurs in the modern lexicon as *mhita* when referring to beads used as currency. Sold at the *feiras,* a *motava* of beads yielded forty *cruzados* in contra-trade. Evidently, beads were a highly profitable business.

As we have already noted, the Zumbo trade with the Rozvi continued undisturbed and expanded during the eighteenth century. Beads were an important commodity in this exchange. Some of these included the so-called *water beads,* a class of large, transluscent glass beads. These and other beads feature prominently in the material culture of the Venda which recognises three distinct classifications of ancestoral beads. Each group comprises several sub-classifications of beads each with a special name and description. One of these is the *dombo,* a Shona and Venda word denoting a large variety of opaque bead. Similar beads occur in eastern Zambia around Petauke where oral traditions associate them with the Zumbo trade of the nineteenth century. During the late eighteenth century dispersal of the Rozvi there was one major migration to the Nzhelele river valley in the Zoutpansberg mountains of northern Transvaal, South Africa. These Rozvi, led by Chief Dimbanyika, encountered remnants of earlier migrants from Great Zimbabwe who had also come in search of new and pleasant lands. They settled near the stone–walled ruins at Dzata, possibly built by their Zimbabwean predecessors, and now form part of the greater Venda speaking people. Water-beads have assumed almost mythological proportions in Venda cultural traditions which speak of a provenance far to the north — the old Rozvi heartlands (69a).

Cowries, the shell of a small marine mollusc scientifically known as *Cyprae moneta,* feature prominently in the material culture of the Tonga people of the upper Zambezi valley. The cowrie was traded in a similar fashion to beads. The major source of the cowries was the Querimba archipelago — a group of small islands off the coast of northern Mozambique. The shells also feature in lists of exports from China and in 1725 a total of 50 *picols* of *cauris* or cowries were shipped from Macau. (70) The cowrie trade never assumed the same economic importance as the Indian *cambay* beads which were cheaper and easy to obtain.

Copper, bronze or brass bangles, bracelets, anklets and beads were also popular and evidence of this was found on the skeletons of five burials at Dambarare excavated in 1967. These brass beads were formed by clipping a short piece of wire over string with the two ends joined together. One of the burials contained a necklace of small copper beads together with four large crystal beads (71). Brass bangles and beads are still a common form of personal adornment in rural Mashonaland and Manicaland where the generic name for brass, *mundarira,* is used. Broad brass bracelets worn by women in the Pfungwe during 1929 were reportedly known in the local dialect as *mabadera.* (72)

According to oral tradition, the brass was obtained from the Portuguese, forged red hot and then drawn into wire by Njanja smiths. Using a special tool with a series of graduated holes or dies the wire was gradually reduced in diameter to the required gauge. In this manner the African craftsmen fashioned arm and leg ornaments (73).

On 24 October 1505, Vasco Soajo, the measurer of wines at the Sofala fort bartered one hundred brass bangles with local Africans in exchange for supplies. The bangles, made from thick brass did not find an immediate market in Sofala as the coastal dwellers preferred a thinner quality. Again in December 1505 beads and brass were sold at Sofala in exchange for foodstuffs (74).

Weaponry

Two cannon, one a bronze breech-loader and the other an iron muzzle-loader with the Portuguese coat of arms were recovered

from Danangombe (Dlo-Dlo) during excavations at the former Rozvi settlement in 1895 (75). A report of 1831 attributable to João Julião da Silva suggests that there were "four big artillery pieces, very rusty on the ground." Three barrels from flintlock muskets were also unearthed. During underwater excavations on the wreck of the *Santo António de Tanna* which sank off Mombasa in 1697, a similar bronze breech-loading cannon bearing the Portuguese coat of arms and the date 1678, was found.

The cannon mentioned above were subsequently removed from the country in the late 1890s on the instructions of Cecil John Rhodes and in 1969 it was established that they were on display at the main entrance to the South African State President's official residence of Groot Schuur in Cape Town, South Africa (76). The use of the *falcão,* an ancient type of light cannon first used in Europe in 1496 is reported in the Portuguese documents (77) during the Barreto campaign.

The Flintlock was developed between 1620 and 1635 in France where gunsmiths perfected the best from the fifteenth century Matchlock design and the later sixteenth century Wheellock weapons. The Flintlock incorporated a more robust ignition method and this weapon quickly assumed the premier position in all the principal armouries of Europe.

It was to endure until the early nineteenth century when the Percussion principle was developed in England by the Revd., Alexander Forsyth. This places the Flintlock barrels at Danangombe any time from the mid-seventeenth century onwards confirming the trading links between the Rozvi and Zumbo during the seventeenth century onwards. Two pieces of lead shot were found during excavations at the Portuguese earthworks of Luanze.

There are numerous documentary references to the *Arquebus* being used by the Portuguese during the Monomotapa campaigns. The name *Harquebus* derives from an early German weapon of the fourteenth century known as *Hakenbusche* and this was later corrupted to *Harquebus* or *Arquebus*. This type of weapon was extensively used by the Portuguese during their interminable campaigns of the sixteenth and seventeenth century. The Harquebus is the generic name for the muzzle–loading weapon known by its firing mechanism using the Matchlock principle based on a permanently burning fuse.

These weapons were developed in the fifteenth century and weighed about ten kilos. The weapon was fitted with a saucer–like depression or *pan* into which the priming powder was placed before being ignited using the saltpetre impregnated slow burning match fuse. These weapons were introduced by the French army and in 1536 the Spaniards incorporated this weapon deploying it in a military formation known as the *tercio* and this was adopted by the Portuguese who may well have used this formation in their limited African campaigns.

When loading, the musketeer or *arquebusier* first had to remove the match while he was pouring the black powder into the muzzle. The charge was then rammed down the barrel with a rod which was kept secured under the barrel when not in use. A lead ball was rammed on top of the charge. The powder for the main shot was of a coarser quality and the primer finer and the two types were kept in separate flasks. The Matchlock was introduced to India and Japan by the Portuguese during the sixteenth century and, as noted, the weapon, successfully used in the Barreto-Homen campaigns (78).

Ornaments and religious artifacts

Ornaments of Portuguese or European origin found at the *feiras* include religious medallions, lockets, rings, badges, aiguillettes in silver and bronze, bronze epaulettes, copper pins, buckles and belt ends. None of these minor objects may be distinguished by a particularly high degree of workmanship, scarcity or value and they are rather ordinary in the context of known sixteenth and seventeenth century wearing apparel. The only items which are clearly identifiable are bronze medallions, two of which were found in burials at Plate 27 Dambarare. (79)

The largest of these depicts a profile of a female head wearing a crown and encircled by a halo with the inscription *S ELISABET R.*

LUSITANIA. On the reverse face is the bust of a cloaked figure of a man contemplating the Christ child with the inscription *S. AN-TONII V* and *ROM.* Elizabeth (1271-1336) was the wife of King Denis I of Portugal. Elizabeth was closely associated with the town of Coimbra and was canonised in 1625 after which time this medallion must have been struck in commemoration. The opposite side represents Antony of Papua (1195-1231) who was born in Lisbon and lived in Coimbra before leaving Portugal. This representation of Saint Antony with Jesus was only popularised in the late sixteenth century and therefore is consistent with the known dates of Portuguese occupation at Plate 28 Dambarare (80).

In 1988 an oval bronze medallion, once gilt, measuring four centimetres by two and a half centimetres was found at map ref TR 763 674 close to the Murowodzi river, Dambarare (81). One side depicts the Virgin in glory with clasped hands and a halo resplendent. This is a representation of the Virgin in the cult of the Immaculate Conception. The other side represents a chalice with rays and kneeling angels surrounded by the inscription *SLIL SA* and *ROMA.*

This find is similar to a medallion recovered during excavations at Fort Jesus in the early 1960s (82). In 1989, a small brass locket Plate 29 and a badge in the form of an eight–point star were found in a field on farm No. 7 Chesa in the general area of Masapa (83). Similar lockets and badges are described in James Kirkman's account of the Fort Jesus excavations.

113

From the artifacts discovered at Danangombe referred to above, the following items are of interest: a gold coin or medallion, a piece of bractea, a bronze oil lamp, a portion of a bronze key, a bell with handle, a Priest's seal, one metre of gold chain (possibly part of priestly regalia) with a mass of molten silver attached to it, a piece of a silver plate embossed with vine leaf decorations (possibly a sacramental plate) and some pieces of embossed silver. Unfortunately, only a few of these items have survived and these are in the Bulawayo Museum (84).

An unusual rectangular tablet of fine clay was found by Peter Garlake during his excavations at Dambarare. It bears an impression of the Virgin, crowned and holding a sceptre. Below is an armorial shield bearing a single crescent-shaped device surmounted by a three-armed cross. The tablet was either placed loose in the grave or was contained in a pouch or pocket which subsequently decayed for there was no visible means of attaching the tablet. This obscure find is not of any importance but merely assists in developing the overall picture of Portuguese occupation of the *feiras*.

Ivories

During the seventeenth century a large number of ivories were commissioned from Indian craftsmen in Goa and most of these works represent the Virgin. An example of this art form has been discovered in Zimbabwe. Prospectors clearing ancient workings at the Bay Horse Mine, near the Mupfure river in the Chegutu district, discovered the ivory statuette in the 1930s (85). This find may date back to the time of the seventeenth century trading *feira* of Maramuca. Although badly worn, the ivory clearly depicts the Christian Icon of Our Lady of the Immaculate Conception and is on display in the Bulawayo Museum. As demonstrated in the text, ivory was embarked for the Far East markets and undoubtably some was sold to Japanese customers by the Portuguese trading settlement at Nagasaki. An interesting piece depicting a Japanese hunter armed with a Matchlock rifle has survived.

Many of these ivory statuettes did not reach Lisbon for, on their return journey home the owners travelled on ships which were often forced to winter in either Mozambique or take the outer passage via

Brazil and the Azores before returning home. It is not surprising therefore that many ivories of this general type can still be found in the Azorean archipelago. Examples of these religious ivories may be found elsewhere in the old Portuguese empire -in the early 1970s an ivory of the Infant Jesus was found in Indonesia (86).

In their original form, these statues were splendid examples of Indo-Portuguese craftsmanship (the carving of ivory was an ancient tradition in India before the arrival of the Portuguese) and bore such characteristics as gilded hair and lace borders or twisted cord fringes, fan–pleated cloaks and necklaces.

From the mid-eighteenth century the depictions of the Virgin became increasingly Europeanised with their Eastern origin evidenced only in secondary detail such as the shape and decoration of the base, drapes, the drawing of the eyes and hair which were outlined in black (87). The Zimbabwean example must have been produced in the seventeenth century and may well have belonged to Gonçalvo João, the Portuguese trader who was driven from his Maramuca concessions around the 1660s.

Ivory was an important export commodity from south-east Africa and both Mozambique and Zimbabwe were suppliers throughout the Portuguese period. Ivory was generally classified according to colour and size. Tusks weighing from 9 kilos were large, up to 8 kilos medium and those weighing less than 2 kilos small. The standard unit of measure was the *bar* equating to approximately 290 kilos of ivory and in the eighteenth century a *bar* of ivory was worth 500 *Cruzados* in the Sofala and Zambezia districts of Mozambique, and we may assume that this would have applied to Zimbabwean ivory too. When available, rhinoceros horn was also traded because it found a ready market as the base for various Asian remedies including an aphrodisiac which contained powered horn. Beautifully crafted transluscent drinking vessels, made from rhino horn, were believed to alter tone and colour if poison was present and served to further enhance popular misconceptions — many of which endure to this day — about this material.

Miscellaneous finds.

Small ivory beads, lead shot, glass bottle stoppers, metal fragments and other miscellany have been found at the *feiras* and these appear consistent with known Portuguese occupation of the sixteenth and seventeenth century. Other finds worth recording include: firstly, brass cups of Indian workmanship, one of which is from the D Troop Mine near the Angwa *feiras* and now on display in the Bulawayo Museum, and secondly a hanging oil-lamp of Portuguese origin. The iron lamp may originate in the northern Portuguese province of Trás-os-Montes (88).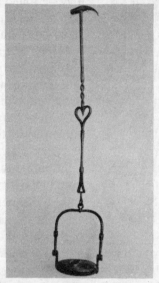

A third relic of possible Portuguese provenance is a curious piece of ironwork which is now the focus of *Chimombe,* a venerated deity of the Chirundu district in the Zambezi valley. The God *Chimombe* is consulted through an acolyte whose task it is to communicate between the living and the spirit world. There are some who contend that this obscure religious artifact may originally have been the stand for an arquebus or an oil lamp but whatever its original purpose it is now the central feature of this African religious shrine and is worshipped by a Tonga clan of the Zambezi valley.

It comprises an upright iron frame and this is decorated with strings of trade beads. A number of elephant tusks completes the assemblage. The more factual origin may not be quite so exotic as similar contraptions occur amongst the Lozi people of western Zambia and examples are on display in the Livingstone Museum, Livingstone, Zambia.

During mining operations in ancient workings at Gaika Mine, Kwekwe, in 1908, a prospector named Burke found two silver bowls nearly ten metres underground. He also recovered a collec-

116

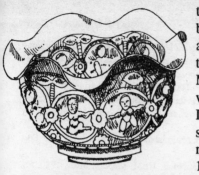

tion of ten soapstone figurines. The bowls were later sent to the Victoria and Albert Museum, London, where the Keeper of Indian Antiquities, Mr. J.C. Irvin identified the silverware as being of nineteenth century Indian origin (89). The bowls have subsequently disappeared but fortunately they were photographed in 1964 and are illustrated in the text. The nineteenth century origin suggests that the bowls are connected with much later mining activity.

An interesting piece of carved coral was found at *Masapa* in 1990 (90) and appears to be the bottom section of a religious statuette representing the christian image of Mary. The white coral is overlaid with a red patina.

This scant account — much still lies buried beneath the ground — of the finds at the Portuguese feiras is extremely important. Considered from a strictly academic perspective, this catalogue effectively allows us to retrace the old trade routes which connected the Portuguese Empire with the Rivers of Gold. At the same time these artifacts bring vivid expression to the pages of history.

References

1. Cuama, archaic name for the Zambezi river. By 1677 the Portuguese were now using the Zambezi name instead of the Cuama - see Carta do Cabo da Boa Esperança até Mombaça com a demonstração do Rio Zambeze aonde foi a frota que mando o Princípe de Portugal este ano de 1677 - map by João Teixeira de Albernaz, from Monumenta Cartographica Portugalia with the original in the Societe de Geographie, Paris, France.

2. On display at Bulawayo Museum, Zimbabwe., see also Hall & Neal, *Ancient Ruins of Rhod.*, Reprint, 1972, p. 140.

3. Sasoon C., *Chinese Porcelain in Fort Jesus*, National Museums of Kenya, 1975. Fort Jesus Illustrated Studies.

4. Trabalhos de Arqueologia e Antropologia, No. 1, UEM, Maputo, Moz., 1980, for discussion of trading relations between Manyikeni and Zimbabwe.

5. Sasoon C., op. cit.

6. There was a well established trade between South China, India, Persia, Arabia and the East Coast of Africa during the fifteenth century. Cheng-Ho, a eunuch, was an admiral of the Imperial navy.

7. Beatriz Basto da Silva, Entre Goa e Macau, *Boletim de Centro de Estudos Maritimos de Macau*, 1989, p. 103-110.

8. Macintosh D., *Chinese Blue and White Porcelain.*, Book Marketing Ltd., Hong Kong, 1987, p. 61.

9. Macintosh D., op. cit. p. 61-63.

10. Macintosh D., op. cit. p. 61-65.

11. Chinese Export Porcelain, 1989, Catologue of *Chine de Commande.*

12. Macintosh D., op. cit. p. 70. Sasoon C., *Chinese Porcelain in Fort Jesus*, National Museums of Kenya, 1975.

13. Macintosh D. op. cit. p. 12,117,118,123.

14. Macintosh D., op. cit. p. 117-119, 134-5.

15. Macintosh D. op. cit., p. 70,88-89,98,118.

16. Mário C. Leão, *Boletim de Centro de Estudos Maritimos de Macau*, No. 2, 1989, p. 74.

17. Dias, Jorge., A Perspectiva Portuguesa do Japão, *Boletim de Centros de Estudos Marítimos do Macau*, 1989, p. 103-110.

18. *Documents* Vol IX, p. 181.

19. *Documents* Vol IX., p. 191

20. *Documents* Vol IX., p. 231-235.

21. Boxer C.R. *Grande Navio de Macau, Fundacao Oriente*, Museu e Centro de Estudos Marítimos de Macau, 1989, p. 161.

22. Boxer C.R. op. cit., p. 161.

23. Boxer C.R. op. cit., p. 161

24. Boxer C.R. op. cit., p. 161. see also Souza G.B., *A Sobrevivencia do Imperio : Os Portugueses na China, 1630-1754.*, 1991, Lisboa, Publicacoes Dom Q.,p. 195.

25. Boxer C.R. op. cit., p. 162.

26. Chauhan R.R.S. *Journal of Goan Archives*, Vol II, No. 1, 1984, p. 14-22.

27. António Gomes, *Viagem*, Beach/Noronha translations, 1980, UZ.

28. Gelfand M., *The Traditional Medical Practitioner in Zimbabwe*, Mambo Press, 1985, p. 36 for details of *Runyoka*.

28a. Diaz, Bernal. *The Conquest of New Spain*, Penguin Classics, 1963. Innes, Hammond. *The Conquistadors*, Fontana/Collins, 1969, p 32-3.

28b. Gelfand M., Mavi S., *The Traditional Medical Practitioner in Zimbabwe*, Mambo Press, 1985.

29. Filipe de Assumpção, *Viagem*.

30. Posselt F., *NADA* No.9, 1931, p. 25-29 in which Native Commissioner Posselt provides details of a well beaten bush path linking the Mount Darwin district to Nyasaland and Northern Rhodesia via the Tete district of Mozambique. Posselt encountered droves of Africans whose journey often took 6 weeks or more. This trail was also known as the **Blantyre Path**. Significantly the path led past an Indian store at the Mukumbura river on the Mozambique-Zimbabwe border where trading was conducted. This same path was also used by Portuguese traders who visited Mount Darwin, Bindura and Shamva to trade for gold until the early twentieth century. The old Blantyre Path was later superceded by a modern gravel road connecting Mount Darwin with Mukumbura and Nova Magoe on the Zambezi river in Moçambique.

31. *Documents* Vol. VIII., p. 271-273.

32. Macintosh D. op. cit., p. 150-151 Appendix A on the manufacture of Blue and White.

33. Macintosh D., op. cit., p. 150-151.

34. Harper, Rosemary., A Study of Ceramics, Mae Nam Noi kiln site, Bang Rachan, Singburi Province, Thailand, West Australia Museum, 1988, for an extensive survey of stoneware jars.

35. Maura, Rinaldi, *Kraak Porcelain-A Moment in the History of Trade*, Bamboo Publishing, 1989, for a comprehensive discussion on all aspects of kraakware and detailed description.

36. Dickinson R.W., surface collection at Sofala and now in QVM, Harare, Zimbabwe.

37. Garlake P.S., excavations at Luanze earthworks, in collection of QVM, Harare, Zimbabwe.

38. Ellert H., field survey at Mount Darwin presumed Masapa site, 1989,90 and 91.

39. Garlake P.S. excavations at Dambarare feira, now in collection at QVM, Harare, Zimbabwe. Ellert H., surface collection at Angwa feira, 1988.

40. Museu Nacional de Arte Antiga, Lisbon, Fort Jesus Museum collection.

41. Museu Nacional de Arte Antiga, Lisbon and shards of similar jar found at Mount Darwin farm No., 3.

42. D. Hein to H. Ellert 19-4-91 and Adhyatman, Sumarah, *Burmese Ceramics*, Ceramic Society of Indonesia, Jakarta, May, 1985, and Rodho, Abu, *Tempanyan Martavans*, revised 2nd edition, Ceramic Society of Indonesia, Jakarta, 1984.

43. Harper R. op. cit., for additional details of Portuguese and Dutch East India Company (VOC) trade with Ayutthaya.

44. História Trágico-Marítima, Portugália, for details of the ship wrecks of the Great Galleon São Joao off the coast of Natal and the Não São Bento.

45. Kirkman J., *Fort Jesus — Portuguese Fort on The East African Coast.*, 1974.

46. Dickinson R.W. survey and collection of ceramic shards from the Sofala shoal and Angoche island archaeological sites, to QVM May, 1975. See also QVM ref. 1639 BD1, 1979, Dickinson, finds of celadon and blue and white shards.

47. Calado R.S., *Faianca Portuguesa* 1600-1660, Lisbon-Amdsterdam and Museu deArte Antiga, Lisbon, Portugal for a complete catalogue of Portuguese faience wares unearthed in Amsterdam dating to the seventeenth century.

48. Calado R.S. op. cit.

49. Calado R.S. op. cit.

50. Garlake P.S. Excavations at Luanze and Dambarare and collection of shards, QVM ref 1730 BD 2, 26 and 27.

51. Garlake P.S. op. cit.
52. Kirkman J., op. cit.
53. Lisboa Quinhentista, Museu da Cidade, Lisbon, 1983 for details of various styles of *barro vermelho.*
54. Personal communication R.S. Calado to H. Ellert, Lisbon, 1990.
55. Garlake P.S., Excavations at the Seventeenth Century Site of Dambarare, Rhodesia , in *Rhod.Sc. Assoc., Proceedings and Transactions,* Oct., 1969, Vol. 54 I, p. 23-
56. Kirkman J., op. cit.
57. Garlake P.S., op. cit.
58. Ellert H., 1989-90. site visit.
59. Mackenzie J.M. The Njanja and the Iron Trade, *NADA,* 1975, p. 200-220.
60. Mackenzie J.M. op. cit. p. 204., this account is the most popular on the origin of the Njanja, a sub-group of the Mbire who moved to the Wedza area and displaced the Hera who were then occupying the area from their southern core of Buhera.
61. E. Matenga to H. Ellert, personal communication, March, 1991.
62. Ellert, H. *Material Culture of Zimbabwe,* Longmans, 1984, p. 61-64.
63. Musonza, Pauros Mugwagwa, Oral tradition, interview with D. Mujeri, Archives, 1979 file ref. AOH/51.
64. Musonza, P. M. op. cit.
65. Gelfand M. *The Traditional Medical Practitioner.,* op. cit.
66. *Documents,* Vol I, p. 289
67. *Documents,* Vol I, p. 293, 341
68. *NADA* No. 7, 1929, p. 24-25.
69. *Documents,* Vol I, p. 271-273.
69a. Personal communication S. Mudenge to H. Ellert, 17-1-1992.
70. Souza G.B. op. cit., p. 195.
71. Garlake P.S. op. cit.
72. NADA No. 7, 1929, p. 24-25.
73. Musonza P.M. Archives ref. AOH/51, 1979., see also *Chisambara* (brass wire work on wooden artifacts), *ukambo* (thin brass wire), *usenga* (very thin brass wire), *njovo* (brass bead bracelet) and *rundarira* (coiled brass wire bracelet.)
74. *Documents* Vol. I, p. 293 & 341.
75. Hall and Neal, *Ancient Ruins of Rhod.* listings of finds. See also Ian V. Hogg, *Illustrated Encyclopaedia of Firearms,* Hamlyn, 1978, p. 24-27.
76. Cooke C.K., Dhlo dhlo Ruins : the Missing Relics, *Rhodesiana,* No. 22, 1970., p. 45-52. Cooke C.K., Dhlo dhlo Relics and Regina Ruins, *Rhodesiana,* July 1972., p. 48, for additional details on the ruins and circumstances of the finds.
77. *Documents* Vol VIII., p. 289.
78. Hogg, Ian V., *Illustrated Encyclopaedia of Firearms,* Hamlyn, 1978, p. 14-19, 20-23, 24-27 and 28-33.
79. Garlake P.S. op. cit.
80. Garlake P.S. op. cit.
81. Ellert H., surface find, Doxford farm, 1988.
82. Kirkman J. Fort Jesus, op. cit. p. 159.
83. Ellert H., surface find, 1989.
84. Cooke C.K., Dhlo dhlo Ruins, the Missing Relics, *Rhodesiana,* No. 22, 1970, p. 45-52.
85. Bulawayo Museum, collection.
86. Da França, António Pinto, *Portuguese Influence in Indonesia,* Lisbon, 1985, Calouste Gulbenkian Foundation.

87. Marfins d' Alem Mar, Museu Nacional de Arte Antiga, Maria Mendes Pinto, 1988.
88. Personal communication R.S. Calado to H. Ellert.
89. Hobhouse to M.A.S. Huffman, QVM, the silver bowls were sent to England by the Editor of the Umtali Post some time prior to the 1964 identification.
90. Ellert H., surface find on farm 7, Chesa, Mount Darwin district, Zimbabwe.

CHAPTER 4

Crops

Description and historical setting relative to the introduction of exotic fauna and flora to Zimbabwe

As the Portuguese established themselves on the coast in the early sixteenth century they started to interact with the African societies of the interior and inevitably new and exotic plants were introduced. These were absorbed into local agricultural traditions. Before reaching a satisfactory conclusion for this hypothesis it is important to review the historical perspective and the supporting evidence.

On 12 October 1492 the Spanish landed in Cuba. Although this event is heralded as the discovery of the Americas it was an earlier voyage of the Portuguese João Vaz Corte-Real in 1472 (1) which provided the intelligence upon which Spanish conviction of a successful landfall in the west was founded. But of more profound importance for the world was the discovery of maize on the island of Hispaniola, as Cuba was then known, a crop later found growing in fertile Mexican valleys of the Sierra Madre Oriental. That maize originates in the Americas there is no doubt although there is some debate that the crop was first recognized and developed in Peru, South America, where a huge variety of this plant species adapted to various climatic conditions is found, and not in Meso-America as initially supposed (2). It is very likely that maize was first established in the Cape Verde Islands, introduced from Bahia, northern Brazil. The Atlantic Islands including Madeira and the Azores quickly followed and soon there were reports of plantings at Sevile in Spain and at Coimbra in Portugal.(3)

Maize was certainly brought back to Iberia in the late fifteenth century and it spread rapidly throughout the known world. The crop may first have gone to Morocco and thence overland to sub-saharan Africa but it would certainly have been transported in Portuguese vessels bound for *Asia Portuguesa* during the sixteenth and seventeenth century. Maize, sweetcorn, sweet potato and groundnuts reached China in the late sixteenth or early seventeenth century. The first known illustration of maize appears in *Delle Navigationi et Viaggi* an Italian translation of João de Barros's *Asia* which was published in Venice in 1563. Maize quickly gained acceptance as a popular food in southern Italy where it is still known as *parlenta* (4).

Other important crops discovered in the New World were legumes which grew in conjunction with maize, providing a rich nitrogenous element in the soil. Maize and beans constituted the essentials of starch and protein in the Amerindian diet (5). The soil too, was enriched by these agricultural techniques of growing the two crops in tandem.

In the high Andean valleys potatoes were discovered as well as a wide variety of squashes. These provided nutritious oil-rich seeds, flesh and useful calabash containers. Other Indian food crops discovered by the Spaniards and brought back to Europe included tomatoes, groundnuts, cacao, cashew nuts, vanilla, avocado, pineapple, cassava or manioc, papaya, granadilla and sweet potatoes (6).

Martin Alonsa Pinzon, a Portuguese captain on one of Columbus's ships, the Pinta, found little red and green piquant fruits

growing in Cuba and Haiti and is accredited with the discovery of the chili pepper (7) *Capsicum frutescens* which has gone on to influence culinary traditions in Africa and Asia. Chilies were first introduced to India in the early sixteenth century and to Thailand, the fabled Kingdom of Ayuthia, in 1511 by the Portuguese. The word chili or chile stems from the *Nahuatl* tongue of Mexico and occurs in both Spanish and Portuguese. The species is entirely indigenous to Central and South America. The capsicum is a member of the family *solanaceae* which includes the potato. The western and eastern world owes a considerable debt to the highly civilized and scientific plant engineers of Central and South America. In particular the gift of maize has had a very profound impact on human society as a major food source.

A review of the traditional food crops in the rural areas of Zimbabwe (the African peasant farming sector) includes a number of plant species relevant to this account of the Portuguese in the Rivers.

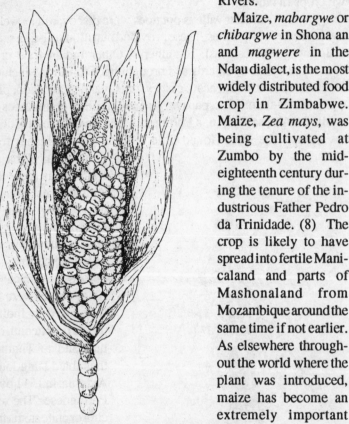

Maize, *mabargwe* or *chibargwe* in Shona an and *magwere* in the Ndau dialect, is the most widely distributed food crop in Zimbabwe. Maize, *Zea mays*, was being cultivated at Zumbo by the mid-eighteenth century during the tenure of the industrious Father Pedro da Trinidade. (8) The crop is likely to have spread into fertile Manicaland and parts of Mashonaland from Mozambique around the same time if not earlier. As elsewhere throughout the world where the plant was introduced, maize has become an extremely important food crop in Zimbabwe. In 1648, António Gomes reported the existence of different varieties of maize and several other food crops including broad beans, pumpkins, watermelons, cucumbers, garlic, onions, eggplant, sesame and cabbage growing within the Rivers (9). Some experts argue that maize was unknown on the coast before 1600 (10). In many rural areas of Zimbabwe, particularly along the border with Mozambique, unimproved varieties of red, yellow and ochre corn are cultivated.(11) A red variety of maize known as *zaburro* was reported growing near Sena in the mid–eighteenth century. (12)

According to oral traditions, maize was generally eaten roasted or boiled and not commonly used to make the staple *sadza* or stiff porridge. Sadza was normally prepared from millet and sorghum. During his 1882-1887 travels through the Makoni district of Zimbabwe Frederick Courtney Selous remarked upon,

> traces of rice and maize fields which can still be discerned in almost every valley, around the sites of ancient villages, long ago crumbled to decay.

Rice, *Orysa sativa, mupunga* in Shona, principally the red variety, is grown in highveld wetlands along streambanks and in *vleis*. There is a type of rice which is believed indigenous to Africa but Asian strains of this crop may have been imported in pre-Portuguese times along with other non-African plants like mangoes *Mangifera indica*, limes *Citrus medica*, sesame, onions *Allium cepa* and sugarcane *Saccharum officinarum*. The rice-plant was scientifically identified and classified in 1562 and is clearly of oriental origin. Sugarcane is believed to originate from wild species of *Saccharum robustum* which occur in New Guinea and which subsequently spread (12a) from South East Asia to India, the Middle East and the Mediterranean during the Muslim conquests. The Portuguese were responsible for its global flowering initiating the first great plantations in Madeira and subsequently Brazil. It is therefore highly likely that the arrival of sugarcane on the East-African coast pre-dates the arrival of the Portuguese. The mango is one of the most attractive of tropical fruit trees providing sustenance and shade. In the northern and eastern provinces of Zimbabwe mangoes constitute an important dietary supplement during the summer rains. There is an early seventeenth century report of sugarcane at Sofala. João dos Santos, who lived at Sofala in the 1580s commented on the extent of sugarcane plantations, orchards of orange

Citrus aurantium and lime trees and a well established system of organised agriculture. Limes were carefully cultivated in Swahili settlements along the east coast of Africa being indispensible in cooking and the preparation of refreshing drinks.

Frei Gaspar de Macedo's report in *Livro dos Moncões* of 1633 about the Manica region which straddles both sides of the common Zimbabwe and Mozambique border, indicated that in "these lands there were many fruits from India such as figs, pineapples, guavas, papaws, oranges, limes, cidras and lemons and excellent melons." He continued his report by stating that "it has been proven by experience that all the wheat planted from April to the end of May developed in such a way that one grain of it would produce fifty ears and some others thirty-seven.(13)" In the 1630s, Filipe de Mascarenhas, then captain of Mozambique, reported that Sena was producing all the wheat required for the Island of Mozambique and that if the Africans could be persuaded to adopt its cultivation there would be an exportable surplus for India. (14)

Lemon, mango and banana have become localized and now flourish over large parts of north-eastern Zimbabwe. Although lemon trees were first domesticated in South East Asia, their introduction to Mozambique and eastern Zimbabwe is likely to have preceded the arrival of the Portuguese. Wild lemon trees, *Citrus limon*, known as *muremani* and *mundimu* in Shona, grow along the Mazowe river. On 26 September, 1889 the British hunter and explorer, Frederick Courtney Selous, crossed the *Umrodzi*, the actual *Murowodzi* river which he followed to its confluence with the Mazowe.

Here, Selous found:

> a great many lemon-trees growing just on the water's edge, many of them loaded with fruit. These lemons were large and thick skinned, and not so sour. The natives had no tradition as to how the lemon-trees were introduced, but that there is a connection between them and the ancient gold-workings seems certain, for wherever lemon-trees grow, old gold-workings will invariably be found in this neighbourhood.

Root stock from these trees was used by plant botanists at Mazowe (15) to graft improved varieties, but this practice has been abandoned because the wood is not resistant to the phytopherine virus which induces root decay. Further trials are being considered using wild lemon trees growing in water-logged conditions in the Dichwe lemon forest (16) of the Umboe district of Mhangura. As the roots grow in water they may be virus resistant and of value to plant geneticists.

During the 1980s, botanists discovered an ancient avocado, *Persea gratissima*, cultivar growing wild in the Rusitu valley of the eastern districts of Zimbabwe. The variety was identified as Mexican - the avocado pear originates in Meso-America – and this cultivar appears to represent a link with the past. Guavas, *Psidium guayava*, have become localised in many parts of the Eastern districts. These trees, producing the vitamin C-rich fruit originate in Central-South America and were first catalogued in 1555 by the Spanish before being imported to the Old World and thence to Africa and Asia where they thrive in tropical conditions.

Other food plants which clearly originate in the Middle East, Mediteranean countries and India including eggplant or aubergine, *Solanum esculentum,* cucumber, *Cucumis sativus,* and possibly sesame are amongst those found by António Gomes and referred to earlier (17). Of these plants, the sesame, *Sesamum indicum*, enjoys fairly wide distribution throughout Zimbabwe as the fresh leaves are cooked as a relish and the seeds used for their oil content.

The tuberous rhizome tumeric, *Curcuma domestica,* is an important Indian condiment giving both the characteristic yellow colour and a special flavour to ethnic cuisines. The plant may have been imported to Mozambique during the Portuguese period. The spice is extensively grown by peasant farmers in the Chimanimani and Chipinge districts. During the season, itinerant peddlers travel throughout Zimbabwe selling the tumeric root to the Asian community.

Tumeric belongs to the ginger family, *Zingiber officinale,* and this piquant condiment is similarly cultivated in the Eastern mountains of Zimbabwe and is sold in local markets or *msikas* as a medicinal cure for constipation, abdominal pains and coughs. The commercial ginger variety has two local counterparts, *Siphonochilus aethiopicus* or mauve ginger and *Siphonochilus kirkii* or rose ginger and these both occur in woodlands of the eastern highveld.

Exactly how and when the prickly pear, *Opunta ficus-indica*, *dhorofiya* in Shona, with its edible fruit was introduced to Zimbabwe cannot be established but these plants originate in the Americas like many others. In Manicaland and south-western Masvingo provinces of Zimbabwe the spiney cactus is grown as an effective hedge. Its introduction to Zimbabwe may well be a much later phenomenon as in the case of the donkey.

Pineapples, *Ananas comosus*, which were first domesticated in lowland areas of South America including Brazil, (18) must also be considered as a strong contender. The spikey fruit was first pictured by *Frei Cristovão de Lisboa* when he published his *Historia dos Animais e Arvores do Maranhão,* an account of the fauna and flora of Brazil recorded between 1624 and 1627. *Chihengi* or *nanazi* are Shona names for pineapples and according to Ndau oral traditions have been under cultivation in the eastern districts of Zimbabwe for a considerable time.

A variety of bean known in Shona as *nyemba, Vignia unquinculata,* is cultivated throughout Zimbabwe and this may have been introduced by the Europeans. Groundnuts, *nzungu* in Shona, are extensively grown and popularly used to prepare *dovi* or peanut butter, a savoury which is relished in a mixture of cooked vegetables or rice. As noted elsewhere in the text, there are strong oral traditions associating the Njanja people of Zimbabwe with groundnuts and the Portuguese. Oil extracted from groundnuts, *Arachis hypogaea,* was traditionally used cosmetically to smear on the body in the same fashion as the extract of the thorn apple seed *Datura stramonium.* A third leguminous crop is *nyimo*

or ground peas, *Vigna subterranea,* which occur as black, brown or yellow kernels and most often eaten boiled. Ground peas are not considered imports and are believed to be indigenous.

Mbambaira and *madima* are Shona and Ndau words for the common sweet potato, *Ipomoea batatas,* and this crop is grown in all high rainfall regions of the country. *Mananga,* Shona for pumpkin, *Cucurbita maxima,* and squashes may have been improved by imported varieties. A decided candidate is *mufarinha,* a Shona derivative of the Portuguese word for flour describing the dryland crop of cassava, *Manihot esculenta.* This plant was introduced to Mozambique from Brazil in 1750 and climatic conditions were so ideal that it quickly spread inland. *Ndodzi,* Shona for dhal or Indian chick peas are commonly grown in some regions of eastern Zimbabwe close to human habitation. The crop appears to originate in India or the Middle East.

Mudhumbe, Colacasia esculenta, a regional culinary speciality, is the large leafy coco-yam or taro-root shrub which is grown in Manicaland for its starch-rich tubers. This is believed to originate in western India and it features in their cuisine. *Mapapaya,* Ndau for papaya, is a common fruit tree in most rural kitchen gardens. The papaya, known in Portuguese as *papaia* and *mamão,* originates in Brazil. The Portuguese propagated this delicious soft fruit throughout their tropical world. They also brought the cashew nut tree to Mozambique and India where it is extensively cultivated for its valuable nut. *Toronga* or *mhiripiri* or *nyungwe* in Shona are the red chili peppers of Pinzon and many varieties of these are cultivated and used as condiments. In some areas of eastern Zimbabwe chilies, *Capsicum annum* and *Capsicum frutescens* are known as *kachoro* in vernacular dialects.

Perhaps the most important general purpose vegetable in traditional Zimbabwean cuisine is the tomato, *Lycopersicom*. During the early 1970s, the writer found degenerate plants with cherry sized fruit growing along stream banks in the Mukumbura, Mzarabani, Dande and in neighbouring Tete province of Mozambique (close to the Serra de Comboio). The circumstances of this extremely isolated cultivation by remote African communities gave rise to strong argument that these plants were faithful to early imported progenitors. In August 1882 Frederick Courtney Selous camped at Chabonga on the Zambezi (south-east of the Msengezi confluence) where his host, a Portuguese speaking African named Jose Miguel Lobo-Chimbuna, indicated vast fields of tomatoes. Wheat was also cultivated along the river banks. In the 1904 edition of *Ancient Ruins of Rhodesia* the authors claim the existance of wild tomato areas in the Mazowe district. Mention is also made of wild figs and wild grape vines in association with many of the stone ruins. Certainly, many different species of *ficus* do occur near these ruins. The wild grapes described by the authors, Hall and Neal, may be confused with *Lannea edulis,* known as *tsambatsi* in Shona, a small bush bearing fruits which taste similar to grapes.

The history of this important plant has not been established with absolute certainty but it would appear to originate from tropical America, possibly in Mexico or Peru. Botanists contend that the cherry tomato is the original type from which modern cultivated varieties have sprung.

The name "tomato" is clearly Southern Amerindian and derives from the Aztec *xitomate*. It was also known as *tomati* and Mexicans grew the plant amongst their maize crop. In the early sixteenth century the tomato was taken to Iberia and thence to Italy where it became as popular as Marco Polo's spaghetti which he brought from China. The first mention of the plant in European botany is in the 1554 *Herbal of Matthiolus* where it is described as the *pomi d'oro* or golden apple. As the seed is readily dried and stored the plant achieved fast dispersal throughout the Portuguese world. The

Shona lexicon records the word *domasi* and *domatisi* for tomato and additionally there is the word *kariri* to describe a mash of tomatoes cooked by themselves and served as a side dish and *sumu* which is a tomato relish. The Shona word *kariri* is clearly a dialect variation of the Portuguese *caril* or curry stew which relies much on tomatoes.

Kovo or *couve*, Portuguese giant stalk cabbage known locally as Giant Rape, is a crop which is propagated from suckers. It is commonly grown in kitchen gardens in eastern and northeast provinces of Zimbabwe. This type of cabbage is known in Shona slang as *terylene*. The association with terylene, a man-made fibre which is suave and of high quality, occurs frequently when describing an item or thing of quality in popular Shona idiom.

During his journey into the Rivers in 1648 António Gomes, the Portuguese priest, noted the presence of tobacco along the Zambezi river in the Sena and Tete regions (19). Albino Manuel Pacheco saw tobacco under cultivation on the lower Mazowe during his trek to

Zumbo in 1861. The Shona word for tobacco, *Nicotiana tabacum,* is *fodya* which appears to be a derivative of the Portuguese word *folha* or leaf. Cultivation of tobacco quickly spread to highveld settlements and by the late seventeenth century, and certainly the eighteenth century, tobacco smoking and the use of snuff were firmly established traditions. Most remarkable was the *nyoka*

131

tobacco industry of the Shangwe people of the Gokwe district which thrived from the seventeenth century until the 1930s when it largely disappeared in the face of modern competition. (20) Yet, in some regions of Zimbabwe the preparation of the *nyoka* tobacco compound (a well pounded mixture of tobacco moulded into a large cone and dried) which is traditionally used in making snuff continues albeit on a smaller scale. Snuff, known as *bute* in Shona with elaborately carved containers feature prominently in the accoutrement of spirit mediums and traditional healers.

The use of tobacco was preceded by the arrival of the hallucinatory narcotic weed, *Cannabis sativa*, known in the vernacular as *mbanje*. This plant was in all likelihood brought to Mozambique and the Rivers territory by Swahili traders well before the advent of the Portuguese. Varieties of this drug are known variously as marijuana, hashish, bhang or Indian hemp. This plant was originally cultivated in the Middle East and possibly the Indian sub-continent before becoming established in the Zambezi valley and the highveld of Zimbabwe. *Cannabis sativa* is known in central and southern Mozambique by its original Indian and Persian (Iranian) name of *mbangui*. (21) The dry leaves of the pistillates, when smoked, emit a pungent smell. Continued use can be habit-forming. The symptoms of regular use are red eyes and excessive thirst. Although the use of *mbanje* is prohibited in Zimbabwe in terms of the Dangerous Drugs Act it has been condoned by Government authorities responsible for the administration of the Zambezi Valley Tonga.

Tonga womenfolk have traditionally smoked the drug using the *nefuko* or Tonga pipe (22) which is reminiscent of the Middle Eastern *hookah*. The habit of drawing the narcotic smoke through water may well owe its origins as much as the drug itself to early Swahili traders. But there is no firm evidence of any external influence in the development of this style of smoking and it is believed that this technology evolved quite independently.

Father João dos Santos comments in his *Ethiopia Oriental*, that the consumption of *mbanje* was fairly common during the sixteenth century noting that:

> Throughout the whole of Kaffraria a certain herb is found, which the Kaffirs sow, and which they call bangue...The Kaffirs are very fond of this herb, and commonly use it, going about half drunk from its effects..

132

Plate 36

Plate 37

Plate 38

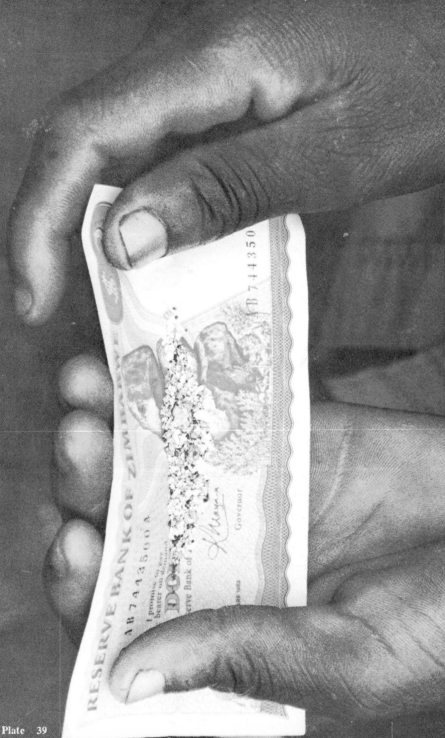

Plate 39

Plate 40

Plate 41

Plate 42

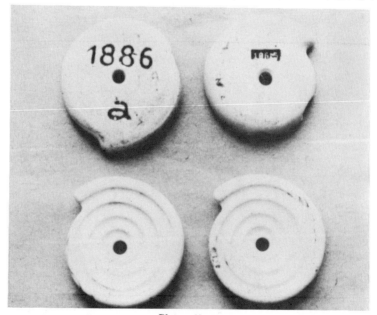

Plate 43

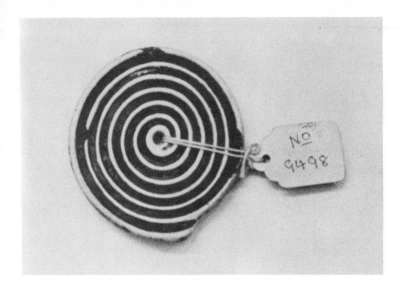

Plate 44

Plate 45

Plate 46

Plate 47

During the seventeenth century Portuguese traders complained that local African cotton looms around Sena on the Zambezi were producing cotton cloth in competition with their Indian imports. (23) It is likely that the raw cotton lint came from *new cotton*, a perennial variety, imported from the Americas where it originates, via Iberia and the Portuguese *Carreira da India*. This disease-prone variety still grows along the Zambezi river as far inland as its headwaters near the Angolan border. (24) American perennials later displaced this low-yielding variety but in the seventeenth century this imported cotton plant formed the basis of an indigenous industry producing *machiras* – thickly woven cloth worn as clothing or used as a blanket. The Portuguese endeavoured to stamp out this activity which posed a threat to their own commercial ambitions. During the mid- seventeenth century Father João dos Santos observed that only the chiefs or notables wore cloth and that the more lowly-born were almost naked or at best had some bark-fibre cloth or skins to cover themselves.

In the eighteenth century Francisco de Mello de Castro reiterated earlier observations that Sena *machiras* competed with Portuguese imports (25). Exact details of how this indigenous industry started cannot be elucidated but there is a species of cotton known as *Sabi Wild*, *Gossypium africanum*. which appears entirely indigenous to Zimbabwe and the Save river valley region in particular, where scattered plants can still be found. This cotton has a very short staple making it almost impossible to gin but as late as 1940 cotton weaving was observed in the Mount Darwin district bordering Mozambique's Tete province.

Spindle whorls were used to spin the lint from what must have been the foreign perennial varieties. Neither is it certain that this cotton industry was based on the American perennial as the seed may well have come from India or the Middle East before the Portuguese. Similarly, the requisite technology may have come from the Indian sub-continent. The resulting thread was then woven on low ground looms into a heavy white cloth — terribly slow and agonising work (26). Soon, better quality textiles were imported and the local industry struggled to survive. But survive it did, albeit in isolated communities of the Zambezi valley and eastern Zimbabwe.

The imported material was unravelled and the coloured threads woven into local cloth. This was done because dyes were generally unknown. Without doubt, these textiles represented articles of incredible value for the Africans and this fact was fully exploited by the importing merchants. Comparable, in a way, is the value that Europeans placed on rich brocades of Chinese silk.

Many of the plants certainly came to Mozambique and Zimbabwe much earlier as in the case of the mango tree, *mangifera indica*. *Zizyphus mauritiana*, *masau* in Shona and possibly a derivative of the Portuguese *maçã* for apple, and the tamarind *Tamarindus indica*, are both considered as indigenous trees and occur along the Zambezi valley and some regions of the highveld. Both plants grow in tropical and sub-tropical western India where they are used for culinary purposes. The *masau* fruit is used to prepare a nourishing dried fruit bread and in this manner it may originally have been transported from Arabia or India. Tamarind seed pulp is commonly used in the preparation of traditional Indian, Arab and Coastal Swahili cuisine enhancing the flavour of spicy meat stews.

The castor oil seed plant, *Ricinus communis*, and *mupfuta* in Shona may also be an import pre-dating the Portuguese. It occurs generally in north-eastern Zimbabwe and is used by traditional herbalists for its oil which has a multitude of medicinal applications. The plant may be a native of the Indian sub-continent. António Pinto da Miranda's 1766 report on Mozambique includes an interesting reference to this plant being used by a doctor Manuel Gomes Nobre in Tete. Nobre's medication was contained in a little gourd and consisted of the castor oil mixed with corrosive sublimate, hippopotamus brains and crocodile bile. Similar preparations were used by a Father Pedro of Zumbo — probably the innovative and legendary Father Pedro da Trinidade — to cure wounds and as an antidote for poisons.

During early Portuguese expeditions to the highveld, African food plants are likely to have featured prominently in Portuguese diet. These would have included finger millet known in Shona as *rukweza*, sorghum *vulgare pers.* or *mapfunde*, large-headed millet or *munga*. The seeds were ground and prepared as the staple stiff porridge or *sadza* and washed down with fermented beer or *doro*.

Their diet would certainly have included any of the following: the Mabola plum tree, known in Shona as *muchacha, Curatellifolia parinari,* which thrives in high water table regions and produces a fruit rich in nutritious syrup; wild figs known generically as *mukuyu* in Shona; the monkey orange or *Strychnos cocculoides;* the baobab or *Adansonia digitata* and the wild loquat or *Uapaca kirkiana* which produces a delicious fruit during the cooler winter months. All of these wild food sources were augmented in the appropriate seasons by game, at least eight different types of caterpillars, beetles, locusts, flying ants, fish and honey (27).

In later years the knowledge of how to distil the fiery alcoholic spirit *kachasu* made from the ripe and fermented *masau* berries is likely to have been acquired from the Portuguese to supplement the imported *aguardente.* The Portuguese word for bottle, *garafa,* has been taken directly into Shona and means, quite literally, a bottle of strong liquor. The distilling of *kachasu* is now a firmly entrenched tradition in north-eastern Zimbabwe. The name stems from the Brazilian- Portuguese *cachaça,* meaning an alcoholic spirit distilled from sugarcane waste.

Other Portuguese related curiosities include the two isolated colonies of Raffia Palms, *Raphia farinifera,* one of which is at the northern end of the Great Dyke within Tengwa State Land and now declared a Botanical Reserve and named Palm Block and the other on the Mozambique-Zimbabwe border. These unique trees, with the longest leaves in the plant kingdom — up to 18 metres in length, may be remnants of once greater distribution (28). In the north-eastern Centenary district of Zimbabwe there is a popular legend that the palms, which grow on the banks of crystal-clear streams and produce exotic waxy amber-coloured seed cones, owe their origins to Portuguese traders. Some country wags also suggest that the palms were planted by Swahili traders as road markers. Craftsmen make use of the great petioles and midribs of the Raffia palm to weave baskets and furniture.

As noted above, Central and South America was the universal source of important food crops which quickly spread throughout the known world. In exchange for these gifts the Spaniards and the Portuguese brought the domestic pig to the Americas and pork gained immediate popularity because of its lard so indispensable in cooking. As the Spaniards were largely responsible for the introduction of the domestic swine to Meso-America so it may be argued that the Portuguese brought pigs to South East Africa.

The pervasive influence of Islam along the East African littoral predated the coming of the Christian Portuguese and would have forbidden the handling of swine. Chinese vessels called on the East coast of Africa until maritime expansion was forbidden by the incumbent Ming Emperor in the early 1400s. These may also have been responsible for the introduction of the domesticated pig.

During the seventeenth century Portuguese vessels of the *Carreira da India* called at the island of St Helena in the south Atlantic and established it as a refreshment station. Fruit trees were planted and pigs and goats were introduced. (29) This provides strong evidence that domesticated swine were embarked for the *conquistas*. Father João dos Santos in his account of the habits and customs of the people of *Ethiopia Oriental* in 1561, included pigs in his nomenclature of livestock suggesting that the animals were by then domesticated by African villagers. However, there is no clear-cut information telling us who brought them to East Africa. However, in 1540,

the Sofala Factor recorded that pigs and other miscellaneous items formed part of an unrehabilitated deceased estate which he was obliged to settle by the payment of ten thousand *Reis* in unminted gold.

This report confirms that pigs were at Sofala by the early sixteenth century (30) from whence the spread inland would have taken place. In 1929 a census of domesticated animals in the peasant farming sector revealed a total of 37 889 pigs (31) and by 1973 this figure had grown to a total of 70 000 animals (32).

The majority of these animals are not penned and they scavenge for food. The pigs in Zimbabwe belong to the family *Suidae* and exhibit traces of foreign origins. They are probably of both European *Windsnyer* stock and Chinese lard pig (33). The original stock may have been imported from Portugal during the sixteenth or seventeenth centuries or in later years from Goa or Macau. Because of the conditions under which these pigs are reared they are only of marginal importance as a protein resource and their distribution in Zimbabwe is confined to the North East districts.

The pigs are extremely prone to *Ascaris lumbricoides*, parasitic worm infestations, but this is not surprising because in the lowlands of the Zambezi valley below the escarpment in the Dande and Mzarabani districts, the pigs forage freely on food scraps, root tubers and fallen *masau* berries. Nevertheless, they appear well acclimatised and seemingly resistant to *trypanosomiasis* or sleeping sickness which afflict other domestic stock and in particular cattle. These animals, known as indigenous pigs to differentiate from later exotic imports can be classified into two types. The first is short and fat with a stubby snout and resembles the Chinese lard pig. The second is the *windsnyer* or long nosed, razor back pig of European origin These animals also exhibit traits of the *akha* pig found in Thailand and characterised by a long snout (34).

All of these pigs are generally black, reddish brown or black and white spotted and the piglets often manifest the longitudinal stripes so characteristic of young bush pigs *Potamochoerus porcus*. There is, however, no evidence that these indigenous pigs have interbred with their feral kin. Very similar pigs occur in Cameroun where they are known in a local dialect as *bakosi* (35). Pigs were reported upon by David Livingstone in 1865 when he visited settlements on the Zambezi river where he described the animals as " horrid, long snouted, greyhound shaped pigs wallowing in fetid mudpools ". During the late 1880s, Frederick Courtney Selous visited Zumbo where he noted that:

> the tse-tse fly swarm on both sides of the river in the immediate vicinity of Zumbo, so that cattle cannot be kept there; but the Portuguese keep great quantities of lean, long-snouted pigs, which, being fed regularly every evening, do not wander far from the houses.

Cured ham or bacon, known in Portuguese as *presunto,* was being made on the Zambezi, above the Manyame confluence, in the 1880s. The art of smoking and curing pork is also known amongst isolated communities of Korekore in the Dande district (35a).

In a report covering the period 1758-1762 referring to Sena, on the lower Zambezi, there is mention of donkeys, cows, goats, sheep and pigs. Ducks, turkeys and domesticated doves are similarly listed. Although turkeys are not common in rural villages of north-eastern Zimbabwe, ducks do occur, and a particularly scruffy type of black feathered muscovy duck may be encountered foraging around rural dwellings. Similarly plumed domestic water-fowl occur in Portugal. In a report on the Portuguese Dominions on the East-African Coast dated 26 December, 1758, Ignacio Caetano Xavier reports on the existence of donkeys, pigs, ducks, mallards and turkeys. Turkeys, known as *peru* in Portuguese after the country of their origin were certainly brought to the Old World by the Spanish and subsequently taken by the Portuguese to their overseas possessions. Turkeys, *Meleagris gallopavo,* are known as *karukuni* in Shona but this may have more to do with the Afrikaans *kalkun* than *Peru.*

There are strong foreign or Portuguese connections with donkeys in the oral traditions of the Njanja and Buhera people of Zimbabwe. In 1929, a census of domesticated stock determined that the horse, donkey and mule population numbered 37 019 (36). Donkeys are much in evidence throughout the southern half of Zimbabwe and in the Buhera district there is an association between donkeys and a particular type of weed known as *chidhongi.* The introduction of these beasts of burden appears to be of much more recent origin and therefore not directly within the scope of this study. However, there is a good case

138

for investigating their introduction by the Portuguese to the Zambezi in the seventeenth and eighteenth centuries. Although donkeys were reported at Sena in the mid-eighteenth century (37) the evidence for their introduction by the Portuguese is still tenuous. The few horses brought to the Zambezi during the ill-fated Barretto-Homem expeditions of the sixteenth century did not fare well and all died from sleeping sickness. Conversely, they may have been introduced from the Gaza province of southern Mozambique or from South Africa in the late nineteenth century. The Shona word for donkey is *dhongwi*, an anglophone borrowing, but the Nguni word *mbongolo* also applies; neither of these suggests any Portuguese heritage.

The ubiquitous whippet type dog which predominates in rural areas of north-eastern Zimbabwe and has traditionally been used for hunting may well have been improved by inter-breeding with dogs introduced by the Portuguese from the sixteenth century onwards. Father João Dos Santos informs us that the Captain of Mozambique, Jorge de Meneses, sent: *"a very beautiful greyhound to Monomotapa, which he had received from Portugal."* The Mutapa truly cared for the dog and as he lay on his death-bed ordered that his canine friend be put to death and so accompany him to the netherworld.

In the absence of absolute proof that much of this exotic fauna and flora was introduced to Zimbabwe by foreign hand the only available evidence is the known place of origin and the historical sequence of events which might have brought them to South East Africa. They could have arrived by way of Spanish and Portuguese possessions in North Africa and thence by Muslim agency to the Swahili coast or directly by the Portuguese in the sixteenth and seventeen centuries. Others, as previously noted, undoubtably made their way to Mozambique and Eastern Zimbabwe during centuries of trade before the Europeans. All the same, maize and pigs remain inextricably interwoven with our account of the Portuguese in the Rivers and are vivid reminders of a Lusophone heritage.

References.

1. João Vaz Corte-Real is believed to have reached the coast of central and eastern north America around 1476 effectively predating Columbus.
2. Harlan J.R., The Plants and Animals that nourish Man., *Scientific American,* 235(3) p.88-97, 1976.
3. Ribeiro, Orlando, *Aspectos e problemas da expansão portuguesa* Lisboa, 1962, pp 26-32.
4. G.B. Ramusio, *Venice,* Vol. 1. 3rd edition, 1563.
5. Harlan J.R. op. cit.
6. Harlan J.R. op. cit.
7. Martin Alonzo Pinzon is believed to have discovered the Chilli Pepper during a foray in the Carribean Archipelago at the time of Columbus's epic voyage.
8. See Desmond. The Portuguesse settlement at Feira. p. 276-279. The northern Rhodesia Journal.
9. António Gomes, *Viagem,* 1648, p. 108-109. Beach/Noronha, 1980, trans. see also p.99.
10. Hair P.E.H., Milho, Meixoeira and other foodstuffs of the Sofala garrison, *1505-1525,* in *Cahiers d'Etudes africaines,* 66-67, XVII (2-3), 1977, pp. 353-363 thinks it improbable that there was maize on the coast before c. 1600.
11. Jeffreys M.D.M. The History of Maize in Africa, *S.A. Journal of Science,* 1954, p. 197-200, see also *Documents* Vol I. p. 747 for purchase of *milho* by the Portuguese at Sofala but it is not certain whether this refers to maize.
12. Beach/Noronha translations, 1980, Info on Sena etc., p. 8., where it is suggested that the *zaburro* maize was similar to varieties which grow in Portugal.
12a. Cobley L.S., *An Introduction to the Botany of Tropical Plants,* Longmans, 1977, p. 64.
13. Gaspar de Macedo, Monções, 1633, Beach/Noronha, 1980.
14. Axelson E. *Port. in SE Africa 1600-1700*
15. Archer J.D. *The Development of Mazowe Citrus Estates,* Heritage, No. 8, 1989, p. 85.
16. Talbot J.N. Dichwe Lemon Forest and its Avifauna, *The Honeyguide,* Nov. 1976 No. 88 p.12
17. Harlan J.R. op. cit. and B. Keevel to H. Ellert, 1991 on visit to Rusitu valley, Eastern districts of Zimbabwe.
18. Harlan J.R. op. cit. Cristovão da Costa, *Tratado das Drogas e Medicinas..* '(1. ed. 1578), 1964, p. 237.
19. António Gomes, *Viagem,* 1648.
20. Beach D.N. History of Tobacco and Smoking on the Zambezi, *Tobacco Today,* 1989, Vol 12, p. 33.
21. Rita-Ferreira A., *Fixação Portuguesa e História Pré-colonial de Moçambique,* Junta de Invest. Cientificas do Ultramar, Lisboa, 1982, p. 50.
22. Ellert H. *Material Culture of Zimbabwe,* 1988, p.
23. António Gomes, *Viagem,* p. 222.
24. Prentice A.N., Our Cotton Heritage, Heritage No. 6, 1986, p. 76-85.
25. Randles W.G.L., *The Empire of Monomotapa,* Mambo, 1981, trans, p. 89.
26. Ellert H. op. cit. p. 87-89.
27. Alvord E.D. *NADA* No.7, 1929, p. 9.
28. Coates Palgrave, Keith., *Trees of Southern Africa,* C. Struik, Cape Town, 1984, p.70-71.
29. Boxer C.R. *Port. Seaborne Empire,* p.123.
30. *Documents* Vol VII p. 15

31. Alvord E.D. *NADA* no.7, 1929. p. 9

32. Holness D.H and Smith A.J., Reproductive Performance of the Indigenous Rhodesian pig. *Rhod. J. Agric.* Res. II, 1973. The original stock was probably introduced by ships of European and Chinese traders calling at the coast of southern Africa between 300 and 400 years ago (Bonsma and Joubert, 1952.) Hence the pigs are probably of both European and Eastern origin, and a sub-type of *Sus domesticus.*

33. Holness D.H. The Role of the Indigenous Pig As a Potential Source of Protein in Africa - A Review. *Rhod. Agric. J.* Vol. 73 (3) p. 59-62.

34. Holness D.H. op. cit. See also Eusebio J.A., *Pig Production in the Tropics,* Longmans, 1980.

35. Holness D.H. op. cit.

35a. Selous F.C., *Travel and Adventure in South-East Africa,* p. 60. Observations near Msengezi Mission, Mzarabani, 1973.

36. Alvord E.D. *NADA*, No.7, 1929. p.9

37. Information on the Portuguese communities on the East African coast — Sena and Mozambique in 1758-1762. Beach/Noronha translations, 1980, p.7-8.

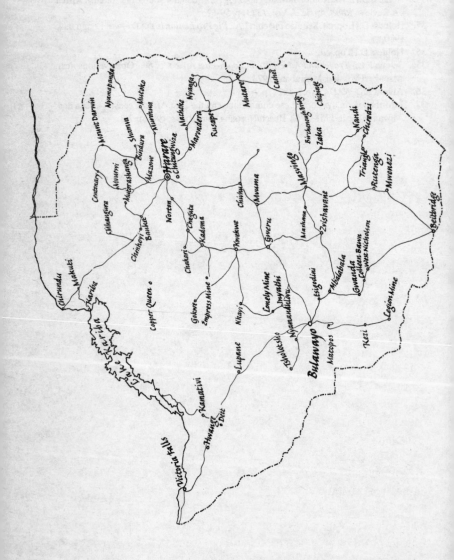

CHAPTER 5

Exports and the economics of trade which focused on gold mining and to a lesser extent on silver, copper and iron but also on ivory and rhino horn.

Gold, followed by ivory, were the principle export commodities of the Rivers. The importance of this trade on Portuguese mercantile operations was decidely more noticeable in the East than in Portugal. In 1547 the Goa mint struck the golden São Tomé, an Indo-European coin, with a value of 360 *Reis* which depicted the seated figure of Saint Thomas. When first minted these coins contained 3,22 grams of gold but this was soon reduced to 2,80 grams. Some of these coins were later minted at Cochin in 1555 (1) and for years to come the golden *pardau d'ouro* was common coinage throughout Portuguese Asia. The early Portuguese spice trade from Malabar and the Banda Islands fuelled rapid commercial expansion in the sixteenth century and Zimbabwean gold must have played a part in this commerce. The importance of the precious metal is as real in modern Zimbabwe as it was during the sixteenth and seventeenth century. Gold production is a major contributor to the national economy. There are presently 450 producing gold mines throughout the country and of these, eleven contribute fifty percent of the national average 12 tonnes output per annum. (2) The rest, so called small-workings provide the balance. More than 6 000 gold deposits have been exploited since the late 1890s producing an estimated 1 566 tonnes of gold. Almost without exception these deposits are located on ancient workings many of which may have been operating during the Portuguese period.

During the early twentieth century several Zimbabwean mines were hailed as the richest producers in the world and these included the Globe and Phoenix Mine at Kwekwe (3), the Cam and Motor Mine near Kadoma and the Golden Valley Mine at Chakari. Significantly all these mines occur within the lands known to the Portuguese as Abatua, Mother of Gold. The development of these mines contributed in part to the mini gold-rush at the beginning of the twentieth century when hordes of European fortune seekers

143

streamed north from South Africa in search of a second *Witwatersrand*. Claims were pegged and mines opened at all the known gold fields of Zimbabwe but principally around Bulawayo, Shurugwi, Kwekwe-Sebakwe, Kadoma, Mazowe, Shamva-Bindura, Makaha, Mount Darwin, Angwa and the Mutare-Odzi gold belts. Most of these mines were extremely profitable because the early miners were able to crush high paying ores or *ancient chips* (4) which had been excavated by ancient miners and found abandoned around the old workings.

Much of the preliminary exploratory work had already been done and the modern miners had only to clear the ancient shafts to gain access to the reef using modern methods. In the case of the Globe and Phoenix Mine, which was developed in 1902, and has been in continuous operation since with a reported yield of 450 tonnes of gold worth an estimated US$ 540 m (5), ancient stopes in the Phoenix claims extend for a distance of 42 metres along the main reef and 10 metres on a parallel reef with average ores of one ounce per tonne (6).

It has been calculated that more than 30 000 ounces of gold must have been extracted from this mine prior to 1902. Ancient workings at the Globe reef at the foot of the Phoenix hill are as extensive as those in the Phoenix but restricted because of the high water table which acted as an effective barrier against all ancient mining activities. Mining work at the nearby Gaika claims in 1902 resulted in the recovery of profitable values in the rubble found at pre-colonial workings here. This golden bonanza paid for much of the subsequent early development of the mine (7). Having depleted the surface outcrops, ancient miners were forced to excavate along the reef-extracting ores. Supporting rock pillars were often left in place

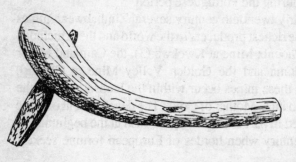

to prevent collapse as in the case of the Gaika Mine but more often than not these techniques were not understood or applied. In a limited number of old gold workings an effective ventilation system was used. Women and children who were generally employed underground were often trapped and killed by rockfall. For labouring in confined subterranean spaces a number of tools were developed including round rock hammers, iron *gads* (a form of short handled pick), wooden wedges, *badza* or hoe blades and wooden scoops for removing the broken ore, were employed. Cracking or exfoliating of ores by applying fires and then dousing the heated stone with water was a commonly used method. (8)

An anonymous Portuguese report of 16 March, 1683 has this colourful account of ancient mining which explains that:

> when the appropriate signs were spotted, news was sent to the Portuguese Captain at Dambarare who would inform the King (Mutapa) who immediately sent two or three envoys to represent him and collect tribute. These ambassadors had authority to conscript and instruct labourers and between 60 and 80 persons appeared. Mining operations would then start with groups of between 4 and 5 men each opening a hole in the ground in the shape of an ordinary well. A shaft, or intura was dug into the ground and after a predetermined depth had been attained in all the shafts the miners started to dig into the middle so that all the horizontal tunnels drove into a central point and joined up leaving a central hanging roof. The roof would sometimes collapse burying 30 or 40 people underground and in such cases there was great jubilation from those on the surface for this was taken as a sign of gold in abundance (9).

Plates 31, 32

Ironically enough, writes the Portuguese narrator, this fateful twist nearly always proved true.

> Immediately after the disaster, news would spread and soon crowds gathered at the mine and within 24 hours the mine had been cleared and the bodies of the dead removed. Mining operations then continued and once the visible gold was discovered it was quickly removed.

The traditional belief about rockfalls and death underground lingers on to this day and it is commonly contended by alluvial gold workers that deaths caused by landslides or rockfalls prove the existence of rich gold. This is an unshakeable belief amongst many rural folk engaged in the precarious trade. (10) An echo from the past was heard in late 1990 when rockfalls killed several miners at an open-cast working near the Sebakwe river in Kwekwe. In a macabre replay of history people rushed to the site convinced that gold was to be found aplenty.

The Portuguese chronicler continued his account of early mining operations at a mine known as Guinzague which was worked for 8 months employing some 75 people removing about 7 goatskins of gold ore per day. The same observer noted somewhat wistfully that one half of this gold was lost in the washing process and the other half which came from the natural mines of Ethiopia, the archaic Portuguese name for eastern Africa including Zimbabwe, and then went into the artificial mines of Hindustan where the *mouros* or Muslims of India put it back into the ground when burying their jewellery-laden dead. Mining at Guinzangue was only brought to a halt by flooding before being abandoned. During its life, the mine was so rich that the African miners approached a Portuguese settlement loaded with so much gold that they had considerable difficulty in disposing of it to the Portuguese who only had a little wax, a wooden bed and the clothes on their backs to offer in trade so wretched was their state of affairs (11).

The same report elucidates Portuguese mal-administration in the Rivers for:

> ...in the first place, the Portuguese stopped informing the Mutapa of the signs pointing to the mines saying that this amounted to a claim and they would begin to dig without the Mutapa's permission...

Official attempts to survey the full extent of the mines and consolidate mining activities were passively thwarted by Portuguese traders and miners. In July 1633 Dom Andres de Vides y Albarado who had earlier conducted a physical inspection of mines in Manica brought a number of Portuguese before the Crown procurator at Sena to give evidence of all they knew about gold and precious metals in the Rivers. (12) Domingos Pais, Domingos Cardoso, Jacome de Carvalho, António Fernandes de Torres, Simão de Figuereido, João Pereira Rebello and Custódio Lopes d'Almo testified under oath all they knew about gold, silver and copper deposits in the Rivers. As long-term residents and traders in the region, they should have known considerably more than vague information concerning Abatua and Manica being rich in gold and recounting stories about huge nuggets and other prospectors' tales. Little of concrete value was elicited from these men. Obviously they were extremely reluctant to jeopardise their respective concessions.

Gold-bearing ores brought to the surface require further treatment to extract the metal from the quartz matrix. A relatively small and simple mortar and pestle technique was traditionally employed to crush the gold ore before it was washed or panned in nearby rivers. Many of these milling sites can be seen in the Kwekwe and Gweru districts and are most often located in living rock formations on the banks of rivers and streams. There is a large-scale milling site (map ref QK 917 022) close to the main Gokwe road some five kilometres from Kwekwe consisting of dozens of rounded mortars or dolly holes which were worn into the rock by continual crushing operations. Examination of another Kwekwe milling site (map ref QK 964 069) suggests that large tree trunks were employed in a rocking motion to provide leverage and pressure against the round pestle to crush the ores in the dolly holes beneath the pivot. The use of this technique is further suggested by the wear on either side of the dolly holes. In 1937 an extensive milling site comprising numerous dolly holes was discovered at the Macardon claims close to the Umzingwani river in the West Nicholson district of southern Matabeleland.(13) Similar milling sites may also be seen along the banks of the Gweru river close to Silobela in the Kwekwe-Nkayi district. The proximity of these sites to streams and rivers strongly suggests the use of water to wash the powdered ores.

Available archaeological evidence points to gold-working traditions dating back more than a thousand years, where the recovered gold was later melted down into rough ingots and beaten into fine gold leaf. This was used to decorate wooden artifacts and attached by means of tiny gold tacks. It was also drawn into wire and used

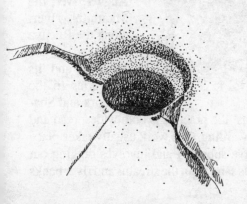

in decorative braiding on ceremonial axes *(gano)* scabbard daggers *(bakatwa)* or fashioned into beads using stone moulds. Evidence of these highly evolved skills in gold-smithing have been found at Great Zimbabwe and at both Kame and Dlodlo ruins in Matabeleland.(14) These traditional skills in working gold were not immediately forgotten or abandoned after the demographic upheavals associated with the end of the Great Zimbabwe society and the rise of the Rozvi-Torwa in the west and the Mutapa dynasty in the east. But they did go into slow decline particularly in the sixteenth and seventeenth centuries when emphasis was placed on the unworked metal as a direct medium of exchange for the coveted imported glass Plate 33, 3 beads and cloth.

Perhaps the easiest method of gold recovery was panning the alluvial sands in rivers flowing through the major gold belts of Mashonaland and Manicaland. In a description of *Oriente Conquistado* by Father De Sousa of 1696 relating to gold deposits and in particular to the recovery of gold dust from river alluviums we learn that:

> The Africans know this special kind of soil and they gather it in the rivers in the summer or in the puddles in the winter and wash it and sift it to separate the precious gold.

Then, as now, Plate 35, 3 37 the methods are virtually identical. Observations carried out in 1987 and 1988 at the Angwa river, the Mkaradzi river, along the Ruenya river and at the Mazowe and its tributaries in the Bindura and Shamva districts determined that the practice is both widespread and occasionally extremely re-warding. The work usually takes place when the summer rains have subsided and involves digging out large quantities of auriferous sand from the streams and river banks and washing it in the river.

In 1614 the Royal Treasury prepared a report for King Phillip III (II) on the mines of Mutapa in which it was emphasized that the gold did not come from underground mines but rather from river beds where it was panned by the Africans. Neither did it come from continuous or verifiable seams but it was drawn from the sands of rivers which flowed through gold belts. Gold was obtained from the *feiras* at Matafuna and Fura districts but not from any mines in the true sense with the exception of Manica where gold ores were extracted from underground.

The report observed that many people were engaged in recovery encouraged by Portuguese who brought trade goods. The gold was then taken to Goa in vessels which normally sailed from India to Africa in January each year returning with gold, ivory and slaves in September .(15)

In June, 1990 the writer visited the Nyaguwe river at a point some kilometres upstream from its confluence with the Mazowe. The

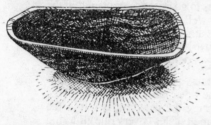

Nyaguwe alluviums are extremely rich in gold and faithful to the traditional methods of extraction, hundreds of men, women and children were busy digging into the river bed and banks extracting the sands. In a process known in the Shona vernacular as *kugeza mudhaka* or literally to wash the sand, women recover the tiny grains of gold. The verb *kuunga* meaning to extract alluvial gold is also applicable. Deep pits had been sunk into the earth and miners descended using simple buckets with bark fibre ropes. The miners follow the gold bearing alluvial strata deep into the earth until their work is impeded by flooding. The alluvial sand is scooped into large wooden dishes known in Shona as *zamba* and these are passed from one to the other before being transported to the river. The golden concentrates or *hundi* are later transferred to a small earthenware dish or *mbiya* Plate 38 which is dried over a wood fire.

Some three hundred people were working at the Nyaguwe river site recovering an average of 19 grams of gold per day. Significantly, the work took place during the winter months when river floods have subsided and the banks were largely exposed yet sufficient water was available to facilitate panning and every *zamba* full of *dhaka* or sand yielded yellow tailings and grains of *goridhe* as the precious gold is known colloquially.

These observations confirm the reports of Manuel Barretto of 1667 when he wrote on the method and time of extracting gold:

> 'The river gold (so they call that which in the winter is washed and carried down by the rivers, where they seek it) is better than the bar gold (as they call that which is dug in mines), nevertheless the gold of the mines of Mokaranga is as good and better than the river gold of Manica, but in Manica nuggets like half an acorn are found, which are equal in quality to the river gold of Mokaranga. The best river-gold of Mokaranga is that of Ongoe, Macana and Mocraz. The gold of Maramuca is generally of inferior quality.'

> A countless number of men, women and children assemble in the place where they chose to open marondos, the chief of each village forms a separate party with his people, and each begins to open his marondo in the fashion of a well. The mouth is so narrow that a man may stand with his legs extended from one side to the other. They make steps to go up and down within the circumference of the well, and on these the people station themselves, passing the mataca, or earth, which is dug away, from hand to hand, which the diggers pass to them in pandes, or wooden bowls.

> The mataca which contains gold is washed in the neighbouring rivers, until the water has washed away all the earth, and the gold, being the heaviest, is left at the bottom of the bowl in small scales or very fine glittering sand.

In the Makaha hills, gold-bearing ores known as *chimkute* are extracted from open trenches or shallow shafts and then crushed and washed to remove extraneous material. The process of extracting gold by crushing quartz ores is known as *kangare* in Shona to differentiate it from the alluvial extraction methods. Streams and rivers flowing through the Makaha area are extensively panned and this activity extends down to the Ruenya river where thousands of people derive a livelihood from this informal industry. A visit to the rural business centre at Makaha clearly substantiates the importance of the gold in the commercial life of the local people. Pla Likely–looking buyers are quickly beseiged by would-be purveyors of gold in open defiance of the Gold Trade Act. Interviews with gold sellers at the Makaha business centre established that regular buyers visit from town. Between 1890 and 1934 approximately twenty European prospectors extracted 322 ounces of gold from the Manyoke and Manuchi rivers which flow past the Radnor Mine and into the Nyamzizi and finally the Ruenya. In 1935 the Manuchi river was surveyed and found to contain 1,4 million cubic metres of alluvial sands. (16)

Experience is important in being able to determine the best point along the river to collect the goldbearing alluviums. This is normally indicated by the meander of the river course and specific points where the heavy gold concentrates are likely to be deposited. The belief that deaths associated with rockfall indicate the presence of gold remains deep-rooted amongst alluvial panners as well as hard rock miners. When suitable deposits are found they are removed to permanent pools where a concentric mud trough is constructed and continually filled with water to wash away the mud and earth from the wooden dish or *zamba*.

During December, 1987, officials of the Zimbabwean Chamber of Mines conducted an investigation into gold panning along the Mazowe. It was assessed that this highly profitable work now attracts thousands of people producing an estimated US$ 7 m worth of gold per annum which is sold into the black market and illegally exported. Unless licensed to operate alluvial gold claims, the activity is considered illegal in terms of the Gold Trade Act and carries heavy penalties for the offenders. The sheer extent of these modern operations clearly confirm the observations of the Portuguese chroniclers of the sixteenth and seventeenth century.

Regrettably, the activities of these illegal gold panners along the fragile riverine eco-systems are having a devastating effect and causing serious stream bank erosion, flooding, drying up of rivers and siltation of dams and weirs. In the case of the Mkaradzi river near Mount Darwin, the impact is extreme. Nearby farmers complain that the river quickly dries and that age-old permanent pools disappear early in the season. This is the same river described by Father De Sousa in his *Oriente Conquistado* of 1696:

> the river Mocaras with its sands of gold in which the
> Africans gather little grains.

After recovery, the gold dust is transferred into the plastic cap of a ball point pen in much the same fashion as the porcupine quills of old and later sold to illegal gold dealers. The operations are lucrative and a fortunate panner can earn thousands of dollars in a month but

151

more often than not the work is back-breaking and provides but a meagre income for the labourer who is obliged to sell his gold well below market prices to unscrupulous buyers. Little has changed since 1614 when it was noted that the gold which is taken from the rivers by the Blacks in such trifling amounts that one person may only earn one and half *Reis*. The *Real*, a low value copper coin, went out of circulation in the sixteenth century.

In the mid-1980s, farmers in the Bindura district reported that seasonal labourers who used to earn money picking cotton now spurn this work in favour of the supposedly more profitable gold recovery. For many rural people, faced with harsh economic realities, gold panning is a ready and immediate solution to their difficulties. Yet the alarming increase in the scale of these operations and the consequent damage to the environment, (meaningless arguments to an empty belly) demand urgent attention at national level if large scale destruction of important rivers is to be halted and controlled.

The recovery of alluvial gold from the rivers of Mashonaland and Manicaland is a long-standing tradition and as late as the 1890s the gold trade continued to flow into Mozambique. During the colonial administration of Zimbabwe, District Commissioners in the north-east authorised villagers to collect gold to supplement their subsistence income during poor agricultural seasons. The Mazowe and Ruenya rivers have long been associated with alluvial gold recovery and in 1965 a Government Mining Engineer was sent to the Ruenya river to give advice to alluvial washers and to purchase the gold at a fair market price. (17)

During the early twentieth century a pair of delicate scales for weighing gold dust were collected from Chief Mangwende's area in the north-east together with the requisite weights (18). These are known in Shona as *mashanu* (five), *mairi* (two), *mana* (four), *nyarupota* (to go round), *nyabadza* (worth a hoe), *nyarusimba* (price of a piece of iron), *tanga* (start), *tanga kadiki* (small start) and *mhopo* a wart. *Tanga* was also a small Portuguese coin of varying value and metal composition current in nineteenth-century Portuguese India. As noted earlier, gold weights were also manufactured from quartz crystal mined in the Odzi district of Manicaland.

It is not surprising that the Portuguese *feira* of Macequece was located where it was. The site of old Macequece lies in close proximity to incredibly rich alluvial gold deposits which occur along the Revue, Chua and Inhamucarara river valleys. There are references to gold extraction from the Inhamucarara and Musa rivers as late as 1795 when the district was featured in a *Description of the Kingdom of Manyika, its Customs and Laws*. These rivers rise in the eastern highlands and within the geological formation known as the Mutare gold belt before flowing eastwards into Mozambique. A major gold mining undertaking to process alluvial gravels, estimated to be up to 30 metres deep in some places, commenced in 1990 with a projected yield of 20 kilos of gold per month. (20)

The Revue valley, including numerous re-entrants and tributaries is extremely rich in gold-bearing alluvial gravel. The gold is found in the form of tiny nuggets which have been flattened by the weight of the gravel and sand. The gold pieces are porous as the silver and copper has long since been leached out by natural solutions of sulphuric acid. As a result, the gold is extremely fine and averages around 920 carats. (20) The sheer extent of the gold in these alluvial gravels suggests that Portuguese reports from the seventeenth century as to the golden riches of this region may well have been understated — a rare occurance indeed, for the Portuguese chroniclers normally exaggerated.

The mining methods traditionally employed were restricted to exploitation of the surface sands and gravels. A thorough geological survey of this region was undertaken in 1989 when it was established that primitive gold mining, panning and sluicing are ongoing activities. Sluicing of crushed gold bearing ores — a traditional method first reported by the Portuguese during the seventeenth century — still takes place on old abandoned claims near the Mimosa Mine situated high in the well wooded mountains overlooking the Nyamakarara river valley in Mozambique. The sluices are constructed from hollowed-out logs fitted with a series of wooden ribs overlaid with sacking or *gudza* bark fibre cloth which trap the heavy gold concentrates as the powdered ores are washed through. The work is done on a co-operative basis with shared effort to construct water channels from diverted mountain streams. Individual "claims" are mined nearby, following the gold-bearing reef or veins deep into the mountain side. The ores are extracted and crushed before being washed through the sluices. (21). Gold recovery by these traditional methods in the Mutare gold belt extending into Mozambique is reaching epic proportions as large numbers of Zimbabweans are now being attracted by the lure of hard currency earnings when they sell their gold dust and nuggets for convertible currencies (22). Clearly, a considerable quantity of gold disappears into the black economy of the border town of Mutare, Chimoio and Beira in neighbouring Mozambique.

The significance of the Manica alluvial gold appears as important today as in those halcyon days of yore when the Portuguese and their Swahili precursors tapped these golden riches. Just as the Portuguese administration of the sixteenth and eighteenth century complained bitterly about the contraband trade in gold (23) and consequent dwindling profits for the Crown, the modern Zimbabwean authority in the Rivers are equally frustrated and seemingly unable to prevent the rampant illegal trade. Conservative estimates formulated by the Zimbabwean Chamber of Mines in the early 1990s suggests that millions of dollars are being lost to the fiscus by the illicit traffic in gold. In the large scale panning of rivers from Filabusi and Gwanda in the south-west; Sebakwe and Munyati in the central Midlands province and the Mazowe and Ruenya systems in the north-east the lamentable story is repeating itself. Hordes of gold panners descend upon the Rivers in a classic re-enactment of history.

A similar situation must prevail in Mozambique as the clandestine traffic in gold is inextricably associated with the economic lifeblood of trading communities in the towns of the Manica and Sofala provinces of Mozambique. The illegal gold trade continues in this century just as it did in the sixteenth and seventeenth century when the Portuguese held sway in the Rivers of Gold.

Silver Mining

The perennial quest for silver, an extremely valuable medium of exchange in China, appears to have obsessed the Portuguese for there is continual reference to their search for this precious metal in documents of the sixteenth and seventeenth centuries. In truth, the

Portuguese never found their African *Potosi* and even the legendary silver mines of Chicoa were never conclusively proven. Some silver may have been recovered from the Manicaland *feiras* and from the Angwa river *feiras* where silver is known to occur in association with gold and copper. The only hard evidence available to support the presence of silver in the Rivers is found in António Bocarro's *Decadas* written in the early seventeenth century. The report reads:

> They say there are some silver mines in the lands of Mocota, a powerful Kaffir, a neighbour of our market of Luanze, and a kaffir brought a large piece of silver ore from them to sell in Luanze, as is related by an eye-witness who is truthful and very worthy of credit.

This is an interesting report because *Mocota* is most likely the Portuguese orthographic rendition of *Mkota*, a remote rural district of north-eastern Zimbabwe, adjacent to the Nyakata mountain at map reference VS 682 564, where deposits of galina, lead and silver were discovered nearly thirty years ago. The prospector did not find any obvious sign of mining however. Still, a combination of the historical records and the physical evidence is convincing and further investigation is indicated. (23) After the expulsion of the Portuguese from the Rivers in 1693, a number of Portuguese Indians, known disparagingly as *Canarins,* were able to insinuate themselves back into the territory. One such man was Domingos Carvalho, a Brahmin from Sanquali village in Salcete, Goa. He befriended a local African chief and established a good business allegedly exchanging silver for cloth. (24)

The African chief or *Régulo* was extremely cautious and did not reveal the source of the silver to the Goan. Around this time, an African servant named Manuel, in the service of Dona Vicência João, widow of Francisco Pinheiro de Faria, absconded from Tete seeking refuge in the Chief's village where he quickly ingratiated himself and by dint of treachery discovered the silver lode. Manuel then fled. The account of this intrigue ends with a note that part of the silver from this mine was later taken to Sena where it was wrought into a religious monstrance for the Parish Church on the orders of Frei António da Conceição of the Augustans (25).

Some thirteen *Arrobas* (approximately 208 kilos) of silver from this mine was allegedly shipped to Goa where a few *Marcos* (a weight of eight ounces) of the metal was fashioned into book-ends and four small candlesticks for the Church of Nossa Senhora das Neves in the village of Rachol, Parish of Salcete in Goa. The silver mine was said to be at a place known locally as *Nhacace* or Nyakasi which borders the lands of Tete and some 30 leagues (150 kilometres by Portuguese reckoning) from a village in a valley near the Zambezi river between two mountains bare of trees. Obviously it was intended that the location of the mysterious mine should remain a secret ! The closest we can come to this obscure location is by reading another report of António Bocarro in which he states:

> One day's journey up this river Mossengueze (Msengezi) along the river Zambezi, in the said Kingdom of Beza, there is a mountain which they call *Nobiry* (Nembire), where there are known to be mines opened and worked, from which the Monomotapa provides himself with what silver he requires. In Chicova, a Dominican friar asked Dom Diogo, the son of the Monomotapa, who was also there with Diogo Simoes Madeira, if he knew anything of those mountains of *Nobiry*, and he replied that he had sometimes seen bars of melted silver brought to his father from those mines.

This is very inconclusive as the geological reports covering the Msengezi river valley and the Nembire district of the Mvuradona mountains do not confirm the presence of silver. (On1 November, 1949 a British South African Police trooper investigated dry stone

wall ruins in the Dotito district and just east of Nembire.)

The Portuguese accounts of silver should be treated as suspect as there are very few sources of free silver in Zimbabwe. The silver specie used by the Portuguese in the

China trade came out to Goa on the vessels of the *Carreira da India* from Lisbon. It was mainly in the form of Spanish, Mexican and Peruvian rials-of-eight (26). Silver coin was also derived in the Nagasaki trade with Japan (27). If any silver did come out of the Rivers and this extremely doubtful — little reliance must be placed on the Portuguese—accounts it must have been insignificant by comparison with the quantity shipped from the Americas to Spain and Portugal.

The metal does occur in Zimbabwe, but mainly in association with copper and gold, and sophisticated extraction methods must be employed in the refining and separation of the metals. It is therefore difficult to believe that silver was ever mined on viable commercial levels by the Portuguese. Perhaps there really is a lost silver mine in north-eastern Zimbabwe or the western Tete province of Mozambique — a popular legend about the lost silver mines of Chicoa has never been substantiated — but this appears the stuff of fiction without basis in fact.

Copper Mining

There is considerable evidence of ancient copper mining at the Umkondo mine in southern Manicaland, at Mhangura and Shamrock mines in northern Mashonaland and at Copper Queen and Skipper Mine in the Midlands Province. (28) Examples of early manufactured copperware in the form of wire and X-shaped ingots support the level of technology and attendant metal-working skills which date from times well before the arrival of the Portuguese. Several copper crosses have been unearthed in the Lomagundi district of north-eastern Zimbabwe and particularly around the Chedzurwi hill, Urungwe. Twenty crosses have been found at this hill feature during land clearing and ploughing. Local traditions talk of jackals with human hands and feet moving over Chedzurwi on moon-lit nights. Agriculture has softened the outline of this mound which has now become more of a hump than a hill. The copper crosses weigh between 1 and 3 kilos and were cast in sand or soapstone moulds. One of these soapstone moulds was found at the headwaters of the Horongwa river. Metallurgical analysis of copper ingots from this region has proven them to be almost pure copper with minute traces of iron, silver and lead.

In a supplement to Manuel Barretto's report upon the State and Conquest of the Rivers of Cuama there is an interesting reference to copper:

> Of the existence of copper there is no doubt, for we have seen it. Among the Kaffirs, it is used as money, which they call massontas, which are two St. Andrew's crosses joined together by a bar in the middle.

A report by Father Luis de Figueiredo Cardozo of 12 December 1680 has details of copper mining in the Manica region of the Rivers where the local Africans dug the copper with great facility producing " some loaves " of the smelted metal. These copper ingots were then traded at the rate of twelve ingots for one *bertangil* of cloth said to be worth two *tangas* of gold. (29)

Iron Mining

The Iron Age society which the Portuguese encountered when they arrived on the highlands of Zimbabwe in the beginning of the sixteenth century already possessed the technology to mine and smelt iron. There is evidence that iron ores were being exported via the port of Sofala as early as the ninth century (30) as there are reports from the writings of Al Masudi of the tenth century about iron at Sofala. Subsequent thirteenth century reports from Ibn Said also mention iron as an export from Sofala. The source of the Sofalan iron exports, as in the case of gold, must have been Manica. Manuel Barretto, writing in the seventeenth century on the Rivers of Cuama emphasised that:

> iron is known. Pewter they use in bartering, like square money with a point in the form of a diamond on one side, which is done in the melting. Some came to my hands in Sena and Tete, and I should be glad if I could remember the name given to it by the kaffirs.

An obvious reference to the *mapadza,* hoe blades, which were extensively used in trade.

There are a number of sites in the Vila de Manica district of Mozambique of which Mavita-Munhinga is perhaps the largest. Examination of this site has produced evidence of open-cast surface ore extraction and nearby smelting. The remains of furnaces, tuyeres and slag evidence a large scale industry in pre-colonial times. (31) Other African iron-age communities on the highveld of Zimbabwe may also have produced pig iron for trade with the coastal entrepôt in pre-Portuguese times. Iron ores are readily available at a number of historical sites throughout Zimbabwe and the most significant of these were centred at Wedza mountain (the Njanja), Shurugwi, Redcliff and Buchwa. The extent of the Njanja iron industry and their association with the Portuguese of the Zambezi valley is extremely important. The Njanja produced a wide variety of iron implements, tools and weapons which they traded with their neighbours. As demonstrated earlier, Njanja folklore incorporates references to the Portuguese. The extreme value of the iron hoe blade, the *badza,* as a unit of exchange and agricultural tool was noted by the Portuguese during their early contacts with the Mutapa. The Portuguese subsequently incorporated a symbolic hoe in their imaginary coat of arms for the *Monomutapa.*

Ivory

The elephant, *Loxodonta africana,* has long been symbolic of the African continent. Yet this majestic and unique order of mammals, the *Proboscidea,* bears a terrible curse. Its ivory has always had a special enchantment and for this reason the unfortunate animal has been hunted and slaughtered for its precious tusks. It was well known in antiquity and its use in India and China dates back to prehistorical times. Ivory is still widely used in the East for making jewellery and in a powdered form, medicinally, as an emetic and a cure for worms (32). The Portuguese quickly recognised the commercial value of ivory and continued exporting tusks to India and the Far East during their tenure in the Rivers. *Marfim,* the Portuguese word for ivory features on a list of merchandise on board Portuguese galleons bound for Japan in 1637. It is extremely difficult to estimate total quantities exported from Zimbabwe during the sixteenth and seventeenth centuries but an analysis of present day elephant populations in Zimbabwe provides some evidence.

Zimbabwe has a significant ivory manufacturing industry which is estimated to be the largest in eastern or southern Africa (33) and this is based on the legal sale of ivory. Zimbabwe has a unique elephant management system which provides for controlled culling of excess populations to prevent environmental destruction In 1991 the estimated total elephant population in Zimbabwe was 70 000 animals of which nearly thirty per cent were concentrated in north eastern Zimbabwe (34). During 1988, Zimbabwe ranked in the top 12 exporting countries in Africa producing 100 865 kilos of raw ivory (35). By the use of imaginative speculation the reader may draw his or her own conclusions as to the total volume of ivory exported from the Zimbabwean highveld during the last milennium. The pattern of trade between the Zimbabwean highveld and the coastal Swahili which pre-dated the arrival of the Portuguese by many centuries included the exchange of ivory as an important commodity. Without doubt, elephant population densities during these times could sustain the seasonal ivory off-takes. With the advent of firearms the kill rate accelerated and peaked in the mid to late nineteenth century when hunters like Frederick Courtney Selous reputedly shot thousands of elephant in Mashonaland alone. During Selous's 1888 visit to Zumbo he reported that:

> the trade is confined to ivory alone, all of which comes from the countries to the north of the Zambezi, on both sides of the Luangwa. Senhor Joaquim Andre Goudinho, the principal merchant said he had sent off two large boat-loads (10 000 lbs) to Quelimane.

Late nineteenth century writers, hunters and adventurers who roamed across much of the Zimbabwean highveld all testify to extensive herds of elephant at that time. All but a few tattered remnants in the Hartley "A" Safari Area of Western Mashonaland have disappeared from the highveld.

Before the introduction of firearms, elephants were hunted and killed by a combination of wit, guile and daring. Portuguese chroniclers of the sixteenth century reported that hundreds of African men, armed with axes, gathered for the hunt. Elephants were ambushed at their favourite feeding grounds and driven into thick bush where lone animals became entangled. The hunters came up and set about the elephants hacking at their tendons until the wounded limbs could no longer support the great body mass. The bones cracked or splintered and the animals fell to the ground where they were finished off with spears (36).

Today, the African elephant is an endangered species and together with the black rhinoceros, *Diceros bicornis*, of which an estimated 2000 only survive in Zimbabwe, (37) remains threatened with extinction. Zimbabwe enjoys the largest surviving rhinoceros population on the African continent with 46 per cent of total and with the largest contiguous population of more than 500 animals occuring in the Zambezi valley of Zimbabwe between the Kariba Gorge and Kanyemba on the Mozambique-Zimbabwe-Zambia border. (38) As noted earlier in the narrative on the extent of intercontinental trade, ivory and rhino horn were and still are in great demand in the Far East and China in particular.

As in the case of present day, rampant, exploitation of the alluvial gold resources along many of Zimbabwe's major river systems and the subsequent terrible degredation of the environment (39) which has now reached epidemic proportions, so has the level of elephant and, in particular, rhino poaching. The slaughter of black rhino in Zimbabwe is the work of influential and wealthy international traders, corrupt politicians, bureaucrats and businessmen who finance a huge network of well armed hirelings who carry out the butchery. (40)

The relatively free availability of weapons - principally the AK-47, SKS semi-automatic carbine, G3 and FN automatic rifles - an awful legacy of regional wars in the 1970s, has greatly facilitated this hideous trade. And for the actual executioners, ignorant peasants faced with harsh economic realities, the work of killing and extracting the tusks and horn, represents a living, albeit precarious and often fatal.

In 1987 the total value of rhino horn introduced to the international, mainly Yemeni and Far Eastern markets was an estimated US$ 4 million annually. (41) The present day value of rhino horn on the Far East Asian markets is around US $ 10 000 per kilo and demand continues unabated.(42) Those responsible for masterminding this iniquitous traffic seem able to evade the law in their own countries (Zambia and Burundi) and appear immune to the efforts of wildlife agencies. (43) As Asian rhino horn reserves are rapidly expended the value of remaining African horn will escalate and unless there is an immediate and international collective resolve to terminate the trade, the remaining African rhino are seriously threatened with extinction.

References

1. Boxer C.R. *The Port. Seaborne Empire*, p. 204. See also Boxer C.R., *O Grande Navio de Macau.*, 1989, p. 315. Strandes, Justus, *The Portuguese Period in East Africa*, EA Lit. Bureau, 1971, p.285 for additional details on golden coins minted in India and comparative values. See also Mitchener, *Oriental Coins*, p. 195 (on Portuguese coins). J. Ferrão Vaz, *Livros das Moedas de Portugal*, Braga, 1973., p. 498. Robert Friedberg, *Gold Coins* of the World, 5th edition, The Coin and Currency Institute, Inc., NY, 1980 p. 247-248. Colin R. Bruce, *Standard Guide to the South Asian Coins and Paper Money* (since 1556), Krause Publications, Iola, Wisc., 1981.
2. Chamber of Mines, Harare, Zimbabwe.
3. Summers R., *Ancient Mining in Rhod.*, 1969, p. 19-22.
4. Summers R., *Ancient Mining in Rhod.*, 1969, p. 22
5. W. Atkinson to H. Ellert, 1988, former mine manager of the Globe and Phoenix Gold Mining Company, Kwekwe.
6. Summers R., op. cit. p. 19-22.
7. ditto
8. ditto p. 163-179
9. Report on the Rivers of Cuama, 16 March, 1683, Beach/Noronha, 1980, p. 159-180 details.
10. Ellert H., verified during numerous interviews with gold panners and miners at Kwekwe, Mount Darwin, Mazowe and Shamva in 1989-90.
11. Report on the Rivers of Cuama, op. cit., p. 179
12. António Gomes, *Viagem*, Beach/Noronha, 1980, UZ, p. 69.
13. Summers R. *Ancient Mining in Rhod.*, 1969, p. 178.
14. Examples of gold leaf, wire, tacks and beads are on display at Bulawayo, Queen Victoria Museum in Harare and at Great Zimbabwe site museum.
15. *Documents* Vol. IX p.
16. The Geology of the Makaha Gold Belt.
17. Summers R., op. cit., p. 33
18. The scales and weights are displayed at the Bulawayo museum having been collected in Chief Mangwende's area during the early 20th century.
19. Interview with D. Sheeren, Geologist with Aluvioes de Manica Lda., Manica, Moz., 1990.
20. ditto
21. Visit to Mimosa Mine, 1990, Ellert and Sheeren.
22. In late 1990 the parallel market rate for US Dollars in the Mutare business community was 4 : 1 whereas the prevailing rate in the Harare black market was 5 or 6 : 1 reflecting the freer availability of US Dollars emanating from gold panners who receive hard currency payouts for their gold.
23. Boxer C.R. An African Eldorado : Monomotapa and Mozambique, *CAHA* No. 2, 1960, p. 3., Professor Boxer points out that "many local Crown officials and particularly the governors, made large fortunes trading in gold. As early as 1511 it was reliably reported that although the gold trade was supposed to be a royal monoply, three quarters of the gold exported from Sofala evaded the royal fiscus ."
23a QVM Arq. ref 1632 D1, interviewed on 18-3-1986 after examination of the museum records, Queen Victoria Museum, Harare, Zimbabwe. Calder, an old time prospector, worked along the Mazowe river in the 1950s.
24. Francisco de Sousa, *Oriente Conquistado*, Description of the Rivers of Cuama, Beach, Noronha trans., 1980, p. 243-245.

25. op. cit. p. 243-245.
26. Boxer C.R. *Portuguese Seaborne Empire.*, p. 217.
27. Janeira, Armando Martins,. *O Impacto Português sobre a Civilização Japonesa,* Publicações Dom Quixote, Lisboa, 1988, p. 119-120 for details of the Portuguese trade with Japan. Evidently, silver and copper were mined in Japan and during the Portuguese period the Japanese acquired updated mining technology.
28. Summers R. *Ancient Mining in Rhod,* 1969, p. 19,212 and 215.
29. Monçoês, Vol 46B, 166-166V dated 12-12-1680, Father Luis de Figueiredo Cardozo, Beach/Noronha, 1980, p. 158.
30. Dickinson R.W., Sofala, Gateway to the Gold of Monomotapa, *Rhodesiana* No. 19, 1968, p. 35-37. MacKenzie J.M., A Pre-colonial Industry-The Njanja and the Iron Trade. *NADA,* 1975 p.200-
31. Barradas, Lereno, *Arqueologia de Manica e Sofala,* IO. Congresso Nacional de Arq., Lisbon, 1959, p. 471. Geologist D. Sheeren confirmed the existence of pre-colonial iron workings in the Manica district during interview 1990.
32. Eltringham S.K., *Elephants.* Blandford Press, 1982. p. 205.
33. Martin E.B., *Zimbabwe's Ivory Carving Industry.*, Traffic Bulletin Vol VI (2), 1984.
34. Estimate by Zimbabwe Parks and Wild Life.
35. *Elephants, Economics and Ivory.* Earthscan Publications Ltd., London.
36. *Documentos,* Vol VII, Br. Baltazar to Fr. Marcos, 16-11-1560.
37. Tatham G.H. & Taylor R.D., The Conservation & Protection of the Black Rhinoceros In Zimbabwe, *Koedoe,* 32/2, 1989, p. 31.
38. op. cit. p. 31.
39. Zimbabwe Government Statutory Instrument 275 of 1991 *Mining (Alluvial Gold) (Public Streams) Regulations, 1991.* This regulation provides definitions of alluvial gold deposits, describes approved methods for working these claims and penalties for offenders. Irrespective of this official action, illegal gold panning escalated nation-wide on a massive scale during 1991-92 reaching epidemic proportions with consequent awful degradation of the riverine environment.
40. op. cit. *Koedoe,* p. 32.
41. op. cit. *Koedoe,* p. 33.
42. Martin E.B. & Ryan T.C.I., in *Pachyderm* (13), 1990.
43. op. cit. *Koedoe,* p. 33.

CHAPTER 6

Conclusion

Concluding remarks with a summary of events from 1693 to the 1930s

The Portuguese period in Zimbabwe's history is too brief and inconsequential to have left any meaningful or visible impact as elsewhere in the old Lusophone world. That the Portuguese ever held sway in the Zimbabwean Rivers of Gold is perhaps difficult to comprehend given the pronounced English speaking cultural imprint on the society. This fact also serves to emphasise how tenuous was their hold. It may be contended that the missionary zeal of the Dominicans, whose parish the Rivers was, did not match that of the elite and wealthy Jesuit order who may have enjoyed more success. The widespread Islamic influence along the Zambezi and the missionaries' apparent lack of ruthless dedication as in Goa, where remorseless tactics were applied, may offer some explanation. Christianity never took hold. Having already been exposed for generations to the concept of monotheism by the Islamic Swahili, the Muzungo religion had nothing new to offer. Lasting edifices were never built on the highveld and with few exceptions the missionaries allocated to the Rivers were manifestly inadequate for the task. It was only in 1884 that the Jesuits built a superb church at the mission of Saint Joseph, Boroma, some 36 km from Tete and the closest point to the highveld. For Christianity to have succeeded on the plateau similar missions and churches would have been necessary.

The central purpose of this book has been to enliven a long forgotten sequence of historical events starting around 1540 and ending in the late 1890s and to illuminate a hidden Portuguese legacy. The introduction of important food crops is perhaps their single most important bequest. The Portuguese influence upon African society is relatively obscure but in unveiling many of the intrinsic Zimbabwean ethnic conventions something of this Portuguese enigma is exposed. The complex jigsaw puzzle of Portuguese inspired fragments can never be adequately assembled as they have been absorbed and infused with an unequivocal Zimbabwean identity.

Although, by the beginning of the eighteenth century, the Portuguese had been effectively driven out of the Rivers, they did continue to enjoy seasonal and intermittent trade until the late nineteenth century when British colonial interests expelled them from their few remaining and isolated trading concessions in Manicaland and Mashonaland. This last chapter summarises our account of the sixteenth and seventeenth centuries and considers the activities of the Portuguese in Zimbabwe during the ensuing two centuries, which, as we shall hear, was largely confined to the western Rozvi trade conducted from Zumbo (until the 1830s) and with the people of Mashonaland and Manicaland (until the late 1890s). This occured at a time when the Rozvi were the supreme authority on the Zimbabwean highveld and the enfeebled Mutapan dynasty had withdrawn to the eastern escarpment and the valley beyond.

The Rivers trade never ranked high in the list of contemporary Portuguese priorities and their settlements on the Zambezi and the Zimbabwean highveld were extremely far down the list after the Indies, Brazil, Angola and even the Guineas (1). This was obvious, considering the absence of permanent and structured settlement and the extremely low level of human resource commitment to the region. Indeed, for nearly the entire period reviewed in this book the Africans were effectively in control of their own destiny with the exception of the seventeenth century when Portuguese influence in the Rivers reached its zenith. The *modus vivendi* actually suited the Africans who co-existed with the Portuguese as long as they behaved within tolerable, acceptable limits, respected traditional custom and paid their dues.

The African hierarchy and upper classes had grown accustomed to commercial relations with the Swahili and therefore accepted their European successors. But with their arrival the age-old system of seasonal and mutually acceptable trading relations was distorted. Between 1576 and the 1600s increasing numbers of Portuguese entered the Rivers (2) and, for as long as they could be integrated into the Shona political economy and play by acceptable rules, they were tolerated. Their trade was valuable, the cloth and beads and later firearms and gunpowder were much in demand by the rulers and therefore encouraged (3).

But the Portuguese were not content with mere commercial

relations and began to meddle in African politics hoping thereby to manipulate events in their favour. This deplorable state of affairs contributed to the political crisis of the Mutapa State during the early 1600s. Grasping the Cross in one hand and the musket in the other, Santiago and Eldorado, they influenced the progression of rulers and with a complete disregard for cultural norms rode roughshod over society with disastrous results. The Portuguese were their own worst enemy and frittered away what opportunity might have existed for permanent settlement and trade on the Zimbabwean highveld. African indignation and determination to rid themselves of the Portuguese steadily mounted in the second half of the seventeenth century and as noted earlier, exploded in the 1690s. The Portuguese were then compelled to leave the Rivers and during the eighteenth and nineteenth centuries their business dealings with the western Rozvi and the eastern Shona were regulated increasingly by intermediaries, the *vashambadzi*, operating from Manica, Tete and Zumbo.

During this period the *prazo* system of settlement on the middle Zambezi assumed important dimensions and became the *foci* of Portuguese activity and trade with Zimbabwe. The *prazeiros* established permanent dynastic lines based on intermarriage, force of arms and most important of all, cultural forbearance and deference. Economic endeavour focused mainly on the ivory, gold trade and slavery. These early *prazos* of the middle Zambezi relied heavily upon their vassal armies, the actual forerunners of the *Chikunda* people - a disparate amalgam of people subsequently transformed by historical imperative into a homogenous ethnic grouping with decidedly militaristic cultural traditions. The name *Chikunda* stems from the Shona verb *kukunda* and *kukura* meaning to erode, overcome or sweep away. During the 1970s nationalist guerrilla war in Zimbabwe, the liberation movement, ZANU, operating from bases in the Tete province of Mozambique, formed a crack fighting unit known as the *gukurahundi*. Meaning, quite literally, the wind which sweeps the chaff from the ground in advance of the rains. This name evoked the *Chikunda* traditions of old.

The eighteenth century *prazo* dynasties, nominally European, gave way to a new order of *prazieros* of the nineteenth century largely Asian in origin. The collapse was precipitated by the demographic depletion during the slave trade occasioned by the growing Brazilian demand for labour. Having exhausted the local African population the *prazeiros* stupidly started exporting their *Chikunda*. This was absolute madness and indicated the dissipated and totally corrupted nature of the old order. Inevitably, it provoked massive resistance and accelerated destruction of the structure, which for decades had underpinned the *prazos,* that of *chikunda* military vassalage.

The arrival of the Nguni invaders from the south during the early eighteen century *mfecane* hastened the break-up as the ageing *prazieros* abandoned their estates for the relative safety of the coastal regions. Chaos ensued, the *Chikunda* dispersed and realigned themselves with the new order.

The economic vacuum was quickly filled. During the late eighteenth and most of the nineteenth century, Goan traders asserted their dominance with the backing of Gujerati *banyan* financiers of Mozambique island and the Querimba archeopelago. By the nineteenth century a new and clearly distinct generation of Asian sired *prazeiros* emerged. These families, founded largely by Goan Indians, now reoccupied the decaying estates on the Zambezi and became legends in the history of nineteenth century Mozambique. Gonçãlo Caetano Pereira, Manuel Antonio de Sousa, Paul Mariano Vaz dos Anjos and Nicolau Pascoal da Cruz were the principal progenitors of these vast new and heavily armed fiefdoms which occupied most of the Tete province of Mozambique. These armed mini-states depended upon their *chikunda* allies. Alliances were formed by inter-marriage with important African families and for most of the nineteenth century these afro-asian *muzungos,* now strongly associated with African interests, effectively blocked Portuguese colonial expansion to the west. Ironically, the creation of the *prazo* system effectively hindered Portuguese re-occupation of the Rivers. This was an intolerable situation as the Portuguese were then anxious to demonstrate title to lands beyond the coastal regions of central Mozambique. After initial disastrous military reverses these *muzungo* warlords were finally subdued. The last great stronghold was that of Antonio Vicente da Cruz (nick-named *Bonga,* the wildcat) at Massangano which fell in 1888 to a combined force commanded by Manuel Antonio da Sousa, himself one of the famous *prazeiros*, and Captain J.C. Paiva de Andrade, known in the Shona vernacular as *Payiva*.

The Portuguese authorities recognised the importance of the various Indian, Goan and/or coloured traders, the *Muzungos* and *Mwenyes*, who ventured beyond the western escarpment to the Rivers beyond. Their interests would be served by asking these traders to carry the Portuguese flag and in the last decades of the nineteenth century many did. Manuel Antonio de Sousa's agents travelled extensively in Manicaland and western Mashonaland but true obedience to the Portuguese Crown was suspect and relied on whether or not it suited African interests. Parts of eastern Mashonaland were subjected to raiding by *vazungo* warlords like Chimbangu, Perizengwe and Sakani from below the escarpment (4). Certainly, in the late 1880s Chief Rusambo accepted the authority of Ignacio Jesus de Xavier, known in Shona as Karizamimba, from Baroma to whom he paid annual tax in gold and grain. (5) These were important considerations and dominated the question of nominal allegiances to the Portuguese.

The extent of *muzungo* raids upon the scattered Shona communities during the eighteenth and nineteenth centuries: and perhaps much earlier, may have prompted the construction of the numerous stonewall fortifications which occur on kopjes and hills over much of the central watershed. Known in archaeological terms as *refuge*-type walling, these hilltop fortifications which bear no evidence of any influence from the Great Zimbabwe traditions, merit greater attention than they have hitherto enjoyed. Eastern Mashonaland is particularly rich in the so-called *refuge* sites. Unsubstantiated reports indicate that a Portuguese named *Rei*, led raids during the nineteenth century on villages around Castle Kopje — a *refuge* site — seizing cattle, girls and boys. (5a)

In 1856 the Portuguese Government published details of mineral deposits and mines within the district of Sena (this included much of eastern and central Mashonaland). The information was obtained by the Brazilian born Izidoro Correia Pereira who by 1850 was a prominent trader on the Zambezi. (5b) Pereira traded, through his *vashambadzi,* with Mzilikazi of western Zimbabwe in the 1850s and in the 1860s he was engaged in the purchase of ivory and cattle. Pereira was reputedly involved in raids upon the Samuriwo people in the upper Mupfure valley prior to the incursions of the Zwangendaba Nguni around 1830 (5c). If these reports are correct Pereira would inevitably have become familiar with large tracts of the central plateau and this is strongly evinced in his *List of mines known in the District of Sena* as published in *Annaes do Conselho Ultramarino, Parte não official, Serie II.* His list is considered fairly accurate and incorporates most of the known goldfields. Copper and iron deposits are also represented. Pereira's original notes describing the *Suri Suri* mention the existance of *"large demolished buildings"* nearby and this may be a reference to the *feira* of Maramuca. As in the case of Gouveia, Pereira's name is likely to have become synoymous with any Portuguese and reports concerning his activities on the highveld during the mid–nineteenth century viewed in that context.

Captain J.C. Païva de Andrade, after his visit to the highveld in the late 1890s, claimed that many chiefs from the Munyati river to the headwaters of the Sabi declared themselves Portuguese subjects and asked for flags (6). Some even pointed out trees planted by his Lusitatian forebears in ancient times. The ruins of Portuguese dwellings and forts were also indicated to the Portuguese official (7). Engineer F. M. Vitor Cordon, during his 1889 exploration to the Zambezi and upper Sanyati, constructed a stockade at the confluence of the Sanyati and Mupfure rivers and for a short time some local Chiefs nominally accepted the Portuguese who could defend them against raiding Ndebele *impi* (8).

In response to these optimistic reports, the Portuguese Crown extended the district of Zumbo to include most of the lands traversed by this energetic Portuguese captain. A Governor and a *capitão-mor* were to be appointed and stationed within the new district (9). These claims, as already explained are suspect and no amount of old lemon trees were to help the Portuguese regain the Rivers. The die was now finally cast.

Still, the Rivers trade did continue as Gouveia's or Kuveya's *vashambadzi* and individual Indians or Goans, known in the vernacular as *mwenye,* a corruption of the Portuguese word *monhe* meaning a Muslim or islamicised person of mixed Arab/Indian and

African blood, persisted with the traditional commerce and these merchants came to established outposts on the Zimbabwean highveld where they sold their trade goods in exchange for gold-dust. In reality, acceptance of the Portuguese crown amounted to little more than a hastily sewn and tattered standard (10) flying from a tree to impress British imperialists, as occurred in August of 1889 at Nyota.

An important Indian trader of this period was Vallji Mussagi Couto, known colloquially as *Variadye,* who operated a trading station near Nyota hill in the modern day Chiweshe district close to the Mazowe gold belt. In 1889, Frederick Courtney Selous met Mussagi and his African wife at Chief Mapondera's village (11). There is evidence that Mussagi was acting on behalf of the Portuguese authorities and reported details of his contacts with chief Mapondera and his relations with the British imperialist agent, Frederick Courtney Selous, known as *Sirewo.* Mapondera was the *de facto* authority on the north-eastern highveld and resisted British expansion in the Mazowe valley until his demise in 1901 (12).

Mapondera was evidently adept at playing the Portuguese off against the British. This was at a time when the era of British colonial authority had not yet dawned on the highveld and the African people of Mashonaland and Manicaland naturally owed their commercial allegiances to the feared warlords and Portuguese traders who brought much needed goods. The Portuguese were instrumental in arming the Shona during 1889 to act as a counter against Ndebele territorial ambitions. This did not endear them to the British when these same guns were used during the later *chimurenga.* At the same time the Shona were induced to accept the Portuguese flag (13). Even after the creation of British Southern Rhodesia, the Rivers trade in gold continued to flow eastwards to Mozambique.

This industry remained largely in the hands of the *mwenye* operating from Tete and Macequece who visited the goldfields well into the 1930s (14). The old *Blantyre trail* along which Mozambican and Malawi migrant labourers walked was the focus of Indian shop-keepers. Outposts, where the alluvial gold was exchanged for goods, were established at Mukumbura, Nura and Magoe. Many of these locations were best known by the name of the Indian who kept shop. The pervasive commercial strength of these Asian entre-peneurs is best symbolized by the adoption of the Indian monetary system of Rupees rendered into Shona as *rupiya*.

The final episode in the story of the Rivers was effectively written by Portuguese speaking Goans, Gujeratis and their coloured progeny, the *mwanamuzungo*. The rise of the *Banyans* or Gujerati commercial class in the history of Mozambique was only halted with the formation of the chartered companies of Niassa, Zambezia and Moçambique financed largely by Portuguese and European mercantile capital. The Indians were driven back into their traditional role of traders and middlemen - the despised engrossers who waxed fat on the backs of the Portuguese. Communities of Indian traders have since become firmly rooted in Moçambique. Significant in this context are the Muslim Indian communities of Chimoio — adjacent to the goldfields of Manica — and that of Mutare. Their own ethnic cultural mores have also permeated African society manifesting itself in culinary traditions, language borrowing and bodily adornments (15).

The eighteenth and nineteenth centuries in Zimbabwe were characterised by generally peaceful trading relations - although these were frequently marred by armed raids - conducted between the Africans and the *muzungos* but as in the case of the preceding two centuries the Africans retained control of the gold trade as an integral part of their intrinsic African economy. They were able to regulate the lucrative traffic and phased alluvial recovery according to their needs. Strict taboos and regulations governed exploitation of this resource and there was minimal ecological disturbance. There was harmony with nature. The rivers were panned in the traditional manner and the tiny golden grains exchanged for cloth, beads and guns. This long established economy was finally broken by the British South Africa Company's commercial expansion of the early twentieth century and an entirely new chapter in Zimbabwean history was to be written. The Rivers were to undergo drastic transformation as the British became masters of the land.

References

1. D. Beach to H. Ellert, 1991.
2. ditto.
3. ditto.
4. Beach D.N., *Mapondera 1840-1904*, Mambo Press, 1989, p. 26,33.
5. Selous, F.C., *Travel and Adventure in South East Africa*, Pioneer Head, Salisbury, Rhodesia, 1972, p. 281.
5a Thornycroft C.E., Report on an Excavation at Castle Kopje, Wedza, *Zimbabwe Prehistory* 20 (29-36), 1988.
5b. Beach D.N., Refuge Arch., Trade and Gold Mining in 19th century Zimbabwe : Izidoro Correia Pereira's list of 1857, *Zimbabwean Prehistory* 20 (3-8), 1988.
5c. Beach D.N., op. cit.
6. Beach D.N., de Noronha H., *The Shona and the Portuguese 1575-1890*, Albino Manuel Pacheco's Tete to Zumbo journey of 1861.
7. op. cit.
8. Axelson, E. *Portugal and the Scramble for Africa*, Witwatersrand Univ. Press, 1967, p. 155.
9. op. cit. p. 156
10. Beach D.N. op.cit. p. 62
11. Selous F.C. op. cit. p. 288
12. Beach D.N. op. cit.
13. Beach D.N. op. cit. p. 23
14. Chakanuka Chihoro to H. Ellert, 2-1-86 report that his father settled on farm No. 2 Chesa in 1958 and knew of a Portuguese Indian who came from Portuguese East Africa to trade for alluvial gold at the Mkaradzi river.
15. Some African women have adopted the Indian habit of piercing their nostril to wear a nose stud.

Indonesia and Japan are two other examples of countries where Portuguese culture has impacted on society (1). This book has examined the complex and multi-faceted historical background to the Portuguese in Zimbabwe, their *feiras*, the substance and provenance of imported trade goods and the extent of commercial and political relations with the Shona-speaking people from the beginning of the sixteenth century until the close of the nineteenth. Vestiges of Portuguese influence although masked by an African face and further obscured by British colonisation, remain discernable. Some of these enigmatic elements are now reviewed.

Indo-Portuguese influence can be found at various levels of Shona society — in the language, family names and in the spirit world. But there is an even more precious gift. Chroniclers recorded details of their interaction with the Shona people from the early sixteenth century and these records, fragmented and inadequate as they are, represent the most priceless of all legacies. Portuguese narratives of the sixteenth century alerted future generations to the word *zimbaoe*. The Portuguese noted that a *zimbabwe* referred to an important population centre, chiefly residence or house of stone. Sure enough, the Portuguese writers of this period did not always faithfully interpret events but the documents which have survived are important source material for scholars.

Outstanding contributions in this regard include that of Father João dos Santos and his classic *Ethiopia Oriental*. Unique in the context of sub-saharana Africa (and with the exception only of Amharic and Arabic records of north Africa) these Portuguese documents on South East Africa and the Rivers of Gold outweigh all other considerations for they open a window, for those who wish to see, into the past.

Proof of Portuguese cultural influence is more pronounced along the eastern border of Zimbabwe amongst the Korekore people of the north-east, Njanja, Zezuru and the Manyika and Ndau people of Manicaland Province which borders Mozambique, although they are certainly not restricted to these regions. Some elements of Portuguese influence upon African society have been examined earlier in the text and we now consider other, more forgotten, remnants of the Portuguese-related culture including Shona adoption of Portuguese words and family names. The use of the Portuguese word *Senhor* as *Sinyoro* amongst the Njanja people of the Wedza district is one example of borrowing from Portuguese. In Mozambique, an African who has attended three years of primary schooling is referred to as *Sinyoro* in recognition of his education and hence elevated status above the illiterate.

If the same person spoke Portuguese the name *Sinyoro* was also applicable. Corruptions of *Gouveia* and *Caetano* occur frequently amongst families of north-eastern Zimbabwe as *Goveya* or *Kuveya* and *Kaitano* respectively. The Shona orthographic rendering of Gouveia relates to Manuel Antonio de Sousa, the renowned Gorongosa *prazo* holder and warlord whose *vashambadzi* or agents operated over much of north-east Mashonaland and Manicaland during the late nineteenth century. Better known as Gouveia or Kuveya, this Indo-Portuguese became a legend in his own time amongst the African people. The Shona have also borrowed the name *João* which is written phonetically as *Zhuwawo*. The same is also true of the Portuguese name Joaquim which is translated into Shona as *Zhuwakinyu.*

The use of these more archaic Shona renditions of Portuguese christian names is being rapidly displaced by the modern English equivalents. The seventeenth and eighteenth century Portuguese word for concessionary grants of land, *prazo,* has arguably been transferred as *purazi.* The Portuguese habit of extending credit for sales of cloth and beads and the subsequent confiscation or seizure of cattle when the debtor was unable to meet his commitments in gold or ivory is a likely derivation of the Shona word, *pinyoro* from the Portuguese *penhor* meaning to pledge and the subsequent *penhora* meaning seizure of goods.

The term *pinyoro* is nowadays used to describe a pledge of money or some item of clothing in lieu of cash during *chabuta* "heads and tails" gambling sessions in beerhalls (2). *Pinyoro* may also relate to a pledge which must be redeemed in connection with payment to a prostitute for services rendered. The *Pinyoro* system was common amongst lower paid farm labourers on large–scale commercial farms during the 1950s and 1960s. The borrowing of Portuguese words, *farinha de pau, ananás* and *folha* for cassava, pineapple and tobacco respectively as *mufarinya*, *ananasi* and *fodya* are all clear examples of language borrowing.

The derivation of *fodya* is the Portuguese word *folha* meaning leaf. The Portuguese word *sombreiro* has fallen into Shona usage as *somborero* meaning an umbrella or sunshade. See table I for a short list of Shona words which owe their origin to Portuguese. This listing is not exhaustive but illustrative nonetheless. We cannot be certain exactly how and when these words were borrowed into the Shona lexicon. Yet, examination of these words certainly suggests a measure of antiquity as in the case of *chumbo* or lead which was used in making shot. In 1929, the word *dinyero*, (3) meaning gold, was reported amongst the Chitonga, a Shona clan. The word comes from the Portuguese *dinheiro*.

Retso which occurs in the Shona dictionary, meaning silken threads, may owe its origin to the Portuguese *lenço*. *Lençóis* (pl) are rolls of kerchiefs in striped or red cloth from Diu and were an important trading commodity in the nineteenth century.

TABLE I

Shona	English	Portuguese
Bakayau	dried fish	bacalhau
Bakayava	dried fish	bacalhau
Chikoti	sjambok (4)	chicote
Chumbu	lead (Pb)	chumbo
Dona (5)	slim, attractive girl, a Lady.	dona
Dhinyero	gold - money	dinheiro
Fodya	tobacco, leaf	folha
Fofo	matches	fósforo
Hadiyo	garlic	alho
Jari	shawl, tasselled rug.	chale,

175

Kadhera	chair, seat	cadeira
Kanjadu	padlock	cadeado
Mbatata	ordinary potato	batata
Mubhanana	banana	banana
Garafa	bottle	garrafa
Kachasu	alcoholic spirit	cachaca
Pasika	easter	pascoa
Mufarinya	cassava	farinha
Mupapaya	pawpaw	papaia
Mwenye	Indian-muslim	monhé
Pesa	roll of cloth	pica-pico (7)
Muparu	cloth, wrap	pano
Muvhakacho	holiday	vacação
Muzezuru	Zezuru	Muzuzuro
Ngarava	ship	navio
Nanazi	pineapple	ananás
Nhavhaya	razor, or sharp blade.	navalha
Njiva bombo	Namaqualand dove	pombo (8)
Pendi	comb	pente
Pinyoro	pledge	penhor
Pesa	roll of cloth	peça (9)
Putukezi	Portuguese	Português.
Retso	*shave* cloth,	retrós or Lenço (10)
Rusariro	rosary or beads	rosário
Rupiya	twenty-cent piece	rúpia (11
Runeta	bugle, trumphet	corneta
Sabhani	soap	sabão
Sinyoro	Lord or Sir	Senhor
Somborero	umbrella	sombreiro
Tsumhu	tomato sauce	sumo (12)
Tapa	lid	tampa
Tizora	scissors	tesoura
Vhinyu	palm wine (13)	vinho

Similar examples are found in the Swahili language along the Kenya coastline :

Swahili	English	Portuguese
Meza	table	mesa
Zeituni	olives	azeitona
Wvinyo	wine	vinho
Sukare	sugar	açúcar
Nanasi	pineapple	ananás
Pasaka	easter	páscoa
Gereza (14)	prison, barracks	igreja

There are a number of Shona words of apparent Swahili origin which are evocative of bygone times and these are *hanzu* from the Swahili *kanzu* meaning a long cotton garment typically worn by the Coastal Swahili to this day. Another word is the Shona *unga* which relates to gold dust or gold powder and may have some connection with the Swahili *unga* which means flour. *Unga* also means gunpowder. The Swahili word for a coin, silver or money is *fedha* and may have something to do with the Shona *fejafeja* game of chance involving money.

The Chikunda language of the Tete province is very rich in Portuguese vocabulary and this is not surprising considering the historical origins of this ethnic grouping. The first half of the twentieth century has witnessed a pattern of emigration by Chikunda–speaking people to Zimbabwe where they have now settled.

The story of Portuguese language transfers to the Shona language has a later sequel. During the Zimbabwean independence war of the 1970s, Mozambique served as an important rear-guard sanctuary for the largely Shona political and military movement, the Zimbabwe African National Liberation Army (ZANLA) and new influences were brought to bear. (15) Because of that country's Portuguese colonial history it was inevitable that a further language shift would take place during the interaction of the Zimbabweans with their Mozambiquean allies. For political and military reasons Portuguese terminology was borrowed by the Zimbabweans and most of these expressions are still being used directly or indirectly.

Because of the similar political ideology upon which the African nationalist forces of the Zimbabwe African National Union (ZANU) and the Front for the Liberation of Mozambique (FRELIMO) were then structured, the adoption of the Socialist or Eastern European-Soviet-Chinese nomenclature of *Camarada* and subsequently *Comrade* were universal in both FRELIMO and ZANLA describing the cadre or common guerrilla fighter. Although the term is now largely anachronistic it retains a strong emotional connotation for those who used it during the liberation war and it is still applied as an honorific title for leading political figures, Ministers and the State President, i.e. Comrade Minister or Comrade President. The term *comrade* is also applied to a broader and more lowly spectrum of society including supporters of the government or ZANU-ZAPU political parties or those perceived to owe such allegiance. In many respects the term has lost its purity. The Portuguese, *Chefe*, meaning a leader or commander has also fallen into contemporary Shona usage and is written as *Chef*. It is still commonly applied in the modern Shona idiom and is equivalent to the word *Boss*. Political slogans used extensively during the liberation war were still widely used during the 1980s in Zimbabwe and these include the Portuguese *abaixo* or *abasha* in Shona. *Abasha* means the same as *Pasi* or down with so-and-so. It is particularly used by politicians to condemn or denigrate some person or organisation. In more recent times it has taken on a more impassioned implication and may be used when calling for the banning of an organisation, removal from office or in a perjorative sense when referring to a specific person.

The Portuguese word for a box, *caixa*, was translated into Shona as *kasha* or *makasha* in the plural and was commonly used to describe a box of one thousand rounds of Warsaw Pact 7,62 intermediate ammunition suitable for the AK-47 assault rifle, the SKS carbine and the RPD machine gun which were the standard issue weapons for nationalist guerrilla forces based in Mozambique (16). When praising a political or military leader the term *viva* or long live was often used and nowadays *viva* is still used in the general preamble of slogans shouted at Zimbabwean political rallies. Another Portuguese expression which has fallen into common colloquial usage in Zimbabwe is the word *nada* which literally means nothing but in the Shona idiom has taken on a slightly different sense. When used in contemporary *mudhoroba* or urban slang-Shona, *nada* suggests categoric refusal or an absolute No !. It is often used in association with the Shona phrase *Nada, kuramba ikoko* so as to emphasise the refusal.

The Portuguese *macaco* or monkey is commonly used in Zimbabwe as an abusive term describing a prostitute or a woman who sleeps with divers men. Strangely enough, the term is also used to describe a break-down recovery vehicle. (17)

APPENDIX II

A fascinating aspect of the Portuguese heritage is to be found in the ethno-history of the Shona speaking peoples of Zimbabwe. As noted earlier in the text, after the expulsion of the Portuguese from the highveld at the end of the seventeenth century, they remained in effective control of trade with the Shona. This monopoly of trade rested largely with the *prazeiros*. The best known of these traders was a Goan, Manuel Antonio de Souza, who came to the Zambezi district around 1852-53 from Goa.

Travelling extensively within eastern Mashonaland, De Souza's *vashambadzi* or agents have become misconstrued in the folk myth of north eastern Zimbabwe as *goveyas* after their master *Gouveia* himself. The only record of Goveia entering the plateau south west of Mutoko is in 1889 and this was perhaps his only visit and it led to his capture by the British as he represented inimical foreign powers. These traders brought their inventory of trade goods including muskets, gunpowder, lead, flints, cloth, beads (18) and conus discs which were highly prized by the Shona as emblems of wealth and importance. Oral evidence obtained by the author from villagers in north-eastern Zimbabwe has established that the conus discs were imported by the *Muzungos,* the Portuguese.

Yet other informants said that the conus discs were brought by the *Goveya,* yet another term for the Portuguese. Of course, Gouveia and his emissaries were not the only traders of this period because the old gold trade at Mount Darwin, Mazowe and Makaha continued. Gold was exchanged for percussion-lock muzzle loaders which now entered the country in huge quantities (19). After the collapse of the old *prazo* system and despite a switch of allegiance to the new armed States formed by the dynastic lines of Caetano Pereira, Vaz dos Anjos, Vicente da Cruz and Manuel Antonio de Sousa, some Chikunda raided up the Zambezi valley and subordinated the upper Zambezi Tonga. (20) The captured slaves were destined for the Zanzibar market .(21) They may also have brought trade goods including cloth, beads, cowries and various different types of *ndoros* to the Tonga such is the propensity for all of these items among these folk to this day. Popular oral traditions indicate they were brought by the *muzungos* and the *chikunda*. (22)

The importance of the conus discs, or *ndoro,* as they are known in Shona, was first observed by Father João dos Santos in 1561 during his sojourn in the Rivers. The succeeding account subsequently appeared in his *Ethiopia Oriental* published in Evora in 1609.

> " *O Monomotapa e Os Mocarangas, seus vassallos traze na testa um buzio branco, como joia, pendurado dos cabellos, e O Monomotapa traz outro buzio grande sobre o peito. A estes buzios chamam Andoros.."(23).*

The Monomotapa and their vassals the Mocarangas wear a white jewel-like shell on their forehead and the Monomotapa wears another large shell on his chest. They call these shells Andoros.

Plates 40, 41

The *ndoro* is an interesting phenomenon occurring amongst the African people of eastern, central and the Zambezi valley regions of Zimbabwe and the Tete and Manica provinces of Mozambique. The ndoro is the bottom or base section of the marine sea shell of the genus *Conus turbo* or *Conus virgo* which are commonly found along the east African coast. The original sea shell discs which have been cut away from the upper cone section are of a heavy, white, calcarious substance and are most conspicuous by their characteristic whorls or concentric spirals on the concave aspect of the shell.

The fact that the Shona and the Gwembe (Zambezi) Tonga placed considerable value on the *ndoro* appears to have provided motivation for their importation as trade goods. At an undetermined stage, probably in the late eighteenth or early nineteenth century, ceramic copies of the original conus discs were manufactured in response to commercial interests. The fact that no ceramic copies of the *ndoro* have been found at the site of Portuguese *feiras* would tend to suggest that they were not being produced prior to these dates. Only one genuine *ndoro* can be linked to a Portuguese site and this was found at Dambarare.

Because oral evidence indicates that the *ndoro* were imported by the *Muzungos* it may be argued that the source of these discs was within some unspecified Portuguese territory. Albino Manuel Pacheco undertook an overland trip from Tete to Zumbo in 1861 and this lead him through the lands of the Chedima largely affiliated to the Korekore people of neighbouring north-eastern Zimbabwe.

181

He commented upon the predeliction for the *ndoro* conus discs and other "goods most needed and easily sold... cotton fabrics from Lisbon or Asia, brick-red, green and yellow missanga or beads, fake coral, buzios or ndoros, cowries, tin, brass wire for the arms and legs and *aguardente* or alcoholic spirit". Just as Gujerat was the source of the textiles it may be possible that the Mount Abu region of western India — famed for its production of glass beads, glassware and ceramics — is a likely source of these unique *ndoros* but clear evidence as to exact provenance still eludes us.

The *ndoro* occupies an important role in Shona tradition and in many families these objects have featured in patrilineal inheritance for many generations. In some cases, where the *ndoro* has belonged to important ancestors, the disc is venerated as a valued possession as it plays an important part in the ceremony preparatory to the appearance of the ancestral spirit in the medium. The *ndoro* must be worn by the medium who would also have other articles which belonged to the ancestor.

The oral history of the Nyandoro clan of the Zezuru, a sub-group of the Shona, indicates that some time in the eighteenth century their ancestors migrated into northern Zimbabwe from the Tete region (most probably Zumbo district) of Mozambique. They settled around the Chihota and Chinoyi districts where many live to this day. *Ndoro* is considered the likely origin of the clan name as their *chidao* is *unendoro* or literally " you have the chiefly medal."

The importance of the *ndoro* in the cultural life of many Zimbabweans continues to assert itself and to this day plastic copies of *ndoro* are sold at open air markets, or *msika* in Zimbabwe. Ceramic copies of the *ndoro* have been manufactured in a variety of sizes and because the author is not aware of any previous attempt to catalogue and identify the various types found in Zimbabwe and adjacent Zambia (where they are known as *mpande*) and Moçambique, a simple classification has been established in Table II.

Table II

Category, type, description & distribution.

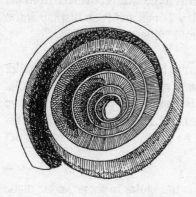

N1

Original sea shell of the *Conus turbo* or *Conus virgo* genus. The disc is formed from the bottom end of the shell which has been cut away from the upper cone. The discs measure on average 50 mm x 11,5 mm and have a central bore of 5 mm in diamter through which a string is threaded. Examples of the genuine *ndoro* may be found in the accoutrement of traditional herbalists and spirit mediums.

N 2 Brown coloured earthenware copies of the original. It has 5 inner spirals, measures 55 mm x 15 mm with a central hole of 7 mm. Found in NE Zimbabwe and the Changara district of Tete province. _{Plate 42}

N 3 Ceramic copy of the original in fine quality porcelain _{Plate 43} with a pure white glaze. It has 5 spirals on the concave face, measures 45 x 9,5 mm with a central hole of 4,5 mm. This is a fairly common type and is readily identified because of a batch serial number stamped on the convex side, *10615*. Examples have been collected along the Zambezi valley Tonga of the Binga district. They have also been recovered from the Tonga on the Zambian side of the border. The concentration of this specific type along the upper Zambezi evidences the extent of Portuguese trade.

N 4 Similar to type 3 but measures 42 mm x 8 mm with a hole of 3 mm. It has 5 spirals and is made from a fine porcelain. This type is not marked with any serial number. This type is also strongly represented amongst _{Plate 43} the valley Tonga.

N 5　Large porcelain copy of the original, measures 75m
m x 11 mm x 5 mm hole. It has 7 spirals and the rear　Plate
faceis stamped 1886 above the hole and with the let
ter *e* or *c* below. This type was recovered from the
upper Zambezi valley Tonga and is on display at the
Livingstone Museum Livingstone, Zambia.

N 6　Ceramic *ndoro*, similar to type 5 but slightly smaller
measuring only 45 mm x 8 mm x 3,5 mm central hole.
It has 5 spirals and is stamped on the rear 1886 above
the hole and with the letter *a* below. An example of this　Plate
type was recovered by the author in the Binga district
of Zimbabwe.

N 7　This type of *ndoro* is triangular in shape and is made
from white or red-coloured glassware. It has no central
hole and is designed to be worn as a pendant from a　Plate
string of beads. It may be considered a stylistic *ndoro*
and examples of this type, in a variety of sizes, has
been found among the upper Zambezi valley Tonga.
This type of triangular-shaped *ndoro* occurs in differ
ent sizes and is usually strung in series interspersed
with coloured glass beads.

N 8　A large ceramic *ndoro*, in a fine white glaze, measuring 75 mm x 11 mm x 5 mm central hole. It is very
similar to type 5 but is not marked with any lettering　Plate
or numbers. It is fairly common and examples are
fairly widely distributed throughout eastern and north
ern Zimbabwe with particular concentrations around
Binga, north-eastern Zimbabwe and the Zimunya and
Manga areas of the Mutasa district of Manicaland.

N 9　*Ndoro* carved from soapstone measuring 46 mm x 10
mm. An example of this type of *ndoro* was unearthed
at Khame ruins near Bulawayo (the site of the Rozvi　Plate
stone city.)

N 10 Plastic and composite materials are nowadays used to produce facsimile *ndoro* similar to type N 3. These are available for sale at the traditional *msika* or open air markets in Zimbabwe. This modern manufacture evidences the continued importance of these objects.

APPENDIX III

List of prazeiros and traders of the nineteenth century associated with Zimbabwe from the 1880s to 1990s. (according to D N Beach.)

Chimbangu	Vicente Jose Ribeiro de Fonseca, *prazeiro.*
Kanyemba	Jose do Rosario Andrade, *praziero.*
Karizamimba	Ignacio de Jesus Xavier, *prazeiro.*
Kuveya	Manuel Antonio de Sousa, *prazeiro.*
Matekenya	Jose de Araujo Lobo, *prazeiro.*
Payiva	Joaquim Carlos Paiva de Andrade, *afficial.*
Perizengwe	Sebastiao Moraes Almeida, *prazeiro.*
Sakani	Vicente Ribeiro de Fonseca, *prazeiro.*
Variadye	Valligy Mussagi Couto, *trader.*

REFERENCES

1. Janeira A.M., *O Impacto Portuguê sobre a Civilização Japonesa.*, Anais, Lisboa, 1988.
2. D. Masango to H. Ellert, 1991.
3. Alvord E.D. *NADA*, No. 7, 1929, p. 95. Other vernacular regionalisms for gold collected at the same time were *ndarama* amongst Chitawara speakers and *mkuwa* with the Chibudya. See also GOLD for additional details.
4. *Sjambok*, an Afrikaans word for a whip made from hippo hide.
5. Dona, a Portuguese title originally given to ladies of quality. The term was corrupted when describing the *prazo* matriarchs of the seventeenth century onwards. In a report dated 1766 by Antonio Pinto de Miranda on the self-indulgent life style of the Portuguese on the Zambezi *prazos* we learn that "all of them (European, native or descendents of Goanese) are haughty and arrogant. All, without exception entitled themselves *donas* and *senhoras*. For instance a married woman is addressed as Sra. Dona Maria, and the same goes for umarried women after the early twenties. The term Dona had little to do with the social position of the person concerned". By virtue of the powerful *prazo* institution and their Donas the term fell into popular contemporary usage to describe virtually all muzungo womanhood in much the same way as the term madam was used in colonial Rhodesia by Africans in a master and servant relationship when addressing the European mistress - even a young European girl would be referred to as a pikinin madam or little lady. An example was Dona Inês Graças Cardoso whose death in 1757 was much lamented by the neighbouring Manyika. See Bhila's *Trade and Politics in a Shona Kingdom*, p. 123. See also a report dated 5 July, 1795 listing numerous residents of the district of Sena, Tete and their respective households all headed by Donas.
6. Padlocks, first invented in Europe in 1478, likely to have been used by the Portuguese in the period under review.
7. See also PICUL and PIKUL. The *pico*, a unit of weight, was current in the Portuguese Far East in the sixteenth and seventeenth century and was worth 100 *cates* or 1.600 *taeis*. It was equal to 133,5 English Lbs avoirdupois. Silk was generally weighed in *picos*. Boxer C.R. *Grande Navio de Macau*, 1989, p. 319.
8. Roberts, *Birds of South Africa*, No. 318, The Namaqualand Dove enjoys wide distribution throughout S.E. Africa including Mozambique and the highveld of Zimbabwe.
9. See note 4.
10. The literal translation is silken threads.
11. From the Portuguese *rupia*, a coin of Portuguese India and originally equal to a two Shilling piece.
12. *sumo* in Portuguese comes from the Arabic *zum*, a sweet juice. The Shona *tshumo* is best translated by the Portuguese *molho* which relates to a piquant onion and tomato sauce spiced with *piripiri* and not sweet.
13. Palm wine, juice extracted from the *Hyphaene gaertn* palm which is widely distributed in S E Africa and exploited as a source of wine with a single tree capable of producing 60-70 litres. See Keith Coates Palgrave, *Trees of Southern Africa*, No. 67. The Portuguese word *nipa*, a strong alcoholic drink, has also been transferred into the regional dialect of South Eastern Zimbabwe. Ilala palm wine is colloquially known as *nhipa* or *nyipa*. Interestingly, the same Portuguese word has been adopted in Japanese and means *drink* (n).

14. The Swahili *Gereza* derives more from the shape of a Church, a large building, than from the intended purpose of the edifice itself.

15. In 1989 FRELIMO abandoned its Marxist-Leninist principles in favour of a demo-cratic multi-party system and free market economy.

16. Ellert H., *Rhodesian Front War*, 1989, Mambo.

17. D. Masango to H. Ellert, 1989.

18. Bhila H.H.K. *Trade and Politics in a Shona Kingdom*, 1982, Longmans, p. 211. See also Albino Manuel Pacheco's diary of a *Voyage from Tete to Zumbo* in 1861 where he came across demand for rifles, gunpowder and flints *(perdeneiras)*. Beach/Noronha transla-tions, 1980 Vol II.

19. Bhila H.H.K. op cit. p. 211.

20. Rita-Ferreira, A. *Fixacao Portuguesa e Historia pre-colonial de Moçambique*. Lisboa, 1982, p. 257-258

21. Rita-Ferreira, A. op. cit.

22. B. Whacha to H. Ellert, 1986, on popular oral traditions amongst the Tonga people around Binga, Zimbabwe.

23. Dos Santos, João, *Ethiopia Oriental*, Évora, 1609, cap. XVI, p. 105.

BIBLIOGRAPHY

Axelson, E., *The Portuguese in South East Africa 1488-1600,* Cape Town, 1973.

Axelson, E., *The Portuguese in South East Africa 1600-1700,* Witwatersrand University Press, Johannesburg, 1969.

Axelson, E., *Portugal and the Scramble for Africa,* Witwatersrand University Press, 1967, Johannesburg.

Abrahams, D.P., Maramuca : An Exercise in the combined use of Portuguese Records and Oral Tradition, Journal of African History, 1961.

Archer, J.D., *The Development of the Mazoe Citrus Estates,* Heritage, 1989.

Baxter T.W., Four Portuguese Settlements or Forts c 1895-97, Zambia/*NR Journal,* Vol VI, 1965

Burke, E.E., Some Aspects of Arab Contact with South East Africa. *Historians in Tropical Africa,* UCR, 1962.

Boxer, C.R., *An African Eldorado* : *Monomotapa and Mozambique, 1498-1752. CAHA.,* No. 2, 1960.

Boxer, C.R., *The Portuguese Seaborne Empire, 1415-1825.,* 1969.

Boxer, C.R., *Grande Navio de Macau.,* Fundação Oriente, Museu e Centro de Estudos Maritimos de Macau, 1989.

Boxer, C.R., *The Dutch Seaborne Empire, 1600-1880,* Hutchinson, London, 1977.

Breve Monografia Agraria, Ministerio da Agricultura, Maputo, Mozambique, 1977.

Beach, D.N. *The Shona and Zimbabwe,* Mambo Press, Gweru, Zimbabwe, 1980.

Beach, D.N. The History of Tobacco and Smoking on the Zambezi, *Tobacco Today,* 1989.

Beach, D.N., *The Changing Traditions of the Mutapa Dynasty,* History Seminar Paper No. 79, 1990.

Beach, D.N., & de Noronha H., *Translations of Portuguese Documents,* Vol I & II, Univ. Of Zimbabwe, 1980, unpublished.

Beach, D.N., *Mapondera 1840-1904*, Mambo, Gweru, 1989.

Bocarro, António, *Decadas*, RSEA.

Bhila, H.H.K., *Trade and Politics in a Shona Kingdom*, Longmans, 1982.

Bruce, Colin R., *Standard Guide to the South East Asian Coins and Paper Money since 1556.*, Wisc. USA, 1981.

Barradas, Lereno, *Arqueologia de Manica e Sofala*, 1 Congresso Nacional de Arq., Lisboa, 1959.

Camões, Luis de, *Os Lusiadas*

Cooke, C.K., Dlodlo Ruins, The Missing Relics, *Rhodesiana* No. 22, 1970.

Chauhan, R.R.S., *Journal of Goan Archives*, Vol II, 1984.

Calado, R.S., *Fiança Portuguesa 1600-1660*, Museu da Arte Antiga, Lisboa.

Coates-Palgrave, Keith., *Trees of Southern Africa*, Cape Town, 1984.

Documentos Sobre Os Portugueses em Mocambique e na Africa Central, 1497-1840, vols. 1-9, National Archives of Zimbabwe, University Eduardo Mondlane, Centro de Estudos de Historia e Cartografia Antiga do Instituto de Investigação Cientifica Tropical.

Dos Santos, João, *Ethiopia Oriental*, Evora, 1609, reprint.

Da Costa, Cristovão, *Tratado das Drogas e Medicinas*, (1578) reprint, Lisbon, 1964.

Drummond & Coates Palgrave, *Common Trees of the Highveld*, Longmans, 1973.

De Carvalho, Pires, *Velha Macequece*, Mozambique, 1946.

Desmond-Clarke, J. The Portuguese Settlement at Feira. *Northern Rhodesian Journal*, 1965.

De Laessoe, H.H., The Zambezi River - Victoria Falls to Chinde, A Boat Journey of Exploration, in *Proceedings of the Rhodesian Scientific Assoc.*, Vol 8. Part I, 1908.

Da Silva, Beatriz Basto, *Entre Goa e Macau*, Bol. de Centro de Estudos Maritimos de Macau, 1989.

Dias, Jorge, *A Perspectiva Portuguesa do Japão,* Bol. de Centro de Estudos Maritimos de Macau, 1989.

Dickinson R.W. Gateway to the Gold of Monomotapa, *Rhodesiana,* No. 19, 1968.

Da Franca, António Pinto, *Portuguese Influence in Indonesia,* Lisbon, 1985.

Diccionario Portuguez-Cafre-Tetense, Imprensa da Universidade, Coimbra, two editions of 1899 and 1900.

Ellert, H. *Material Culture of Zimbabwe,* Longmans, 1988.

Ellert, H. *Rhodesian Front War,* Mambo Press, Gweru, Zimbabwe, 1989.

Ellert, H. Feira of Masapa, Portuguese Settlement in Zimbabwe during the 16th and 17th Centuries, Mount Darwin District, *Zimbabwe Science News,* Vol 22, No. 5-6, 1988.

Ellert, H., Indo-Portuguese Imports and Trade Goods in Zimbabwe, 1570-1900., *Journal of the Goan Archives,* 1988.

Eltringham, S.K., *Elephants,* Blandford Press, 1982.

Elephants, Economics and Ivory, Earthscan Publishers, London.

Fernandes, A.P., Portuguese Trading Company, 1694-1699, *Journal of the Goan Archives,* Vol. II, 1985.

Fothergill, R.J. *The Monuments of Southern Rhodesia,* 1953, Commission for Preservation of National and Historical Monuments.

Ferrão-Vaz, J., *Livros das Moedas de Portugal,* Braga, 1973.

Friedberg, Robert., *Gold Coins of the World,* Coin and Currency Inst., N.Y., 1980.

Garlake, P.S., 17th Century Portuguese Earthworks in Rhodesia, *SA Arch. Bull.* Vol XXI, No. 81-84, 1966.

Garlake, P.S., *Some Early Portuguese Relics from Dambarare, Rhodesian Scientific News,* Vol II, No. 12, 1968.

Garlake, P.S. *Report on Tafuna Hill,* Sa. Arch. Bull. No. 26, 1971.

Garlake, P.S., The Value of Imported Ceramics in the Dating and Interpretation of the Rhodesian Iron Age, *Journal of African History,* 1968, 9.1.

Gelfand, M., *The Traditional Medical Practitioner in Zimbabwe*, Mambo, Gweru, Zimbabwe, 1985.

Gibbs, P., *The History of the BSAP*, Vol I., Salisbury, 1972.

Harper, Rosemary, *A Study of Ceramics, Mae-Nam, Noi Kiln Site, Thailand*, Western Australia Museum, 1988.

Hall, R.N. & Neal,W.G., *Ancient Ruins of Rhodesia*, Methuen, London, 1904.

Hogg, Ian V., *Illustrated Encyclopaedia of Firearms*, Hamlyn, 1978.

Hanlan J.R., The Plants and Animals that Nourish Man, *Scientific American*, 1976.

Hair, P.E. H., Milho e Meixoeira, *Cahiers d'Etudes Africaines*, 1977, Vol. XVII.

Holness, D.H. & Smith A.J., The Reproductive Performance of the Indigenous Rhodesian Pig, *Rhodesian Journal of Agriculture*, 1973.

Holness, D.H., The Role of the Indigenous Pig as a Potential Source of Protein in Africa, *Rhodesian Journal of Agriculture*, Vol. I, 1973.

Jeffreys, M.D.M., The History of Maize in Africa, *SA Journal of Science*, 1954.

Janeira, A.M. *O Impacto Portugues sobre a Civilização Japonesa*, Publicacoes Dom Quixote,Lisboa, 1988.

Kirkman, J., *Fort Jesus : A Portuguese Fort on the East African Coast*, Oxford, 1974.

Lobato, A., *A Expansão Portuguesa em Mocambique 1498-1530*, Lisboa 1954-1960 Vol. I, II and III.

Lopes, Fernão, *As Cronicas, Antologias Universais, Lisboa, 1969.*

Leao, Mario C., *Reflexo de Portugal na Cultura Goesa*, Bol., Centro de Estudos Maritimos de Macau, 1989.

Livingstone, D. *Travels*

Mudenge, S., *A Political History of Monomotapa*, ZPH, 1988.

Mudenge, S., *Christian Education at Mutapa Court*, ZPH, 1986.

Mandivenga, E.C., *Islam in Zimbabwe*, Mambo Press, 1983.

Monclarro, Francisco, RSEA, Vol III.

Macintosh, D., *Chinese Blue and White Porcelain,* Hong Kong, 1987.

Maura, Rinaldi, *Kraak Porcelain : A Moment in the History of Trade,* London, 1989.

Mackenzie, J.M. The Njanja and the Iron Trade, *NADA,* 1975.

Musonza P.M., Oral Records in the National Archives of Zimbabwe, Ref. ADH/ 51, 1979.

Mitchener, *Oriental Coins.*

Martin, E.B., Zimbabwe's Ivory Carving Industry, *Traffic Bull.,* Vol. VI, 1984.

Martin, E.B. and Ryan T.C.I., *Pachyderm,* 1990.

Newitt, M.D.D., and Garlake P.S., The Aringa at Massangano, *Journal of African History,* Vol. VIII, 1967.

Newitt, M.D.D., *Portuguese Settlement on the Zambezi,* Longmans, 1973.

Pinto, Maria Mendes, *Marfins d'Alem Mar,* Museu da Arte Antiga, 1988.

Phillipson, D.W., Kasoko : A Portuguese Entrepôt in the Middle Zambezi Valley, *Zambia/NR Journal,* Vol VI, 1965

Reynolds, B., *The Material Culture of the People of Gwembe Valley,* Manchester, National Museums of Zambia, 1968.

Ribeiro, Orlando, *Aspectos e Problemas de Expansão Portuguesa,* Lisboa, 1962.

Rita-Ferreira, A., *Fixação Portuguesa e Historia Pre-Colonial de Mocambique,* Junta da Investigação de Ultramar, Lisboa, 1982.

Summers, R. *Ancient Mining of Rhodesia,* Museum Memoirs, 1969.

Selous, F.C., *A Hunter's Wanderings in Africa,* London, 1893.

Selous, F.C., *Travel and Adventure in south-east Africa,* reprint, Pioneer Head, Salisbury, Rhodesia, 1972.

Sasoon, C., *Chinese Porcelain in Fort Jesus,* National Museums of Kenya, 1975.

Souza, G.B., *A Sobrevivencia do Imperio : Os Portugueses na China (1630-1754)*, Publicacoes Dom Quixote, Lisboa, 1991.

Strandes, Justus, *The Portuguese Period in East Africa*, EA Lit. Bureau, 1971., translation.

S.R. Geological Bull. No. 45, 1956, The Geology of the Odzi Goldbelt.

S.R. Geological Bull., No. 32, 1937-64., The Geology of the Umtali Goldbelt.

Tracey, Hugh,. Antonio Fernandes, Rhodesia's First Pioneer, *Rhodesiana*, No. 19.

Tredgold, Margaret H, and H.M. Biegel, *Rhodesian Wild Flowers*, Museums and Monuments of Rhodesia, Thomas Meikle Series, No. 4, 1979.

Theal, George McCall., *Records of South Eastern Africa*, Vol. II, III and VI. Govt. of the Cape Colony, 1899.

Talbot, J.N., *Dichwe Lemon Forest and its Avifauna*, Honeyguide.

Tatham, G.H. and Taylor R.D. *The Conservation and Protection of the Black Rhinoceros in Zimbabwe*, Koedoe, 1989.